Patterns
of
Development

George Sternlieb

CENTER
FOR URBAN
POLICY
RESEARCH

Published in the United States of America
by the Center for Urban Policy Research
Building 4051—Kilmer Campus
New Brunswick, New Jersey 08903

Library of Congress Cataloging-in-Publication Data

Sternlieb, George.
  Patterns of development.

  Includes index.
  1. Housing—United States. 2. Cities and towns—
United States. 3. United States—Economic conditions—
1981–   . I. Title.
HD7293.S73 1986   307.7'6'0973   86–6876
ISBN 0–88285–117–9

Patterns
of
Development

Contents

Contents

III. The Changing Shape of the Economy

Exhibits

Chapter 9: *Housing in New York City: Matrix and Microcosm*

Figures

Preface

Revolutions come in two forms. First, and perhaps more transient, is the classic palace revolt: the sun sets with one ruler; it rises in the presence of another. But history teaches us that these changes rarely are much more than cosmetic, witnessed by alterations in the signature on the currency—and frequently little else.

Far greater in significance are those that result from long-term sweeping changes in our folkways and in the parameters—social, economic, demographic, political—that shape them. The history of America is that of a continuous rolling evolution exemplifying this latter type of phenomenon. The axioms and unquestioned postulates of one generation are cleared away by the next. Agriculture gives way to manufacturing, gives way to services, gives way—to what we are not sure—but the very receptivity to new development has been one of the great strengths of our society.

Certainly the rituals of society continue well past their functional bases, but they are properly backwatered, revered for a while, laughed at for a while, and ultimately smiled at into oblivion. Much of contemporary economic thinking is more the deification of things past than a forecast of the future. And being a prisoner of history is far from unique to economists!

Turner's thesis at the turn of the century—that the existence of the frontier and the flexibility that it made possible was responsible for the singular freedom of American folkways and adaptive capacity—has proven false. Regardless of the significance of the frontier, its disappearance did not hinder the freedom and adaptive com-

petence of American society. Our openness to immigration, for example, has no parallel in the rest of the world. And while fears of the
present and future are sometimes reflected in legislation, the basic
thrust has been acceptance of the adventure of change and a belief in
progress. Not all adaptations have proven beneficent, and even those
which have been most productive in the long run have often been
accompanied by trauma and pain. But the acceptance of transience is
an essential corollary of adapting to innovation.

Within the continuity of this dynamism, however, there are
specific areas which provide terminal points of the old and observation
posts for the new. While the perceived discontinuity at the end of an
era sometimes is not borne out by statistics, they are useful nevertheless as motivators for self analysis. Ours is just such a time. The
changing role of government is still to be fully mirrored in the federal
budget, but its very threat has caused a reexamination of the fifty-year
cycle initiated in the early days of the New Deal.

Similarly, the industrial and economic hegemony of the United
States, first displayed in World War I days and confirmed dramatically
by World War II, now is challenged by the increasing worldwide
homogenization of labor force and industrial sophistication. The
phenomenon of the baby-boom generation and with it the cult of
youth of the 1960s and early 1970s reached its high-water mark with
Woodstock and perhaps the turbulence of the Democratic convention
in Chicago in 1968. It now has passed into history and leaves behind
it an America suddenly conscious of its aging, of shortfalls in capacity.
The shortages of housing which dominated a generation ago have
given way to unparalleled housing affluence for most Americans. And
yet in the midst of it there is an increasing uncertainty on the shelter
provisions of the poor as the consensus on housing priority begins to
falter.

The essays presented here are a modest effort to view the man-
ifestations of change in central cities, in housing, and in the economy
itself. They are the perspectives of a moment in time—all of them
completed within a two-year period. The uncertainty of some of
them, the pessimism of others, hopefully will be found faulty in the
future. But so may some of the over-optimism. I have avoided the
temptation of updating the articles. Interest rates have fallen, the
economy currently is improving, the immediacies are much more positive than just a short while ago. But none of the long-term issues have
been resolved. The problems and prospects cited here will revisit us.

Real change comes so rapidly as to leave observers, professional and amateur alike, lurching in its wake. Our generalizations have difficulty coping with the present—much less forecasting tomorrow. But this is not unique to our time. And if nothing more, it is important to be reminded of past mountains that have been scaled. The dreads of the Depression years, the fears of automation of the 1960s, the oil crunches of the 1970s have receded in detail. They have left residues, however, in our thinking; and, at the very least, provide lessons on meeting future stress. Yesterday is not tomorrow. But it provides heartening evidence of our survival capacity.

As a practicing academic, I am continuously amazed that society is willing to pay me to be a professional observer. A barrage of desperate complaints about the onerousness of my duties is used to cloak the joy lest I be found out. Even in the midst of this camouflage, however, the pleasure of working with my associates can never be dimmed. The work presented here was developed in full partnership with my co-authors and all the members of the Center for Urban Policy Research. It is dedicated to them.

PART I

Housing

The study of housing—its provision, support structures, levels of priority, changing sponsorship and actual physical forms—provides most-useful insights into the total society. There are few spheres of activity that tie into our lives, both in the economic and noneconomic sectors, with as much potency. In order to understand housing, from forecasting starts to zoning, a breadth of societal analysis is required. And this is far from a one-way relationship. Housing, in turn, helps shape the broader reality.

It is in this light that the first piece in this section was generated. Its concept is that housing, at least in American society, has been much more than a synonym for shelter, but rather, certainly for the last half-century, an important binder for the society as a whole. The vision of the implicit social compact described here is a very simple one—a safety net for the poor whose structure and comfort level may be disputed, but whose existence is generally accepted, a capacity for the working class and moderately incomed, if they are willing to work and save their money to buy the symbols of the good life—principal among them homeownership. In return, both groups may unite in envying the rich, but they do not hate them.

While the specific form of the thesis presented here is from an article in *Society* in 1984, with James Hughes, entitled "Structuring the

1

Future," it went through a number of permutations and was strongly influenced by the drastic downturn in housing starts of the early 1980s. In a startling hint into some of the potential structural problems of our society, housing starts at the time were at their lowest levels since World War II.

There has been a fair amount of dispute over the issue of whether Americans have overinvested in housing at the cost of more "productive" inputs into industrial infrastructure. Without getting into the arithmetic of this situation—which can be utilized to support both sides—I would suggest that they both suffer from a failure to understand the true significance of homeownership within our society. This must be kept in mind in the years to come. Despite the return to the comparative housing affluence of the mid 1980s, I still believe strongly that housing ownership should be of great priority in the future national agenda. And there is little input, except on a parochial base of special-interest pressure groups, to place it within an appropriate context.

Given that belief, it was a privilege to be invited by the *Journal of the American Planning Association* to write a brief piece on the twentieth anniversary of the launching of the Department of Housing and Urban Development (HUD). This was part of what, in a more positive context, probably would have been a "Happy Birthday" party. Under the circumstances of the low ebb of the Department, it resembled a series of ritual dirges.

HUD was the chosen instrument for providing social housing. Its failure can be viewed as an indictment of our system—or a tribute to the success of that very same system in providing housing for the center of the voting pork chop.

The role of personalities, of leadership and personal interplay versus the "spirit of the times," is difficult to ascertain in any public arena. Would HUD have done better with different managers? Or were the political cards stacked against it? And, what do we do now? In a very modest compass the paper attempts to suggest some of the parameters that I think underlie the mixed success of HUD's youth— and some of the necessities of realpolitik for the future.

Much more substantial in formal content is the paper which follows it, which focuses on efforts to provide housing for the low-incomed. This was put together by my associate, David Listokin, and myself, for a housing conference organized by Peter Salins under the sponsorship of the Lavanburg Foundation.

It is all too rare to have the opportunity of extending a broad historical net over a subject as dominated by current trauma as is housing. The field has suffered from the priority given immediacy of analysis and the weight accorded "instant action" results. The cost is a loss of broader perspective. There are dozens of aphorisms on the dangers—or inconsequence—of neglecting history. In the housing field I would lean toward the former. Even at the length of this paper, the richness of the topic, moving from legislative reports of 1857 to the new federalism of today, can be more than a little bewildering. Professor Listokin joins with me in hoping that this essay provides some clarification of past policy and specific action that is of use as we debate tomorrow. Certainly the vagaries of federal housing subsidy programs over time are noteworthy. Perhaps equally intriguing, however, is the increasing role of local government as federal priorities shift after the 50-year focus on housing launched by the New Deal.

But the enormous progress made in physical housing standards for nearly all Americans, including the poor, was as much or more a function of housing plenty for middle America as it was of directed housing efforts targeted specifically to the poor. While abstract criticism can be made of the filtering process, the hard facts of housing, as best we can examine them, certainly certify its historic competence. When this process was fostered by omnibus housing production programs supporting a broad spectrum of housing starts, the yields were truly monumental.

The potency of housing has many dimensions, but one of its most significant forms is the feedback of housing cost and availability on household formation and configuration. In the last article in this section from *American Demographics*, James Hughes and I attempt to look at this linkage. In the process, we posit a reversal of accepted calculus. Most housing economists take household formation as a given—and move from there directly to housing starts. We suggest as an alternative that it is the availability of housing—and at an affordable price—which makes for household formation. If the flow of housing suffers from constraint, the capacity to set up housekeeping on one's own must soon falter with it. This in turn can have very important impacts not only on the economy, but societal folkways as well. Again, the early 1980s gave some warning of this; the price of disregarding its implications may be substantial in the years to come.

1

Structuring the Future

George Sternlieb and James W. Hughes

The United States is in the process of dismantling the very apparatus that has woven together our social and political fabric since the Great Depression. The 1980 census, indicating that 64.4 percent of the nation's householders own their own homes, may well mark the high point of the incredible ascension that moved the America of 1930, a land primarily of renters, to one of owners—and owners of a product that is the envy of the rest of the world.

The importance of housing is not merely as a refuge from the elements; rather, we suggest, it is an essential tool binding together the implicit social compact that gives coherence to an America of enormously varied humanity. Home ownership glues people to the system. We are one of the few countries in which the rich are not hated—they may be envied, but they are not life-threatened. This results from the success of the social compact: on the one hand, a safety net for the poor; but even more important, an implicit promise that if the middle classes maintain the work and thrift habits of yore, they can enjoy the central material symbols of belonging—and chief among these is the real potential of home ownership.

But we have reached a historic turning point in home ownership. According to the statistical evidence at our disposal, ownership is beginning to decline, a decline that is the deliberate result of an implicit public policy assault. The seemingly immortal housing boom of the post-World War II era was abruptly terminated in 1978–79 in an attempt to cope with the fiscal excesses accumulated over the preceding decade. Housing was removed from its sheltered credit-market standing, seriously threatening the capacity for future home ownership. But we are not merely altering the shape of the shelter industry—rather, we are threatening the harmony that has broadly characterized the last half-century. This is a development that may have very unpleasant consequences for the nation in the 1980s.

The genius of America is not to create social philosophy in the abstract, but to engage in a process of experimentation to find mechanisms that work. At present, however, we are reinventing the housing finance disasters of the past. A step back to the beginning of the era of the New Deal in housing makes this sobering fact most evident.

The ebullient 1920s were wafted along on a tide of rising presumptions of prosperity without end. Expanding incomes and surging automobile ownership were translated into the achievement of a new ideal: middle-class home ownership, particularly suburban ownership—an emulation of the pattern established by the rich a generation earlier. The net additions to America's housing stock, and indeed to home ownership, were then without parallel. Nearly 60 percent of the net additions to the housing stock during the decade of the twenties was for home ownership. Such shelter advances were achieved despite financial terms that would be unbelievable to young American householders four decades later (but shockingly familiar to their counterparts ten years further in the future): typical mortgages secured from commercial banks or insurance companies had five-year terms. There was no amortization; at the end of the five years, the full amount of the principal was due. They were rarely written for more than half the nominal value of the properties and, thus, encouraged a host of second and third mortgages to make up the gap. These latter were, again, very short term and involved interest rates that reached the 20 percent mark. But such short-term credit structures created a very fragile base. The necessity to renegotiate at maturity, and the potential of financial and institutional inadequacy, were overlooked. In the words of stock market analysts of the time, it was "a new era"; all the laws of economics had been repealed. And the real estate boom of the 1920s was furious.

The Crash came and the Great Depression began. Not only were aspiring home buyers denied their dream, but home owners had to struggle furiously, often with little success, to keep theirs. Housing starts plummeted; waves of foreclosures took place, eroding the capital position of most Americans and feeding back on the entire economic system. Deflation, both real and anticipated, smashed consumer buying, with an enormously deleterious effect on the total economic fabric. Indeed, in the decade of the 1930s, the proportion of home owners declined dramatically and the progress of the previous decade was aborted. There was a virtual collapse of the shelter system which had evolved. Riots and lynch mobs attended efforts of banks and municipalities to foreclose property because of unpaid mortgages and taxes. A near revolutionary situation was evident.

It was the emergence of a new social compact, somewhat inaccurately referred to as the New Deal, which served to reduce social tensions. Emergency financing measures were put in place to reduce the immediate fear of foreclosure; but even more important, in the midst of national economic havoc—measured only in part by a decline in the gross national product of nearly 50 percent—was the creation of new opportunities to secure ownership of part of the system. Housing had long been viewed as crucial to this goal and, when coupled with its vitality as an economic stimulus, became a principal element.

This was far from a unique inspiration of President Roosevelt. In 1931, his predecessor, President Hoover, had established a planning committee on housing, stressing that "nothing contributes more to happiness or sound social stability than . . . homes." Even before the convening of the committee, Hoover announced his intention to recommend to the Congress what he called "a system of home loan discount banks." But it was not until 1933, when the Home Owners' Loan Act was passed, that the Federal Home Loan Bank System was established. That system, noted Milton Semer, was

> conceived broadly and simply... to have a dual function: first, to provide a means for accumulating long-term savings of individuals and families, encouraging such savings; and second, plowing the capital thus accumulated back into housing in the form of first mortgage loans for the building or purchase of homes. The instrumentalities were not conceived of as banks in the ordinary sense and were clearly distinguished from commercial institutions. Underlying this approach were two closely related propositions: first, the encouragement of long-term savings and habits of thrift was in the best interests of people and stability generally, especially homeownership, and second, that long-term individual savings were a particularly appropriate source of funds for home mortgage investment. They were thus distinguished from the more volatile flow of funds into and out of the general investment markets.

The concepts of stability and trust permeated the structure and terminology of the member institutions. Account holders were considered members or shareholders, rather than depositors, and the funds themselves were referred to as shares, rather than deposits. Similarly, the earnings credited to shareholder accounts were considered dividends, rather than interest. Checking privileges and other general banking services were considered to be completely outside the range of normal operations—stability, not flexibility, was the emphasis.

The matrix of enabling legislation which emerged thus had as its central instrumentality specialized long-term lending institutions, and this marked the true emergence of the thrift industry. It rationalized and strengthened institutions which had existed for at least a century, generally under the rubric of "building and loan associations." New, federally chartered savings and loans emerged; state-chartered savings and loans were able to secure federal insurance under the Federal Savings and Loan Insurance Corporation. Generous tax-exemption provisions were provided for these institutions in return for their concentration on housing. This certification provided assurance to depositors. At the same time, the Federal Housing Administration (FHA) provided insurance on mortgages, revitalizing the confidence of depositors as well as lenders. The development of the long-term, self-amortizing loan swept the nation and became the standard not only for government-insured mortgages but for uninsured ones, as well.

The model mortgage of the 1930s was written for a period of twenty years, with interest rates (set by FHA regulations) not to exceed 5 percent. The first mortgage covered 80 percent of the total house value. While these parameters changed over time, the shifts were slight. The concept of long-term lending at fixed rates with relatively low down payments became the principal instrument to provide stability to the housebuilding industry—to revitalize the economy but, most important, to provide access to meaningful property to the vast ranks of middle America.

The financial sins of the past had been burned into the public consciousness. The new tools were shaped in the fire of the Crash and, as shown in FHA model advertisements, were promulgated to an America that found them completely compatible with their desires. Americans joined in a happy process of following the literal Latin meaning of amortize—"to kill," by easy stages, their home borrowing.

In the heart of the economic darkness that was the Great Depression, we moved, Republicans and Democrats alike, to strengthen and revitalize a concept as old as America—the ownership of real property—shifting from the rural scene to the urban and suburban one. We supplemented the vision of the independent farmer, viewed by Jefferson as the backbone of the nation, with a reality of the home owner whose acreage may have been relatively minute, but whose sense of dignity and honor was equally enhanced by the new shelter emphasis.

Throughout this period, a concept established first in the short-lived income tax passed in 1862 to help finance the Civil War—that deductions were to be permitted for payments of state and local taxes and for interest on personal indebtedness—was continued. In the earlier era, this reflected the long-term agrarian interest of the United States; in recent history, it symbolized the national importance of home ownership for an increasingly urban America.

If we can borrow from an advertising line for *Forbes* magazine, home ownership became an acknowledged "capitalist tool" in the very best and most honorable sense of the phrase. Certainly to detractors of the system, housing's potency is viewed as an insidious weapon generating stability where they would prefer the onslaught of the revolution and class warfare. Thus, in Marxist theory, home ownership was seen as a plot to subvert the workers and those of moderate income. Engels (in 1887) viewed worker ownership of housing as immobilizing them and therefore making them prey to wage and working-conditions exploitation. But the American ideal was rather an acknowledgment of working-class property interest, their implicit right to join in this most important of symbols of the good life.

Recouping from the Depression was a long and painful process. The new housing tools did not create a millennium, but they did provide a source of inspiration—not only to those who could take advantage of them, but also to others who could hope and aspire to a future which would include a home of their own. And the trauma of World War II generated a remarkably homogeneous set of shared values about the future to come. In a perhaps romantic retrospective, William Manchester recounts, in *The Glory and the Dream*, the yearning that emerged:

> The dreams of different soldiers were remarkably alike . . . a home that was not in the Army. . . . Betty Friedan, then fresh from Smith, later recalled that "women as well as men sought the comforting reality of home and children." . . . Possibly because there was so much correspondence between the front and home, the girls and the men in the ETO (European Theater of Operations) and the Pacific not only longed for the same future; they often agreed about its most minute details. The house would have a white picket fence. It would be within

walking distance of a school. The girl would have a chest of silverware,
the ex-GI a den. They would garden together. He would probably commute to work, because they lived in a quiet suburb.

The enormous buildup of home-front capital also enabled the era of
the American dream house to unfold. The liquid dynamite of GI and
defense-worker savings—greatly underestimated by wartime economists—combined with the dreams and aspirations of home ownership,
long frustrated by the economic constraints of the 1930s and war, to
set the stage for America's "golden housing era."

But this could not have reached reality without the basic financial
infrastructure which had been set in place in the 1930s. The specialized housing-loan institutions, fortified increasingly by secondary financial markets which provided them with greater liquidity, were essential
to this process. The conventions generated in the 1930s, in regard to
the long-term, fixed-rate, self-amortizing mortgage, were key to this
process. While Congress rewarded the returning victors with eased
stipulations of mortgage down payments and the like, the basic enabling structure remained constant.

The Golden Housing Era

The America of the late 1940s and 1950s believed in housing,
believed in growth, believed in development. Without this credo,
there could not have been the emergence of the large-scale homebuilders and land developers who provided an efficiency and economy
(to say nothing of delivery system) that overcame the housing shortages bedeviling the rest of the world and provided housing which
most Americans could afford. Certainly, in many cases, we were
building on the installment plan, building stripped-down developments. It was not the house that was stripped down, but the
infrastructure—the basic support elements. Home purchasers ultimately would bemoan the additional costs that later were required to
provide the schools, sewage treatment plants, and the like. But, in
turn, this cycle of construction and improvement was done in a
fashion commensurate with the consumer's income life cycle. We
minimized front-end costs and thus permitted more Americans to at
least secure a first bite into home ownership.

Between 1950 and 1970, the nation's overall housing inventory
increased by 50 percent—21 million units—while median family

incomes virtually doubled in real terms (see Exhibit 1). The positive relationship between housing cost burdens and growing affluence permitted home ownership rates to soar beyond 62 percent (see Exhibit 2). And the nation's minorities also partook of these gains. Between 1940 and 1970, the home ownership rates of black and "other" households surged from 24 percent to 42 percent. The housing momentum of America was unprecedented. Every major consumer survey confirmed the dominance of home ownership as *the* personal goal and symbol of economic achievement. A Roper poll undertaken in the early 1970s exemplified this in revealing that nearly 85 percent of the survey respondents considered home ownership to be the major part of the "good life."

The advances registered in the twenty years previous to 1970 served only as a prelude to the frantic activity of the following decade. Between 1970 and 1980, we secured almost 20 million net additions to the nation's shelter stock, replicating in one decade the achievements of the previous two. The 1970s turned out to be the most prolific housing decade ever.

EXHIBIT 1

Median Family Income, 1950–81

	Current Dollars	*Constant 1981 Dollars*
1950	3,310	12,549
1955	4,418	15,003
1960	5,620	17,259
1965	6,957	20,054
1970	9,867	23,111
1973	12,051	24,663
1980	21,023	23,204
1981	22,388	22,388
Gains in Real Income*		
1950–60	$4,710	37.5%
1960–70	$5,852	33.9%
1970–73	$1,552	6.7%
1973–81	−$2,275	−9.2%

*Constant 1981 dollars.

Source: U.S. Bureau of the Census, Current Population Reports. Series P-60, No. 134, *Money Income and Poverty Status of Families and Persons in the United States: 1981 (Advance Data from the March 1982 Current Population Survey).* Washington: U.S. Government Printing Office, 1982.

EXHIBIT 2

Home Ownership Rates, 1920–80
(Owners as % of Householders)

	All Householders	Whites	Blacks and Others
1920	45.6	48.2	23.9
1930	47.8	50.2	25.2
1940	43.6	45.7	23.6
1950	55.0	57.0	34.9
1960	61.9	64.4	38.4
1970	62.9	65.4	42.0
1973	64.4	67.1	43.4
1979	65.4	68.4	44.5
1980	64.4		

Source: U.S. Department of Commerce, Bureau of the Census, *Statistical Abstract of the United States: 1981.* Washington: 1981.

Not only were unsurpassed quantities of housing delivered to America's citizenry, but the quality of the product reached levels inconceivable to consumers of an earlier generation. The middle class moved from a house that was an 800-square-foot tribute to modesty—often sneered at by intellectuals as virtually indistinguishable rabbit hutches (remember all those *New Yorker* cartoons of new home owners or inebriates not able to tell which house was theirs?)—to a format twice as large that could be classified only as a complete machine for living. The finished kitchen, a rarity prior to World War II, had become a technological marvel. The single bath, possibly with roughed-in plumbing for another half, had given way to a mode of two and a half, with sybaritic aspirations often replacing functional necessities—and this for households whose typical size was diminishing quite sharply.

But all this was achieved during an era whose basic contours began to shift in ominous ways. By 1973, the year of the oil embargo, the long-sustained march of ever-increasing affluence for the American family halted. Median family income peaked in 1973 and—after having increased in real (1981) terms by an average of over $500 per year since 1950—began to decline. By 1981, the median family income in America was almost $2,300 below the 1973 high. Housing production, however, accelerated. And this occurred despite the massive cost increases attendant to new amenity levels and despite the institutionalization of "front loading" all possible future development impacts, as virtually armor-clad subdivisions completely supplanted their stripped-down forebears.

Land costs moved from a mode of 12 percent of total house costs to 20 or 30 percent and even more. It was not that Americans had run out of land, but rather that restrictive zoning practices made *developable* land a relatively scarce commodity. When the increases in raw land were compounded by the rise in locally mandated requirements for infrastructure—with sewer hookup charges in some jurisdictions moving into the $3,000-$5,000 range, accompanied by requirements for land dedication to service future generations—the result was to help inspire inflationary bonfires in housing price.

Lagging real incomes, a sagging dollar in the international arena, unprecedented inflation, along with deepening personal tax bites and accelerating housing prices, reinforced the classic belief in housing as a safe port. And consumers, rather than government, adopted this notion with a vengeance. Housing was seen as a rare refuge in an increasingly uncertain and hostile environment. Driven to this sanctuary, people perjured themselves filling out mortgage applications, and were willing to pay exorbitant shares of income to board the housing train. A "postshelter mentality" developed. Housing in America became much more important as a form of investment, of forced savings (and tax savings), and as a refuge from inflation than as a refuge from the elements.

What permitted a scared America to achieve such sanctuary was the continued availability of New Deal-originated mortgage instrumentalities—designed for stable noninflationary economic environments—in a period characterized by strikingly new contours. This made housing borrowing an unprecedented bargain and fed an insatiable housing demand, which in itself directly served to escalate the upward surge in housing costs (a demand-pull phenomenon).

Much bemoaned, but unacted upon in this process, was the increasing failure of the industry to provide new product for first-time home buyers. Only those with a "trade-in" could afford the market. Housing speculation was augmented as shelter itself began to assume the role of middle-class collectible. At the same time, housing and the old financial order were subjected to additional stresses; the house became a vehicle for maintaining consumption patterns in the face of stagnating incomes. The recapture of inflation-induced equity gains via second mortgages by home owners became commonplace. Home ownership became not only the symbol of the good life, it became a means for financing its continuance. Who needed a formal savings account when the house had become the chief repository of personal stored wealth? The consumption ethic conquered the habits of thrift assiduously cultivated in the original social/housing compact. Government policy made losers of savers and winners of speculators.

Disintermediation—the flow of savings out of thrift institutions into more rewarding havens—was far from a novelty. To a substantial degree, it was a built-in regulator of the total economic system. As funds flowed out of the thrifts, housing and related industries would in turn be slowed, thus braking the economy—and reversing the process. Thrift administrators, attempting to stabilize their annual operating statements, had long argued for a broadening of their deposit-gathering capacities, which were limited by the much-maligned Regulation Q. The Carter administration, faced with the grim reality of "stagflation," crumbled in a crisis of nerve and, seemingly over a weekend, invented the certificate of deposit, or CD. This destroyed the wall that had been erected between general market interest rates and the specific functioning of the housing market as we had known it for decades past. Within very short order, thrift institutions' lending money came not from the conventional sources of the past but rather from CDs and a swiftly augmented range of other money-market types of borrowing. For money availability at high cost, we had traded interruptible but low-cost funds for low-cost housing. Instead of stemming inflation, we fed it.

The Federal Reserve, with its October 1979 switch to monetarism, signaled the explicit retreat from the "excesses" of the recent past. In its view, the cost of borrowing for speculation generally—and housing unquestionably—had to be brought to a level higher than inflation; a real cost was attached to "nonproductive" investment. The federal government attempted to curb the housing demand hysteria that it created and for which it was responsible. "Too much capital for housing" and "reindustrialization" were the new catch phrases voiced in a variety of quarters. Housing's priority status within the nation's credit markets was terminated. We moved toward a nondifferentiated, homogeneous financial market.

The transition was not a gradual and orderly one. The financing gusher was violently capped. Mortgage costs soared into a stratosphere that had never been visited before, with long-term interest rates moving up to the 18 percent level. Fewer and fewer potential buyers, regardless of their desperation, could qualify for a loan at these levels. The thinning down of the basic market that had taken place—which placed at the center of new housing demand buyers who were dependent upon resale—proved particularly vulnerable. Each new house required a chain of sales, sometimes three or four houses long. These chains tended to crumble. Developers began to report the necessity for three or four nominal sales in order to yield one real one. Housing as one of the most "leveraged" of all consumer goods was uniquely vulnerable to the sweep of the financial markets. As a result, annual average housing starts during 1981 and 1982 were only half the 2 million annual starts achieved in both 1977 and 1978. The vagaries of national policy had seemingly exhausted the options; the Federal Reserve was left alone to give credibility to the American dollar.

The issue is not the curbing of past excess, but the failure to restructure tomorrow appropriately. Within that context, there is a void of enormous proportions—and of potentially great cost to our total system. The assault on the excesses of the 1970s has shattered the long-term social compact. We have not created adequate housing-finance replacement mechanisms; instead, we have retreated to past inadequacies.

Reinventing Disasters

When current housing mechanisms are examined, there is a dreadful feeling of *déjà vu*. In essence, we have spent the last four years reinventing just those perils and shortcomings of the market which were thought long cured. Before the Home Owners' Loan Act of 1933, for example, it was customary for a home buyer to obtain two or three separate mortgage loans. This was necessitated by the low level of coverage on first mortgages. The latter, in turn, were relatively short term, many running for five years or less. They were not amortized, and the balloon payments fell due at the end of the short term of the mortgage. Today, those who aspire to own a home find such strictures commonplace. We have reinvented the housing equivalent of the Dark Ages.

The peaks and troughs of housing starts are far from a novelty. Housing has long been used as a countercyclical tool, at the price of periodic credit crunches, with an occasional inability to secure financing as the result. But our current situation is much more consequential. It is not an acute attack that will pass in a year or two, but gives every evidence of being a chronic wasting disease. We have changed the shape of the housing-delivery system by submerging its financial requirements. The American home buyer cannot compete with the Fortune 500, much less with the borrowing requirements of the federal government.

The issue of inflation is often used as a catch-all explanation for all the ills on the domestic scene. Certainly this is most strikingly the case in terms of housing. "How can one expect to continue (or for that matter even justify) the old savings account of yesteryear?" "The CD was essential within the context of inflation." And so on. Certainly, the words of one of World War II's price controllers, Leon Henderson, float uneasily in memory: "A little inflation is like a little pregnancy; the individual glows at the beginning of the process, but ultimately—there is a baby." We suggest, without minimizing inflationary stresses, that the disease is in the process of being cured. It is the height of foolishness not to couple the recuperation with appropriate structural rebuilding.

The full measure and future implications of this reality are just beginning to be felt. As yet, the owners in residency—particularly if they are long term—are living so cheaply as to be relatively unaffected. The newcomers to the scene, however, arrive at the station just as the train has departed. Certainly there are substitutions in consumer behavior, and they will continue to take place, but they are also much more limited. And hedonistic expenditure does not provide a full-frame surrogate for housing. It does not require an overly active imagination to forecast a rising tide of discontent and the questioning of a system which cannot provide the trophies of hard work and a disciplined approach to living.

Recognition of the fragmentation of America has been widespread. The ravages of sustained inflation and income stagnation have, from a marketing perspective, diminished the vast middle market. In its stead, consumer segmentation has become the new religion; the isolation of affluent elite enclaves—characterized by the new buzzword "upscale"—is the task of the new missionaries. The social fabric of the nation has been subject to terrible stress. Lost in the shuffle, rhetoric to the contrary notwithstanding, is the broad middle.

In most of the world, the predominant need is for housing as shelter—as protection against the elements and as a means of providing basic physical security. Most Americans, however, are fortunate enough to move within a postshelter society, one in which housing standards have risen to the point where they serve much more significantly as focal points for the good life, prestige, and as measures of success.

The new Spartanism which seems to afflict fringes both on the Left and the Right tends to deprecate these elements, to view them as trivial. The elite of the Right join with the Left in viewing the needs of the middle class as unimportant. The environmentalists sneeringly refer to the ticky-tacky tract house to the applause of the children of affluence. While the Old Left of Engels' days viewed housing ownership as a capitalist plot, the new elite sees it as a distresser of the environment, on the one hand, and an impediment to economic revitalization on the other. The end results, however, are equally deleterious.

The measure of capitalism's success is its record in delivering the goods. The function of private enterprise and business consists in the provision of an improved standard of living. Failure in this regard is not merely a matter of denied comforts but, rather, has a capacity to threaten the very roots of the system.

The purge of excesses that has taken place over the last several years was much needed. And, clearly, the American electorate still agree on the need for belt tightening. We would suggest, however, that the sins of omission and commission have less to do with today's policy than with the failure to address tomorrow with anything much more than wishful thinking. The ideals of a homogeneous marketplace, where each and every good seeks its own level, have a harmony which would delight medieval philosophers. But logic in the pure, when applied to a political economy as complex as ours, has a willful habit of getting lost.

We still have not worked out a road map that can guide the patterns of shelter purchasing, of lifestyle, of symbol and reality away from those which evolved historically and toward the requirements and limitations of the intermediate future. The failure to generate policy within a more adequate, fuller range of priorities is evident— and will be even more costly tomorrow unless a more creative conceptual apparatus is hitched to the government/business nexus. The ameliorative measures in housing do not require a wholesale return to the patterning of yesterday. There are immediate approaches that could produce significant results without relighting the inflationary bonfire.

It should be noted in this context that the bulk of the "new creative mortgages" avoid the realities. Most of them presume a continuance of inflation, which will support relatively low payment levels at the beginning of their tenure—and much higher ones later on. The potential of this type of vehicle to encourage mammoth "walks," literally fleeing from property in which the resident no longer has equity, is worthy of much more analysis than it has been given.

All the forms of renegotiated-term mortgages suffer from the lack of projectability that they impose upon the borrower. The recent Harris poll commissioned by the Federal National Mortgage Association (*Buying a Home in the 1980s: A Poll of American Attitudes*) contains an understandable cleavage in its actual findings versus the accompanying text. The latter suggests that Americans are open to a variety of indenture forms. The numbers, however, speak otherwise and support the market necessity of fixed, long-term mortgages.

In the midst of much lamenting that the long-term mortgage is dead, we would suggest that there are opportunities to revive it. These could include such elements as permitting IRA accounts to be used, without penalty, for first-time housing purchase. This type of approach has become a very fruitful staple in many of the industrialized nations. The IRA adapted to this purpose would make a most important beginning in reinventing the savings/housing social compact.

Currently, the IRA asks young people to put money in virtually untouchable accounts which can be secured only in their late middle age. If anything, it is antihousing. The proof of the pudding is that the typical IRA user so far tends to be well-advanced in years. IRAs are avoided by our youth, and very properly. By providing housing investment as an exception, we could reverse this imbalance. (The amortized house is a form of old-age security which has been proven in practice.)

The working couple, putting $4,000 a year in their IRA account, achieves a reduction of taxes on this sum plus exemption on the earnings of the principal. This is an enormously potent locomotive that should be attached to the housing train. It should further be noted that this vehicle could be structured so that the rates of return are fully compatible with the requirements of a mortgage—thus avoiding the wait for the millennial return of mortgage interest rates to the low single-digit level.

Within the context of a need for a half-step housing mechanism, given the reduced shelter-buying power of Americans, further attention to the possibilities of rental/condominium conversion is clearly warranted. Here, certainly, is an area in which the Reagan administration's commitment to reducing government infringement would pay great dividends—given local strictures that have risen on condo conversion.

The inexpensive condo must be joined by modest-cost, one-family housing in order to balance the reduced housing-buying power that has characterized post-1973 Americans. This will require not only going through the motions of putting together red-tape-slicing task forces, but a broad commitment on the part of all players on the field. The target is worthy of this level of effort.

Systems that do not deliver the goods invite alternatives that promise more. Americans have a marvelous capacity to rally around the flag at times of stress—and they have done so. It is time now, however, to structure tomorrow and the day after tomorrow. The time for belaboring past sins and/or sinners must give way to a more positive assertion of priorities.

The ideal of home ownership is older than the republic. Its fortification and enhancement were seized upon a half-century ago to provide a strengthening of the American system, which we have labeled the "social compact." Failure to comprehend fully the vital role of ownership in the continuance of the system has such powerful negative implications as to require much more attention that it has yet received. We are still dealing with the housing situation as if this were a chronic attack of indigestion—an uncomfortable year or two until the system readjusts. The reality is that we have come to the end of a fifty-year cycle of institution building. It is not enough to bemoan the past—we must structure the future.

2

HUD—A Study in Power and Piety

George Sternlieb

The formation of HUD was painful, its infant years disrupted by the siren call of the urban riots and Great Society promises. The department is now twenty years old—and has yet to find a solid place in the Washington firmament. To secure the latter requires power as well as piety.

The rise and fall of HUD deserves much more study than it has received. It is important both as a study of realpolitik and as a microcosm of an era. But for perspective we must step back in time.

Ten years before HUD was launched, William C. Wheaton was writing his belated doctoral thesis about the potential of a federal department of *urban affairs* ("The Evolution of Federal Housing Programs," University of Chicago, 1954). The postwar euphoria about cities had abated; it would be reignited (literally) only by the urban fires of the 1960s. Clearly, new impetus was required if the federal government's role in urban affairs was to be formalized at the Cabinet level.

Wheaton, one of the most prescient thinkers of our time, was deeply aroused by the plight of cities. He believed, however, that the urban dilemma by itself was not a strong enough issue to provide the basis for a new department that could compete effectively among the

From the *Journal of the American Planning Association*, Autumn 1985, pp. 481–483. Reprinted with permission.

power baronies of Washington. It would have to be linked to another issue that was politically attractive enough to generate a broad and powerful constituency. Public works was Wheaton's first choice as a partner issue, but it was spread among a variety of departments and was too crucial and too basic to their patronage (and their clout) to be considered. Instead he proposed housing, an area that would provide the leverage, the trading counters, with which to secure legislation for the urban domain.

Housing had an undisputed priority in America's political calculus: its patrons and clients were powerhouses of Capitol Hill. The thrift institutions were thriving; the homebuilders were national heroes, although the shadow of the scandals attached to earlier shelter programs lurked just behind the fence. The mortgage bankers certainly were not unenthusiastic, even though that industry was a mere seed of its later maturity. Tract suburbia was in full flower, and Congress could not do enough for the returning war heroes—the World War II tide had been augmented by veterans of Korea, and the Vietnam anomie would not develop for another generation. Housing would be the blocking back, Wheaton thought, and urban redevelopment would follow in its powerhouse wake.

But even then Wheaton had some misgivings. Pleased as he was with this potential coupling, he still closed his thesis with the admonition that if the urgency of Americans' need for shelter ever abated perceptibly, there might well be substantial friction about the federal role in providing housing—and with it, a decline in the potency of housing as the draft horse for the reformulation of the aging city.

If anything, he was overly optimistic! The new department had a stormy birth. President Johnson hopelessly contaminated its launching by making it evident that Robert C. Weaver was not his choice for HUD secretary but rather was being forced upon him. The housing lobbies were accustomed to doing business with the monied ends of the regrouping that became HUD, particularly the Federal Housing Administration, and succeeded—at least initially—in keeping those functions somewhat segregated from the balance of the department. The Farmers Home Administration was carefully kept out of the department, further weakening HUD's patronage capacity.

The frail entity called HUD was barely afloat before the urban riots unfolded. There was not time to develop an institutional/patronage power base. As the department's urban mission was broadened in response to crisis, its link to housing in general (as against social housing) atrophied. The half-life of fear and indignation generated by burning cities—and the consequent interest in the trauma of the central city—lasted only a couple of years. Its most substantial bureaucratic monument was a thin residue of legislation, such as the Model Cities program, that soon shriveled on the urban vine.

When President Nixon imposed the moratorium on subsidized housing in 1973, the mourners were few. Conspicuous by their absence were the really heavy political hitters—the thrift institutions and the mortgage bankers.

By that time, nearly two-thirds of all Americans owned their homes. They had become much more concerned with preserving and elevating their financial worth than with the problems of the less fortunate. America was changing from a shelter society into a post-shelter society; capital gains had become far more important to most Americans than sound roofs and good plumbing alone. "Housing," that enormously potent seven-letter word that had had a premier place in the politician's lexicon just a few years before, suddenly became far more limited: it meant social housing for the poor, it meant "those people living next to me," it meant the potential for high tax rates and fear of change. Americans would continue to plow ever-increasing proportions of their income into houses—but that concept was a long way from "housing."

The main thrust of federal involvement in housing in general had been moved out of HUD's domain. The Federal Housing Administration's share of the market had shrunk dramatically, the former professionalism of its staff drastically watered down by high-ranking, inexperienced newcomers fleeing from jobs in the shrinking Model Cities program.

The HUD of Secretary George W. Romney, who had performed forcefully to enlarge the department despite a conservative governmental frame, was disemboweled by the new urban reality: the department's image had been transformed from the savior of cities into the principal slumlord of Detroit, from a rejuvenator of housing into a hapless financier of phony housing rehabilitation projects. And that image change came on the edge of the "stagflation" that was to dominate the 1970s, when real family incomes in America were to shrink drastically for the first time since the Depression. HUD represented charity; HUD represented waste; HUD was not central to the thinking of middle America.

Under President Carter HUD was the vehicle—the container—for social activism. It shared that role with the Department of Health, Education, and Welfare, but the latter had far more potent weapons in its armory. HUD, by comparison, was relatively patronless. It had become, and still is, an easy target.

One easily could view the peregrinations of the department as comical; but that would be a very sad mistake. There are functions of great importance within HUD's potential domain, including all the elements of the built environment. In order to secure fulfillment of them, however, we need to take a harder look at what went wrong in the past, and we need to conceive a thorough restructuring with which HUD can face the future.

In the search for a new structure for HUD, however, we must distinguish carefully between what was and was not important in HUD's identity crisis, based on its mixed history. The Department of Agriculture, after all—with a far smaller constituency—has enjoyed an incredible level of success over the years (though its aura now may be wearing thin). All the waste at HUD is trivial compared to any major weapons system; yet the Department of Defense seems to have a built-in dynamic of its own. Scandal leads to slaps on the wrist and nominal fines, not to the obliteration of programs. And one could go on in this vein.

The issue is this: What has caused HUD, despite its enormously important province, to be relegated to the backwaters of the power hierarchy? None of the several answers to that somewhat rhetorical question is appetizing, but I think they must be faced.

First and foremost is the issue of race. While President Johnson's hesitation in accepting the political necessity of appointing Weaver as HUD secretary may have had a number of antecedents—and, in the light of my own knowledge of Robert Weaver, all of them wrong!—it dramatized HUD, just as it was being launched, as a department that had, in the view of white America, a skew toward minority groups.

Second, with the exception of Romney, the leadership of the department has never been in the hands of someone who came from Capitol Hill—or, alternatively, directly from a position of high confidence with the Chief Executive. That may be of relatively small importance in departments whose functions are well defined and whose role has powerful flywheels built into it. It is of overwhelming importance, however, when a department's domain must be marked out.

Third, and most important from a power-base point of view, is the necessity for the department to become more central to *all* of housing, to have lines of patronage that feed into the nation's jugular, rather than the attenuated sectors of specialized low-income groups.

America's flirtation with painful social justice came to an end a decade ago.

The lines of force laid out by William Wheaton some thirty years ago still must be reckoned with. Americans are too spasmodic in their guilt, and the levels of financial contribution they will make to assuage it, too erratic to be depended on. And the city is fading from the central focus. If HUD is to help the poor, it must have a far broader constituency. HUD's program spectrum also must be broadened if it is to be central to urban development. Putting together a meaningful, powerful constituency will require a change of course that undoubtedly will outrage many of HUD's traditional clients—and, indeed, those who have suffered along with HUD through the years. But in the Washington of today—and, I would suggest, of tomorrow as well—the department must do well in order to do good!

3

Housing: A Review of Past Policies and Future Directions

George Sternlieb and David Listokin

Introduction: Housing Past and Future

It is nearly a hundred years since the pioneering 1892 congressional study commission report on slum conditions in America's larger cities; more than eighty years since President Theodore Roosevelt's housing commission recommended federal intervention in the cause of shelter improvement; a half-century since the Great Depression brought the federal government front and center into the era of housing. We are more than a generation from the crest of the wave of enthusiasm on urban renewal and the infinite perfectability of central cities; a decade since the Nixon-imposed housing moratorium; and a year from the depths of despond in terms of the production capabilities and reality of the private housing sector. Gone from all but the memories of scholars and historians is the vision of 26 million housing units in a decade with a fifth of them to be allocated to low- and moderate-income families—a goal enunciated by the 1968 Housing Act.

The casting off of old initiatives and the emptying of the pipe-lines of programs which were the accompaniment of the housing slump in the first two years of the Reagan administration provide a breathing space; the abrupt change from the housing initiatives and priorities of post-World War II America gives cause for a reevaluation.

What lessons can we secure from the past? The rules of the

This paper was first delivered at a conference on Expanding Housing Opportunities for Low-Income Families, sponsored by the Lavanburg Foundation in March 1984.

game, as well as knowledge of what has worked and not worked and why, are crucial not only to understand the issues of today, but also to serve as a matrix in planning policy for the future.

The difficulties of capsulizing housing are evident. It is both a reflection of the totality of our society as well as being a vital input into the very making of that society. The complexity of its relationships is evident to any observer in the field.

The factors which have shaped housing policy are thus the sum of our history and must be viewed in practically every dimension: physical, political, and economic. (So important is tax policy that it must be studied not merely as a subset of this latter parameter, but as a vital input in and of itself.) America's housing is a reflection of its wealth, and the division thereof within our population. And while the physical parameters of our dwelling units have been remarkably unaltered by technology, certainly the latter—in terms of forming a matrix of settlement and resettlement—has had enormous impact. Finally, the issues of race and region continue to exert enormous formative pressures.

But this is far from assuming a purely deterministic approach. As the history of housing is viewed, the noise factors—the influence of personalities, of institutions both governmental and private which have sometimes generated a life force of their own—cannot be disregarded. Whether the bureaucrat building up an organization such as the Farmers Home Administration, orchestrating the power blocks of Congress in a fashion which has yielded results quite unlike those initially envisioned in the enabling legislation, or the initial difficulties of gestation and birth of HUD and its immediate submersion in the urban turmoil that soon followed, these are elements which are difficult to measure but nonetheless consequential in their effects. The field is deserving of much more longitudinal analysis than it has received, not merely in terms of the bare bones of production numbers and the role of subsidy mechanisms and the like; the "countables"—housing production by type, area program, etc.—cloak perhaps more than they reveal of the institutional forces and dynamics that have been and are at work.

The paper which follows, in an attempt to provide some partitions for a relatively seamless—if disorderly—web, begins with a broad-brush chronological treatment of the evolution of federal housing concerns and involvement. It focuses on the assistance offered by the Department of Housing and Urban Development and its predecessors, as opposed to other agencies such as the Farmers Home

Administration. Following the historical review, attention is targeted to some of the conceptual approaches and issues of program development. The final section is aimed at providing a perspective on the present, and some vision of alternative futures.

The Federal Housing March
Through the Twentieth Century

Early Twentieth Century—The Limited Role of Government

It is difficult in this era of 3 million federal employees, of near-trillion-dollar budgets, to step back in time to the turn of the century when practically all of the central cabinet staff was compressed into the old Executive Office Building. Its gingerbreaded, calm exterior encapsulated all but a very few of the executive branch agencies. The federal government was actively pursuing the Indians, debating the future of public lands, conducting international affairs—and at least from current perspectives, remarkably little else.

Housing as an official member of the cabinet family would have to wait for two-thirds of a century to be admitted into the sacred portals. The *Statistical Abstract* which has just celebrated its hundredth year was still counting teepees and wigwams, and attempting to define rental multifamily housing as something other than tenements.[1]

This is not to suggest that there was a lack of awareness of America's housing issues. Pioneered by New York, there had been nearly a half-century both of investigations, and increasingly legislation attempting to govern the harsh inadequacy of central city tenements.[2] Thus, a legislative report of 1857 spoke of the

> . . . hideous squalor and deadly effluvia; the dim, undrained courts oozing with pollution; the dark, narrow stairways, decayed with age, reeking with filth, overrun with vermin; the rotted floors, ceilings begrimed, and often too low to permit you to stand upright; the windows stuffed with rags—the gaunt, shivering forms and wild ghastly faces in these black and beetling abodes.[3]

But a half-century later, Jacob Riis's *The Battle with the Slums*[4] sadly enough reported the same conditions. Reform government groups and concerned individuals were faced with population increases which make those of Central America or Africa currently seem relatively

mild, as Europe decanted its landless peasantry and urban slum dwell-
ers into the New World. While tenement laws were passed, their
effects were limited in their application as well as their design.[5] Those
of good will were armed only with a sense of outrage, but certainly little in the way of conviction in terms of the governmental role.
Government in the fashion that we know it today had yet to be
invented in the United States. As late as the beginning of the 1930s
with one exception, there was no state legislature that met annually—
typically it was biennially.

The very concept of a federal role, in what were viewed as
congeries of local problems, was foreign to the American political
geist. It was Theodore Roosevelt who, based on his exposure to
reform movements in New York and the realities of the slum conditions familiar to him from his tenure as police commissioner
(described so effectively in Lincoln Steffens's *Autobiography*),[6]
impounded a Senate commission on the topic.[7] The report which
resulted in 1902 suggested the taking of unsanitary housing and
purchase/or improvements through financing by government. Their
recommendation that "... all unsanitary and unsightly property should
be condemned and purchased by the government, improved in a uni-
form manner and inexpensive and healthful habitation erected for the
poor, who could rent or purchase their homes on installment plans at
low rates of interest,"[8] was completely incongruous to the limited
nature of the federal mandate of the time. It remains a curio incar-
cerated in the ledgers of the Senate. It would be more than fifty years
before a significant approach along the lines envisioned by the task
force at the turn of the century would begin to be implemented—and,
as we will see, even then in a far-from-sweeping fashion.

World War I: The Reluctant Warrior

The first World War provided both incentives and political backing for advances in the federal government in all the spheres of
economic life. Principal among them were actions taken in housing.
The enormous increases of industrial production for the war, and
resulting sweeps of population concentration, generated a need for
housing. The federal government authorized housing loans for ship-
yard employees; while the action was somewhat belated and the pipeline relatively slow, over 10,000 units were produced under this mandate.[9] Perhaps even more consequential was the unprecedented organization of the U.S. Housing Corporation to actually build and manage

housing for defense workers.[10] Under its aegis, over 5,000 units were produced.

While the productive and supervisory structures generated in order to fulfill these needs were dismantled (the housing units were quickly sold off to the private sector in the war's aftermath), the concepts and to a certain degree the precedent, remained. They were to serve in the next great era of national emergency.

Between them, however, was one of the great boom periods of America's housing. The wealth accumulated in the prosperity of the wartime era survived the sharp recession of 1919 and was evidenced in a housing boom. The physical volume of residential construction nearly quadrupled from 1920 through 1925, despite the primitive nature of the financing system which was available (see Exhibit 1). Loans typically were open-ended, with no provision for amortization, and written for relatively short terms. Not uncommonly, first mortgages were available for only 30–50 percent of the value of the prop-

EXHIBIT 1

Housing and Industrial Production: 1920 to 1939

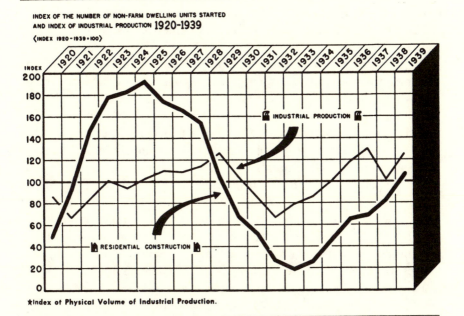

INDEX OF THE NUMBER OF NON-FARM DWELLING UNITS STARTED
AND INDEX OF INDUSTRIAL PRODUCTION 1920-1939
⟨INDEX 1920-1939·100⟩

★Index of Physical Volume of Industrial Production.

Source: National Housing Agency. Cited in Mel Scott, *American City Planning Since 1890* (Berkeley, CA: University of California Press, 1971), p. 279.

erty; a flourishing second, indeed third, mortgage market was the consequence.

In the years of the 1920s, migration off the land served to substantially alleviate many of the housing issues of rural America uncounted by all but a few socially involved individuals. Housing in urban areas tended to improve, in part as a function of reform movements. New York City once again had led the reform thrust through the 1902 Tenement House Act and was followed by many of America's urban areas.[11] Perhaps even more important, however, were advances in transit mechanisms which permitted and fostered an early wave of suburbanization, thus providing an acceleration of the filtering down process for rural immigrants. By today's standards, much of urban America's housing would have been considered dreadful. By contemporary standards, for most of its inhabitants, it represented an upgrading of facilities—while the housing available to America's burgeoning middle class had few parallels in the rest of the world.

The Age of Shelter: The Depression Era

The era of the 1920s ended with a proverbial bang. Black Monday and Black Thursday on the 1929 stock market were followed shortly by the resounding failure of the housing market, and not coincidentally, of practically all of America's industry as well. By 1931, nearly a thousand home mortgages were being foreclosed daily.[12]

It is striking to note, in Exhibit 1, that the decline in housing volume preceded the great crash with industrial production actually following housing. The sheer precipitousness of the decline has no parallel in current times. We moved from the peak of nearly a million housing units constructed in 1925 to less than a tenth of that number in 1933. By that year on-site construction throughout the country employed only 150,000 persons.

The clash between old institutions and indeed nearly religious beliefs and the new exigencies were highlighted by then President Hoover's Conference on Homebuilding and Homeownership of 1931.[13] In language which was to be repeated over and over again, practically without end, by subsequent presidential committees, task forces and the like, there is a substantial documentation of the inadequacies of the housing industry, of the ineconomies of the building cycle, of the limitations of financial institutions, and again, in a most prescient fashion—of land-use controls. It should be noted that this last element occurred barely a half-dozen years after cities had first experimented with zoning—drawing from the 1923 model act published by the Department of Commerce.[14]

But in the face of this list of woes, the major action injunction was a plea to private industry as well as local government to clean up their acts. In the face of a near-revolutionary situation, with lynch mobs attacking the courts in the Midwest in order to stop foreclosure proceedings, this was overly weak medicine for a near-revolutionary era.

The arrival of the New Deal, particularly in its first phase, represented a response to challenge. Precedent was largely thrown out of the window in the face of immediate need. It is striking to note that the first phase of the New Deal institution building resulted in mechanisms which, though shortly blunted by court injunction and indeed some measure of a political backlash, were to serve as precedent for much of the post-World War II housing and urban renewal initiatives. Thus the Reconstruction Finance Corporation was authorized in 1932 to make loans to low-income/slum redevelopment housing corporations.[15] Its mandate can be viewed as one of the foundation blocks, in somewhat different form, of urban renewal.

This is particularly relevant when coupled with the 1933 National Industrial Recovery Act which authorized federal financing of low rent/slum clearance housing and indeed financed almost 40,000 housing units before its use of eminent domain was declared unconstitutional.[16] There was so little in the way of state and local government competence and capacity that one finds, in these early days of the Brain Trust, a level of direct federal initiatives which is far in advance of anything implemented (whether properly or otherwise) even to the present day.

Faced with the virtual collapse of the nation's financial institutions and structures, the Homeowners Loan Act of 1933 and the 1934 National Housing Act brought the federal government and its entities directly into the mortgage market with a reinvention of thrift institutions, now dedicated to the financing of housing on a long-term regulated base.[17] The National Housing Act of 1934 in its multiple titles, which are summarized in Exhibit 2, is a very familiar matrix which has continued with minor conceptual shift to the present day.

Amidst this plethora of activity there were warning signals. Analysis of the congressional hearings and indeed public statements of the Administration indicate the limitations of the housing priority. While President Roosevelt spoke forcefully of a nation, one-third of which was ill-housed, the basic legislation was passed on the grounds

EXHIBIT 2

A Century of Federal Housing Programs/Actions

Date	Legislation/Other	Activity/Authorization
I. Early Studies		
1892	Congressional study commission (Pub. Res. 52–22)	Investigate slum conditions in cities over 200,000 population
1902	President's (Theodore Roosevelt) Housing Commission	Recommended condemnation of unsanitary housing and purchase/improvement/loan financing by government
II. World War I Responses		
1918	Loans for shipyard workers (P.L. 65–102)	Federal loans authorized for housing for shipyard employees; over 10,000 units produced
1918	U.S. Housing Corporation (P.L. 149–164)	Build, organize, and manage housing for defense workers; over 5,000 units produced
III. Depression Era Responses		
1931	President's (Herbert Hoover) Conference on Home Building and Home Ownership	Document housing industry inadequacies (e.g., financing, land-use controls, etc.)
1932	Reconstruction Finance Corporation authorized by Emergency Relief and Construction Act of 1932 (P.L. 72–302)	RFC authorized to make loans to low-income/slum redevelopment housing corporations; $8 million advanced to Knickerbocker Village in NYC, $.15 million for Kansas rural housing
1933	Home Owners' Loan Act of 1933 (P.L. 73–43)	a) FHLBB authorized to create Home Owners' Loan Corporation (HOLC); HOLC refinanced distressed mortgages with long-term, amortized loans (over one million loans were refinanced). b) FHLBB authorized to provide for the organization, operation, and regulation of Federal savings and loan associations — the latter were extended tax and other benefits in return for focusing on local home financing.

EXHIBIT 2 (continued)

Date	Legislation/Other	Activity/Authorization
1933	National Industrial Recovery Act (P.L. 73-67)	Authorized federal financing of low-rent, slum-clearance housing; financed over 40,000 housing units; NIR use of eminent domain declared unconstitutional
1934	National Housing Act (P.L. 74-486)	Federal Housing Administration (FHA) created and given numerous powers: *Title I* – FHA insures home improvement loans *Title II* – Sec. 203 – FHA insures long-term, amortized, high loan-to-value ratio, one-to-four family loans *Title III* – Authorizes establishment of national mortgage association (Federal National Mortgage Association – FNMA – chartered 1938) *Title IV* – Federal Savings and Loan Insurance Corporation created to insure savings accounts
1937	Bankhead-Jones Farm Tenant Act (P.L. 75-210, July 22, 1937)	Authorized Secretary of Agriculture to make long-term, low-cost loans for purchasing, refinancing, and/or repairing farm properties
1937	Housing Act (P.L. 75-412)	Authorized public housing program/U.S. Housing Authority. The latter could make loans or capital grants to local public housing agencies (PHAs)

IV. *World War II Responses*

Date	Legislation/Other	Activity/Authorization
1940	Defense Homes Corporation (P.L. 588 and 611)	DHC authorized to provide housing in Washington, D.C. and other defense locations
1940	Landham Act (P.L. 76-849)	Authorized provision of public war-housing accommodations; almost 1 million units ultimately provided

EXHIBIT 2 (continued)

Date	Legislation/Other	Activity/Authorization
IV. *World War II Responses* (continued)		
1941	National Housing Act (P.L. 77-24)	Title VI added to provide insurance for mortgages on one- to four-family homes in critical defense locations (Sec. 603); over 350,000 units insured
1942	Emergency Price Control Act (P.L. 77–421)	Authorized federal rent controls
1942	National Housing Act (P.L. 77–559)	Sec. 608 added to Title VI of the Housing Act to provide mortgage insurance for multi-family rental housing for defense workers (Sec. 608 was extended after the war for non-defense purposes).
1944	Servicemen's Readjustment Act (P.L. 78-346)	Veterans Administration authorized to guarantee liberal mortgages made to veterans
V. *Early Post-War Responses*		
1949	Housing Act (P.L. 83–560)	*National Housing Policy and Goal* – Declared importance of providing sound housing and realization of that goal through private enterprise *Title I* – Authorized $1 billion in loans and $500 million in grants to aid local slum clearance programs *Title II* – Increase in Title II FHA mortgage insurance authorized *Title III* – Increase in public housing (to 800,000 units authorized) *Title IV* – Secretary of Agriculture authorized to establish programs to improve farm housing
1953	Advisory Committee on Government Policies and Programs (E.O. 10486, September 1953)	Committee recommends that government expand efforts to deter housing deterioration and foster rehabilitation

EXHIBIT 2 (continued)

Date	Legislation/Other	Activity/Authorization
1954	Housing Act (P.L. 83–560, August 1954)	Among other changes (e.g., restrictions on Sec. 608 to curb abuses), the Housing Act introduced programs to encourage rehabilitation/upgrading in urban renewal areas. A "workable program" requirement was introduced to foster planning which would now be assisted by Sec. 701 grants. Sec. 220 authorized FHA insurance for one- to four-family dwellings in urban renewal neighborhoods; Sec. 221 insured mortgages on sister multi-family projects. To foster a secondary market for these new mortgages, FNMA was authorized to provide "special assistance functions (purchases)." (These special assistance functions ultimately became the responsibility of the Government National Mortgage Association — GNMA — when GNMA was split from FNMA in 1968.)
1959	Housing Act (P.L. 372, September 1959)	Section 202 authorized direct low-cost loans for rental housing for the elderly
VI. *New Frontier – Great Society Responses*		
1961	Housing Act (P.L. 70, June 1961)	Section 221 program broadened to include low and moderate, not just displaced families; Sec. 221(d)(3) program authorized to provide below-market rate mortgages for rental housing; new home improvement loan programs — Sec. 220(h) and 203(k) authorized in urban renewal areas
1964	Housing Act (P.L. 88–560, September 1964)	Section 312 low-cost loans authorized for rehabilitation

EXHIBIT 2 (continued)

Date	Legislation/Other	Activity/Authorization
VI. *New Frontier — Great Society Responses* (continued)		
1965	Housing Act (P.L. 89–117, August 1965)	Rent supplements for privately owned housing authorized. The supplement would pay the difference between the fair market rent and one-fourth of the tenant's income. Section 23 also authorized public housing authorities to lease private units.
1966	Demonstration Cities and Metropolitan Development Act (P.L. 89–754, November 1966)	Authorized demonstration programs for inner-city neighborhood upgrading.
1967	National Commission on Urban Problems (Douglas Commission)	National Commission appointed by President Lyndon Johnson
1968	Housing Act (P.L. 90–448, August 1968)	The Act authorized many new housing programs and established a 10-year housing production goal of 26 million units with about one-fifth allocated to low/moderate-income families. Section 235 subsidized low-income rental projects; Section 236, multi-family. Both programs provided mortgages with interest rates as low as one percent. The existing FNMA was partitioned into two separate corporations — FNMA, which would continue market operations, and GNMA, which would focus on special assistance functions. In addition, the Housing Act authorized a National Housing Partnership, riot insurance, and flood insurance, and guarantees of obligations issued by new community developers.
1969	Housing Act (P.L. 91–152)	Rent in public housing limited to one-fourth of tenant income (Brooke Amendment).

EXHIBIT 2 (continued)

Date	Legislation/Other	Activity/Authorization
1970	Emergency Home Finance Act of 1970 (P.L. 91–432)	Purchase authority of FNMA extended to conventional mortgages; new secondary market institutions – Federal Home Loan Mortgage Corporation (FHLMC) – created.
1970	Housing Act (P.L. 91–609)	Secretary of HUD authorized to conduct experimental housing allowance programs

VII. *Reappraisal and New Directions*

Date	Legislation/Other	Activity/Authorization
1973	Impoundment of housing subsidy and community development funds	Effective January 1973, a moratorium on housing/community development assistance is imposed.
1973	*Housing in the Seventies* study (October 1973)	HUD report criticized equity and cost of existing housing subsidies. (Note: This report was critiqued by the Congressional Research Service.)
1974	Housing Act (P.L. 93–383)	Title I replaced many categorical housing/community development programs with Community Development Block Grants. A new Section 8 program replaced the Section 23 leasing subsidy. Section 8 provided payments equal to the difference between the fair market rent and the amount affordable by low/moderate-income families (first 25, then increased to 30 percent of gross income). Section 8 could be applied for new, existing, and rehabilitated housing.
1977	Housing Act	Urban Development Action Grants (UDAG) authorized communities in "distress" to submit applications and compete for UDAG awards. UDAG can be used for both residential and nonresidential purposes.

EXHIBIT 2 (continued)

Date	Legislation/Other	Activity/Authorization
VII. *Reappraisal and New Directions* (continued)		
1983	Housing Act (P.L. 91-181)	Section 8 voucher demonstration program authorized as well as Rental Rehabilitation Grants, and Housing Development Grants (new construction and substantial rehabilitation).

Source: Committee on Banking, Currency and Housing, Subcommittee on Housing and Community Development, *Evaluation of Role of the Federal Government in Housing and Community Development – A Chronology of Legislative and Selected Executive Actions, 1892-1974* (Washington, D.C.: Government Printing Office, 1975); Barry G. Jacobs, et al., *Guide to Federal Housing Programs* (Washington, D.C.: Bureau of National Affairs, 1982).

of jobs and economic recovery. Thus Harry L. Hopkins spoke first of unemployment in endorsing the 1934 Act:

> The building trades in America represent by all odds the largest single unit of our unemployment. Probably more than one-third of all the unemployed are identified, directly and indirectly, with the building trades. . . .

> Now, a purpose of this bill, a fundamental purpose of this bill, is an effort to get these people back to work. . . .

> . . . There has been no repair work done on housing since 1929. . . .

> And finally, we believe it is essential that we unloose private credit rather than public funds in the repairing of those houses and the building of new houses.[18]

Certainly the agenda of housing per se—the alleviation of shelter scarcity—was far from hidden, but in and of itself, at least in the professional judgment of some of the most skilled politicians then in America, it was not adequate. It was necessary to build a broader constituency, and the magic words in the 1930s—ones which would be heard again and again—were "jobs" and "economic reinvigoration."

Even the 1937 Housing Act, which authorized the public housing program, basically was sold under the same rubric of job stimulation and economic growth.[19] Again, let us reiterate: while certainly the sponsors of this program were true believers in housing provision as being central to the good life, theirs was a faith which was inadequate to turn the wheels of Congress and the budget process independent of the broader economic thrust.

A Second Wartime Emergency: World War II Responses

The second World War, from a housing perspective, lasted fully five years in the United States. The defense buildup which finally moved the nation out of the Depression doldrums was fully underway by 1940. Even as late as 1938, for example, the physical volume of housing was barely half that of the 1920 peak (see Exhibit 1). The shift of war workers and mobilization which ensued with the institution of selective service generated a demand for housing. Under wartime pressures, the federal government acceded to them.

Usually the initial responses were essentially elaborations of those pioneered in the first World War period. The scale, however, was much more substantial: the number of units produced moved into the seven-figure area. The mortgage insurance premiums pioneered in the 1930s were now focused on critical defense locations—a forerunner of targeting to come. Similarly the Section 608 program, later to become infamous in terms of the scandals attached to it, specifically provided mortgage insurance for multifamily rental housing for sheltering defense workers.[20] It was extended after the war and served as a progenitor for many numerical titles to come.

Finally (and from a New Yorker's perspective, not least among the federal activities) is the implementation of emergency price controls which put in place rent controls—and certified them as an appropriate act of government in the face of emergencies.[21] While New York had pioneered in this regard immediately after World War I, this was the nation's first taste of what real estate developers viewed as an insidious poison, but consumers saw as a certification of housing as an essential good.

The Early Post-War Responses: Hail to the Returning Heros

Perhaps equally influential in terms of the wartime housing responses was the 1944 pioneering effort to assure returning veterans of liberal mortgage accessibility.[22] The concept of housing and/or land for the returning veteran certainly dates back to the classical era. Those who have visited Blenheim Palace can see the rewards of a nation grateful to the Duke of Marlboro for his success several hundred years ago. Now America moved into the forefront in this regard. Once again, one of the motivating elements was not merely gratitude, but the fear of a resumption of economic malaise once the wartime stimulus was over. And this was merely one element of post-war planning which was implemented as victory drew near; the spectre of the Depression was still fresh in the minds of the political leadership.

The first great housing act of post-World War II America was that of 1949.[23] It set in place many of the initiatives which have continued to the present day. Particularly striking among them was the response to downtown merchants and other real estate entrepreneurs of the central city vaguely disquieted by the beginnings of suburbanization, and perhaps even more troubled by the increasing shabbiness of America's central cities after the long period of underinvestment that dated back to the 1920s. Thus Title I of the 1949 act authorized one billion dollars in loans and 500 million dollars in grants to aid local slum clearance programs. The economic centrality of major cities and their basic vigor were viewed as unimpaired. All that was required was cosmetic cleanup—sometimes viewed as moving the poor, and increasingly the blacks—to less obtrusive locations. Public housing, which had established its credibility in the late 1930s, was substantially augmented with authorization for 800,000 units, in a program which received surprising backing from both sides of the political spectrum. The conflict that arose on the location of these facilities, however, documented in the classic Myerson and Banfield study, was soon to dynamite this unity.[24] But in 1949 the vision of demographic and ecological reality in the central city was yet to take these complexities in hand.

Much more significant to the reality of the new areal configurations of America were the substantial increases authorized in FHA mortgage programs and the relatively innocuous—at least seemingly so—implementation of a program under the Secretary of Agriculture to improve farm housing.

It is intriguing in this context to review those programs which did not make the cut in the post-war era. Principal among them, but specifically rejected after much discussion, was a program of rent certificates to needy families. These were endorsed by the real estate boards of the time, but were viewed as being too open-ended in terms of their cost and counterproductive with respect to improving housing quality:

It has been argued before the subcommittee that such families should be assisted by rent certificates just as grocery stamps have been furnished to needy families. The number of families entitled to rent certificates upon any such basis would be infinitely larger than those requiring other relief. It is not at all certain that such a plan would bring about improvement in the bad housing accommodations that now exist. In fact, the scheme might work to maintain the profitability of slum areas and, consequently, to retard their elimination. It would certainly require a detailed regulation of private rental quarters both as to condition and rent.[25]

The issues of regulating both the costs and the quality of such accommodations in the presence of rent subsidies were elements which echo to the present day. While there was some language addressed to the possibilities of leasing private facilities in the cause of the needy, these also were rejected as imposing too much in the way of risk. The basic formula, therefore, was the institutionalization of aid to the poor through public housing, a dependence on mortgage insurance to increase the total supply of housing to the new middle class, and urban renewal to revitalize the urban core.

The increased overlay of federal housing intervention brought issues, and often conflicts, of administration to the fore. As we move through time and program, the issues of targeting through the *central government* with all of the incongruities sometimes of matching *local* need to administrative requirement, provide a constant tension. The central cities, at least to the present day, were and are concerned perhaps as much or more in terms of regeneration, of restoring the dominance of the middle class which was their old hegemony; wanting freedom to move from rehab to new construction, to infill, to tailor activity to the intimacies of local conditions. The federal government or its bureaucracy, increasingly viewed as the spokesperson for the poor and needy, attempted to ensure that at least some significant portion of the results of its funding activities would benefit its clients.

Overarching all of this are the continuous difficulties of management or of programs whose functions, though sometimes spelled out in legislation, actually had a broad agenda—some of it unwritten. The conflict between housing as a shelter for the needy and those underhoused by the conventional wisdom of sanitary standards and the like (as we will note again and again), is in conflict with the provision of improved, more luxurious, better-sited housing, for those with more affluence.

But certainly as the succession of housing acts of the 1950s and early 1960s indicates, there was a broad constituency for housing incorporating not merely the builders and other entrepreneurs in its provision, but also the panoply of middle-class elements as well as the poor and minority groups. The very vigor and success of this thrust in turn generated major new opportunities—and indeed major new career paths for planners, housing advocacy groups and the like, who further strengthened the flywheel of housing activity as powerful, political entities.

America agreed that Americans were housing short. "Something should be done" for our older cities, and the response should take the form of the federal government having a direct line responsibility in these interrelated matters.

The uneasy relationship between the government in Washington and local officials continuously breaks into the clear. Thus in 1954, the drive toward the requirement of workable programs—in part buffered by the assistance of the Section 701 planning grants.[26] The legislation that we see in this halcyon area is omnibus: There is something in it for everyone. The same 1954 housing act, for example, authorized FHA insurance for one- to four-family dwellings in urban renewal neighborhoods. (The early vision of urban renewal was of land of such great value that a simple sweeping away of the encumbrances of time and title would suffice to bring development running in without additional incentive. This proved then, and unfortunately has proven to the present time, to be far from universally true). At the same time, however, the drumbeat of FHA authorization and facilitation of suburban development continued to outpace efforts at central city restoration.

The 1960s: The Acts of Contrition

By the early 1960s, one of the new frontiers was the city. America was wealthy, the American standard of living was thriving, Kennedy was in the White House—and all could be made well with the world. Median family incomes of Americans in the 1950s in real terms grew by 38 percent. The now-romanticized era of stagnation under Mr. Eisenhower had given way to Camelot. The Section 221 program initially put in place to rectify the sins of urban renewal by housing those displaced, now was broadened to include all low- and moderate-income families.[27] It was followed in fairly short order by a variety of provisions including Section 312 low cost loans for rehabilitation. And perhaps even more importantly in terms of present policy initiatives were the beginnings of authorization—initially as limited demonstration programs—of the rent supplement approach as well as the Section 23 leasing arrangement for public housing authorities which were put in place in the mid 1960s (see Exhibit 2).

The era of the urban riots, the tragedy of Martin Luther King's martyrdom, and the impetus of Lyndon Johnson's political skills combined to produce an explosion of new programmatic activity as the 1960s passed the halfway mark. Notable examples include the Demonstration Cities and Metropolitan Act of 1966, and even more consequentially, the Housing Act of 1968.[28]

The latter, in retrospect, represents the high-water mark of the structural approach (at the risk of a play on words) to America's problems of human ecology and to the art forms pioneered in the Depression years; toward bridging the gap between housing need and the pockets of potential occupants. To the classic tools not only now of insurance of loans—which at a time of more salubrious relationship between incomes and costs had been adequate to generate housing—were added below-market interest rate programs. These had been set in place for specialized purposes earlier in the decade (e.g., by the Sections 202 and 221 (d)(3) programs; see Exhibit 2), but now were brought to their terminus with interest rates as low as 1 percent. Section 236 offered this low-rate financing for multifamily construction. A sister Section 235 program offered the same to foster low-income homeownership—a then-popular and in retrospect overly simplistic approach to revive core areas. Sections 235 and 236 also encompassed a stretchout of mortgage amortization to a somewhat hubristic level of 40 years. A new invigoration was given the secondary mortgage market through the partitioning of FNMA in order to sustain the flood of financing requirements which were to be generated under the banner of 26 million housing units in the decade, with a goodly share of them to be subsidized.

Again in retrospect, this very culmination of the art form, fostered by a belief in housing as the key to resolving social issues, masked the beginnings of the dissolution of the old housing alliance. The stresses of race, complicated by class conflict, and the increased awareness of the cost of the programs began to splinter the former coalition. In a more positive vein there were the beginnings, under the Housing Act of 1970,[29] of new alternatives, and of experimental housing allowance programs. Even the use of vouchers and the like, hitherto a verboten topic, was now discussable in liberal company.

The 1970s and Beyond: The Mid-Life Housing Crisis of America

The housing initiatives of the 1950s and 1960s were in part victims of their own success. Fostered by the broad panoply of financing mechanisms that had been set in place, new housing starts by 1972 peaked at nearly 2.4 million units; nearly 400,000 of these resulted from HUD-subsidized program activity (see Exhibit 3). If rehabilitated units were added to this facility, then the total federally subsidized production volume reached almost 500,000 by the early 1970s (see Exhibit 3).

But a number of countervailing forces were at work which were to make these data the high-water mark rather than the beginnings of a new era of productivity. If decennial census data are viewed, family incomes, in the 1960s again discounted for inflation, rose by fully one-third. The reality, however, is some measure of peaking prior to the failure of city revival: The dissension in the face of racial conflict and, perhaps most of all, the Vietnam War, splintered the old housing coalition.

By January 1973, newly re-elected President Nixon imposed a housing and community development assistance moratorium while calling for formal reevaluation of housing and urban programs. The intriguing phenomenon is not the reality of his act, but the limited level of protest that it engendered. The homebuilders, once strong advocates of federal housing programs particularly in central cities, were present at the hearings—but not in full vigor. The thrift institutions, increasingly involved with suburban housing using PMI (private mortgage insurance), no longer were dependent upon Washington and indeed viewed the latter's interventions as strong negatives. And while certainly the pipeline of subsidies continued for several years thereafter, by 1974 they were at a level roughly one-quarter that of their peak (see Exhibit 3).

The disenchantment with the housing programs of the previous years was widespread. It was symbolized by the criticism of the Section 235–236 efforts by one of its prime sponsors, Congressman Ashley of Ohio. HUD had become one of the nation's leading owners of housing through default. Exaggerated fears of foreclosure and scandal were rife in the subsidized housing sector. In their place, in a radical shift of emphasis, he structured the Section 8 program. This involved a major shift from more or less direct supply emphasis to increases in effective demand through rent subsidies.

This was merely part of the revolution implicit in the Housing

EXHIBIT 3

Total and Subsidized New Housing Production:
1950 to 1985 (Estimated)

Year[a]	Total New Housing Units Started (in 000s)	Total Subsidized New Housing Units Started (in 000s)	Total New Subsidized Units as % of Total New Units
1950	1,952	44	2.2
1951	1,491	71	4.8
1952	1,505	59	3.9
1953	1,438	35	2.4
1954	1,550	19	1.2
1955	1,646	19	1.2
1956	1,346	21	1.6
1957	1,222	47	3.9
1958	1,376	62	4.5
1959	1,529	34	2.2
1960	1,272	42	3.3
1961	1,365	36	2.6
1962	1,492	39	2.6
1963	1,635	48	2.9
1964	1,561	55	3.5
1965	1,510	64	4.2
1966	1,196	72	6.0
1967	1,322	91	6.9
1968	1,546	163	10.5
1969	1,500	197	13.1
1970	1,469	431	29.3
1971	2,085	441 (483)[b]	21.2
1972	2,379	388 (430)	16.3
1973	2,057	290 (332)	14.1
1974	1,353	142 (172)	10.5
1975	1,171	111 (129)	9.5
1976	1,548	118 (138)	7.6
1977	2,002	191 (217)	9.5
1978	2,036	232 (265)	11.4
1979	1,760	237 (273)	13.5
1980	1,313	208 (266)	15.8
1981	1,100	170 (211)	15.5
1982	1,072	178 (204)	16.6
1983	1,713	124 (143)	7.2
1984	Not available	99 (114) − est.	NA [c]
1985	Not available	70 (78) − est.	NA

Notes: (a) Subsidized new housing starts from 1971 onward are shown by *fiscal*, not calendar year. (Total new housing starts are always shown by *calendar* year.)

(b) Data in parentheses indicates *total subsidized housing* production (new construction *and* rehabilitation).

(c) NA = not applicable.

Source: Data on *total new housing starts* derived from: (1) U.S. Department of Commerce, Bureau of the Census, *Historical Statistics of the United States − Colonial Times to 1970* (Washington, D.C.: Government Printing Office, 1975); (2) U.S. Department of Commerce, Bureau of the Census, *Statistical Abstract of the United States, 1982-83* (Washington, D.C.: Government Printing Office, 1982); (3) U.S. Department of Commerce, Bureau of the Census, "Housing Starts December 1983 Construction Reports C20-83-12," January 1984. Data on *subsidized new housing starts* were derived from different sources: 1950 to 1970 data obtained from Anthony Downs, *Federal Housing Subsidies: How Are They Working* (Lexington, MA: D. C. Heath, 1973); 1971 to 1982 data from U.S. Department of Housing and Urban Development, *1980 and 1982 National Housing Production Report* (Washington, D.C.: Government Printing Office, 1983); 1983-1985 data from estimates provided by HUD, Office of Economic Analysis.

Act of 1974, with its stress on the replacement of categorical programs by Community Development Block grants;[30] similarly with the
doing away with support for new construction under the old mechanisms of mortgage subsidies, and putting in place the approach of
enhancing the housing buying power of the needy. The government
was moving out of the supply business after a generation. This was
the accepted wisdom in 1974. In hindsight, it was to take another
decade for the federal government to significantly move from the
housing-supply side of the equation to bolstering housing demand/
consumption by giving vouchers.

Inflation, foreign affairs, and increasingly the issues of the economy and governance took central stage in the 1970s. Middle America
had achieved its housing goals—and at the very same time cities in
the broad had lost much of their priority in America's political
pantheon. Housing, which in the 1950s had developed its constituency as something for everybody—particularly in Middle America—
had by the 1970s increasingly been synonymized with the interests
and necessities of a small, and not particularly favored, group of the
poor. It could not survive this attrition of its political base.

The Housing Act of 1974 set the foundation for the present
situation. The elements of the Reagan housing program were all
firmly in place prior to his accession to office.

The Current Nostrum: The Housing Voucher

As envisioned in 1974, the Section 8 program was to serve the
role of a housing purchasing power enhancer—not as a housing supply
vehicle. In reality, for much of the next decade Section 8 was applied
as one of the most potent housing supply subsidies of all time. The
Section 8 commitments were given to developers of mostly new housing rather than to tenant beneficiaries.

With the Reagan administration sweep into power in 1980, the
housing voucher has been brought to functional reality. While funding
for Section 8 new and substantially rehabilitated housing has been
nearly terminated, administration support for vouchers has remained
steadfast. The Housing Act of 1983 brings vouchers from a demonstration experiment to operating-program status. What has been
wrought?

The housing voucher program has antecedents going back at
least fifty years to the debates at the beginning of the New Deal. Its
heritage is evident in the Section 23 leasing program which provided a

government agency, in the guise of a public housing body, seeking out and entering into arrangements for privately owned and operated housing units. In the act of doing this, however, the agency certified their quality.

The Section 8 program brought the heritage of vouchers even farther into the present. The federal agency in the effort defined appropriate cost structures, as well as quality standards; the potential consumer, however, within these parameters of cost and quality, acted as a relatively independent shopper.

The realities of Section 8, however, very quickly moved well past the hopes and expectations of its formulators. While originally envisioned as a program to assimilate the poor into the broad spectrum of society and shelter with a limitation of no more than 20 percent of the units within a structure to fall under the aegis of the program, this proved impractical in practice—or perhaps wasn't tried hard enough or long enough. Instead, Section 8 rapidly became a take-out mechanism for earlier governmentally funded programs, particularly Section 236 and state housing finance agency-sponsored efforts which could not secure rent levels adequate to support them.

The issues that have been raised on vouchers are complex. In our opinion, principal among them is one which has bedeviled the field of social services since their inception: Is a poor person—plus money—equivalent to, let us say, a moderate-income consumer of equivalent buying capacity? Or is there something uniquely different, in terms of either competence, or the receptivity of general society to such an individual, as to require structured guidance?

Within the domain of housing per se, is there enough adequate housing available? Can the consumer, without structured guidance, find it? Will landlords accept such individuals and households? Will housing services continue to be provided? And, most hopefully, will the new economic status and buying capacity of the poor person engender a wave of improvement in heretofore unsatisfactory facilities so as to bring them up to an appropriate status?

After one of the largest social science experiments in our history with multi-volume reports,[31] and critiques without end,[32] there is no generally accepted answer to any of the several questions voiced above.

The thrust of the experience of the 1970s is reflected in viewing the alternative, i.e., structured project subsidization by the federal government, as a very expensive, very wasteful, process. Can and should housing vouchers play a role? Certainly. Can they handle the job exclusively? Clearly this will vary from market to market. For example, ten years ago New York State had 60,000 mental patients in institutionalized facilities, and now has one-quarter of that number occupying the equivalent. The rest must be housed elsewhere—but where? While certainly the societal initiatives of mainstreaming are important to a great many of these people and most worthwhile, there is a very substantial residue which requires much more than a rent-certificate program per se can offer.

Food Stamp expenditures have received criticism as to their dietary frivolousness or "trade-in," as the case may be; the range of variation in housing is far greater and certainly more complex in terms of the potential shopper. And certainly, at no level of voucher that has been proposed is new housing specifically for rent-voucher persons and households economically likely.

A broader context, perhaps, is also worth observing, and that is the question of housing's priority within the personal and household budget of the low-incomed individual. Since Glazer's seminal article in *Public Interest,*[33] the virtually unthinking acceptance of housing's importance to low-income individuals—of improvement in shelter-serving as an upgrade to all of the other trauma that might affect the poor—has been opened to question. The era of certitude that generated the unique generation of public housers of the 1930s was based upon absolute need, of current levels of trauma associated with multi-families occupying single rooms; of sanitary facilities that did not deserve that term, and the like. Though some of these circumstances still survive in rural pockets as well as the grim heartlands of some of our central cities, they are relatively isolated. The issues, therefore, are much more complex.

Within this context, some critics of the housing voucher program suggest that the issue is not the shelter allowance, but rather the back-dooring of an income subsidy—in a very ineffectual fashion.

The monumental studies of the housing allowance experience can buttress each and every one of the several competing theses. We would suggest, however, that the housing voucher, in one form or another, will now be central to housing programs to come. Nonetheless, the debate over the proper housing subsidy format will continue.

With the evolution of housing subsidies over the past half-century described, it is opportune to turn from the mechanics of their operation to the sweep of what has been accomplished and the emerging themes and influences.

The Mid-Life Housing Crisis:
The Mirror of the Numbers

The old saw that "man is what he eats" can be paralleled (with equal lack of precision) by an equivalent: Countries, governments, and cultures are what they subsidize. A measuring stick of the latter element is shown in Exhibit 3.

Much has been made by housing task forces without end (the Douglas and Kaiser Commissions[34] particularly come to mind) of the erratic nature of total housing starts in the United States; peaks to troughs regularly show differences of 50+ percent. But these are comparatively modest when the vagaries of subsidized new housing units (at least as provided by direct federal subsidies) are considered. From 1950 through 1967, the scale consistently remained well below the 100,000 mark. In turn, while the relationship to all housing construction varied with the peregrinations of the latter, it rarely moved above the 5-percent level until the mid-1960s.

It is the era of the Great Society which drastically altered this balance. Starting with almost 200,000 subsidized new housing starts in the late 1960s (about one-seventh of total new production), the pace rose rapidly to a peak in the early 1970s of almost 450,000 new subsidized units—about one-fifth of total production (see Exhibit 3). Indeed, analyses of the metaphysical relationship between median incomes and median housing costs have been bedeviled by base years formulated at this period which do not take into account the leavening influence of subsidies which artificially (at least in the context of later events) lowered housing costs.

The years immediately after the 1973 moratorium show the impact of the latter event. By the mid-1970s, subsidized new housing production dropped to a low of almost 100,000 units—a quarter of the subsidized production volume achieved in the early part of the decade. The change in administration in 1976, and the subsequent years of the Carter administration, are mirrored in a level of increased new housing starts under direct federal subsidies, reaching about 200,000 units in 1980 (some one-sixth of the total new production, but in a very bad housing year). Even then the absolute number of subsidized new housing production was little more than half that of the earlier peak.

With the advent of the Reagan administration in 1980, the drift toward lower subsidized housing production accelerated. The magnitude of change is evident from Exhibit 3. Subsidized new housing starts dropped to about 180,000 in 1981–82, roughly 125,000 in 1983 and are projected to fall to 100,000 in 1984 and 70,000 the following year. The latter figure represents a return to the modest subsidized production volume of the mid-1960s (see Exhibit 3).

What is most striking is the "successful failure" of the Reagan administration, faced with a housing industry driven back to levels of production that had not been seen for two generations—*not* moving to the conventional wisdom of housing as the key countercyclical tool. Instead, the brakes were applied (with little in the way of Democratic outcry, it should be noted). The old political magic of direct subsidies to housing as a federal commitment had been shattered. The era of the Great Society in shelter, at least as viewed from a Washington perspective, was over. The processes set at work under the Nixon administration in its second term had put in place a new dynamic barely interrupted by the post-Watergate interregnum.

This is not to belittle the wave of innovation which has evolved in the last dozen years, particularly of *local* efforts at reducing housing costs through a variety of interventionary mechanisms. The Community Development Block Grant (CDBG) provided a stimulus for local communities—many of them reinventing variations of the federal Section 312 program—with less of the bureaucratic red tape that had been involved in the latter.

While the standards used by local communities varied enormously, with nominal local rehabilitation productivity reports sometimes incorporating items as trivial as repainting, the growth was impressive indeed. In FY 1976, CDBG funding was responsible for the rehabilitation of approximately 28,000 units; by 1982, for 225,000.[35] Similarly, the status of tax-exempt financing was exploited with such great vigor as to virtually necessitate a reduction in its utilization for housing by local authorities. It is noteworthy in the regard that the Ullman Amendment, which called for the elimination of this tool, was sponsored not by the Republicans—but by the now suddenly fiscally aware Democrats. Regardless of the vigor of these and other local efforts at housing, the message of the cessation of national commitment—and national targeting as well—is obvious.

Old Ends—New Beginnings?

The rediscovery of housing as the key economic locomotive and its sheer capacity to serve that end (as shown in the recovery of 1983) have outrun the projections of every economist regardless of his political beliefs. The old nexus of fixed-interest deposits, going into specialized housing lending institutions—the thrifts—and yielding relatively low-cost, fixed-rate mortgages with long periods of amortization, have been dynamited into history.

Much to the amazement of housing observers, after some period of shock, the variable-rate mortgage, coupled not uncommonly with more modest-scale housing, has served to reinvent the market. At the moment, fostered by an unparalleled level of federal deficit, the economy is at full (and in the opinion of some observers too full) tide. Housing has led the procession. Thus, many of the private sector housing–political powers-that-be are far too busy—and too profitable—to form a new alliance for low-cost housing for the poor, at least in terms of equivalent historic organizations.

This is a field in which prosperity, however, has often been shortlived. In the happy breathing space that is now available, it may be worthwhile to recap some of the learning of the past and some potential themes for the future.

Housing: Review of Past Policies and Future Directions

Federal intervention in housing is only highlighted in Exhibit 2. It has been elaborated in programs, practices, administrative guidelines, and variations in approach practically without end. There are, however, some basic generalizations in terms of results which are evident.

1. *Calibration.* Housing, by its very nature, is a cumbersome good. Recent studies by the Center for Urban Policy Research indicate a modular three- to five-year gap between the inception of one-family housing developments and units coming on-stream ready for occupancy; in multifamily housing, the time span can be substantially greater. Therefore, the efforts to use structured housing programs, i.e., those mandating locational and/or cost and/or configurational and/or tenantry limitations and the like as countercyclical tools, have a certain musical-comedy character to them. The subsidy mechanism is generally invoked at the depths of a recession; the administrative requirements may take a year or more to be approved, and the housing stimulus comes into being just as the economic cycle is reaching a potentially overheated level, requiring some calming down. The results are that the housing intervention, rather than being countercyclical, serves as a somewhat disturbing accelerator when stimulated by federal special programming.

2. *Longevity.* With the possible exception of mobile-home use, invoked periodically as a form of disaster relief, the federal government's focus has been on conventional housing. And it is an enormously expensive good. Its lifetime of use, if the programs are to make any economic sense, has to be computed as at least forty years. Housing is definitely *not* an appropriate element for short-range need, therefore, but rather must rest on a market base of continued future usage. Unfortunately, this frequently has been lacking.

Thus, a number of major housing projects in central cities, which have been losing population quite rapidly, now suffer from the same abandonment as their private neighbors. In general, however, the latter, given better market awareness by the private sector, are much older; those built with public subsidy may reflect much more the political urgency present at their initiation rather than the demographic underpinnings required for their economic viability. Certainly this is a phenomenon which is not unique to housing, as witness the closing of local schools in the face of the baby bust generation; but perhaps both of them epitomize the somewhat spastic character of political action.

3. *Costs.* In general the costs of governmental initiatives in housing have been vastly understated. Without getting into the issues of nominal off-the-balance-sheet financing, it is clear that the use of this seemingly "painless" approach can represent a raid on the federal treasury staggeringly larger than the nominal price tag sometimes put on a program by its advocates.

The political temptation of avoiding the realities of lump-sum costs has tended to generate extraordinary long-term assaults on the public fisc. Thus, for example, under the Section 8 program, as well as earlier predecessors similarly dependent for their success on depreciation tax cover, there has been every incentive to maximize costs; hence the tax write-off capacity of a project, and every disinclination for efficiency. Maximum-cost strictures have quickly degenerated into minimum-charge thresholds.

In interviews with developers conducted by the Center for Urban Policy Research, for similar work in government- and non-government-funded arenas, respectively, cost discontinuities in excess of 200 percent were frequently cited: i.e., rehab jobs done for one's own account, $15,000; under Section 8 substantial rehab, more than $40,000.

Equally consequential, though perhaps less noted, is the price of economic failure. Thus, the abandoned public housing projects cited above are paralleled by the experience in the below-market interest rate programs. More than one-quarter of all the structures subsidized by the Section 236 below-market interest-rate program for multifamily housing have gone through at least one renegotiation of mortgage, and not uncommonly several. Each has resulted in much greater levels of costs to the federal pocket than were recognized in the passage of the original enabling legislation. Write-downs of 50 percent or more of the value of government-insured mortgages have been joined in by interest moratoriums, project subsidies and the like, which make a mockery of nominal accounting procedures.

Within the domain of costs, the very nature of federal legislation and political realities tends to maximize the financial exactions required for the development of the unit and minimize the throughput of a finite number of dollars. The interpretation that has been placed on Davis–Bacon legislation involves labor costs on government projects which average substantially above the market and tend to accelerate inflation for the entire construction industry.

4. *Targeting.* The concepts of vertical equity—that subsidized housing programs should treat people differently depending upon their incomes—and of horizontal equity—equal treatment of those who have approximately equal income—are easily stated but much more difficult to implement. Certainly, however, low-income housing efforts by the federal government have been much more a lottery: a minority achieving success, the majority being left at the station.

The issue of vertical equity must be viewed in the context of realpolitik, of the necessity of securing breadth of advocacy— sometimes at the cost of specific targeting. Even within this context, if one applies a full cash-flow analysis not merely to the housing occupancy as one of the goods flowing from the government initiative, but also to the flows of funds, subsidies, profits, tax covers and the like that emerge from the program, the analogy of feeding the sparrows by assuring oats for the horses comes to mind.

Complexity Versus Sophistication

It was Maitland who pointed out, in his studies of the origins of the English common law, that the primitive is always complex; simplicity arises only from sophistication. Thus, in the very beginnings of formal law, a specific law seemingly is required to deal with every situation, with each and every one of the latter in essence viewed as practically unique in its circumstances. Only with increased experience are the underlying fundamentals made evident; the generalizations and a more simple typology emerge.

We would suggest that the complex numerology of federal housing programs passed may well have been a necessary anteroom—a learning period for a greater level of simplicity, much of which may revolve around a housing allowance to increase the market potency of those in need, combined with a strong thrust toward minimizing the strictures on housing construction.

The Federal System Versus the Federal History

Activist critics of federal housing policy have synonymized the latter with the direct activities portrayed in the national budget. Under a federal system, however, this may very well be a reflection of centralization past. Even at its most centralized, with minor variation, federal housing programming, while using centrally secured funds, has acted through local entities—and with some measure of local control as well. While rhetoric periodically was given to greater flexibility, the old Marxist theme that "the sponsor defines the art form" tended to hold true. Nonstructured programs give way to federal directives in the face of advocacy groups—and scandal as well. It is very difficult, given the vigor of the weight of history, to envision new revenues secured by the federal government being turned over to local entities without a maturing supervisory role accompanying them, though after some measure of time lag.

The New Federalism has called for a short-circuiting of this process—a turning over of certain hitherto federal fund-raising capacities to lower levels of government. And certainly within this juxtaposition the capacity of the latter to govern with greater freedom in terms of the scale of housing ventures, their particular fabric, and the like, would probably expand. The New Federalism, however, as pointed out by Richard Nathan and other scholars of the current administration, has been much more a figment of desire and a theoretical statement than a functional reality. Given the fiscal imbalance that has evolved, it is questionable whether this will be altered markedly in the near to intermediate future. The example of tax-exempt financing earlier cited, and the abruptness of its demise, exemplify the stresses of the situation.

Infrastructure

Perhaps of even greater importance is the rapid attrition in federal provision of infrastructure, not only in terms of highway subsidies, but also—of most importance for housing—of water and sewer funding. This too represents an abrupt break with the pattern of post-World War II reality.

The potential role of the individual states acting as surrogates of the federal government is thus very substantially enlarged. By default of federal inputs, a score of local approaches are at least being discussed in terms of infrastructure provision, such as infrastructure banks and a variety of new taxation forms.

Even more striking, however, is the realism which now pervades local government. When federal funding was relatively generously available for water and sewer development, for example, the goal of local government was to spend it as rapidly as possible—in many cases at a most redundant and wasteful level. With the cutback of federal infrastructure largesse comes the search for who now will pay. The initial local government response is to pass the burden. The concept of user charges and front-end loading development in terms of securing subsidies from developers (and ultimately from occupants), though far from a novelty, now has become a widespread reality and is the fastest-growing form of municipal income.[36]

In retrospect, a strong case can be made that the federal response to increases in housing costs was *not* to attack their roots. Though much fluttering about was done through housing task forces and reports, the sum of their results seems to have been the much-derided, miniscule Breakthrough Program.

Thus, a variety of locally mandated cost-raising inefficiencies in terms of limitations on land use, subdivision controls, building codes, and the like were overcome not through reform of these elements, but rather by a literal "papering over" through federal subsidy mechanisms. With the decline of the latter, the bare bones of these practices are much more fully exposed. Now the housing buying power reality is reflected by land-use techniques, which have been hitherto present solely as gleams in the eyes of planners and fiscal experts. We have reference here to such elements as the patio house, zero-lot-line construction, great changes in terms of use of materials, and the growing acceptance of factory construction.

But important as these shifts are in providing an enabling ladder to bridge the gap between conventional housing and the pockets of consumers, they are far from adequate, particularly for households with low or moderate income. A whole new generation of conceptual approaches has been spawned in the vacuum left by direct government subsidy. *Inclusionary zoning* and *development charges* are two prominent members of this new generation of *local* measures to foster the production of lower-cost housing.

Local Initiatives to Produce Low-Cost Housing—Inclusionary Zoning

Inclusionary zoning is a "process intended to set aside a portion of the total number of units in a development at below-market prices in order to expand housing available to low- and moderate-income persons."[37] While it has been applied in other contexts, inclusionary provisions typically have the objective of expanding housing[38] opportunity. They usually have a triggering specification (e.g., development of a particular size, type, or location). The inclusionary program may be either mandatory or optional on the developer; in the former case, the builder must comply, in the latter he is encouraged to do so. In either case, the inclusionary requirement is usually stated as a share of the total new housing production, usually 10 to 25 percent. To allow or encourage the developer to comply, many inclusionary programs offer a density bonus or other inducements (e.g., reducing subdivision/ parking/set-back requirements, or offering lower-cost financing).

We can obtain a better sense of the inclusionary approach by briefly surveying its history. Inclusionary programs in the United States date to the early 1970s. In 1971, Fairfax County, Virginia required builders of fifty or more units to commit at least 15 percent of their production for low/moderate-income families.[39] In 1973, Arlington County, Virginia enacted a 10 percent inclusionary goal which if realized would result in a 10 percent density bonus.[40] In the same year, Montgomery County, Maryland, adopted a mandatory inclusionary requirement for builders of 50 or more units that they set aside 15 percent of their production for moderate-income families.[41] To facilitate compliance, up to a 20 percent density bonus was authorized. And in response to the *DeGroff*[42] decision, which declared Fairfax County's 1971 inclusionary requirement an unconstitutional taking, Fairfax amended its requirement in 1973 to provide for a density bonus.[43]

The inclusionary spirit soon leaped the continent. In 1973, Lakewood, Colorado required that 10 to 15 percent of the units in housing projects of fifty or more homes be offered at below-market prices.[44] Shortly thereafter, Boulder, Colorado added a similar provision.[45] It was in California, however, that inclusionary mechanisms became most commonplace. As a result of a series of state statutory requirements relating to expanded housing opportunities (e.g., mandating that local governments "make adequate provisions for the housing needs of all economic segments of the community," requiring municipalities to provide "regulatory concessions and incentives" to foster such housing, and preparing model local inclusionary ordinances),[46] scores of California municipalities adopted inclusionary approaches. In 1973, Palo Alto required that developers of twenty or more units provide that one-in-five be low- or moderate-cost units.[47] Others soon followed suit.

The most extensive California inclusionary program in terms of the housing production affected, is found in Orange County.[48] It requires that 25 percent of all units in developments of five or more houses located in most areas of the county (only locations already fulfilling their inclusionary mandate are exempt) be affordable by low- and moderate-income families (those earning below 80 percent of the local median), another 10 percent for "medium I" households (those earning between 80 and 100 percent of the median), and a final 5 percent for "medium II" households (those earning between 100 and 120 percent of the median). Developers can satisfy their inclusionary requirement by: (1) building the one-quarter share in each project, (2) "overbuilding" (going above a 25 percent share) affordable units in one of their developments and then transferring the excess as a "credit" to a project which is under quota, and (3) through other means, such as land donation or in-lieu cash payments to the county. However it is satisfied, the inclusionary requirement is costly to builders. To compensate, developers are offered density bonuses, modifications to subdivision requirements, accelerated processing, and tax-exempt financing.

Orange County's inclusionary program has resulted in a considerable amount of affordable housing being planned and/or produced. As of 1982, there were commitments to build over 5,000 such units; 800 of this total were already built and occupied.[49] The bulk of this was in exclusively low-cost development. More affluent developments subsidized them by buying their fair-share obligation off-site. It should be pointed out, however, that Orange County has recently rescinded its inclusionary housing provision.

While the Orange County decision represents a setback for inclusionary zoning, this land use measure received a strong affirmation in the 1983 New Jersey State Supreme Court decision, *Southern Burlington County NAACP vs. The Township of Mount Laurel* (commonly referred to as *Mount Laurel II*).[50] *Mount Laurel II* declared that "every municipality's land use regulations . . . must provide a realistic opportunity for decent housing for its indigenous poor . . . [and] for a fair share of the region's present and prospective low- and moderate-income housing need."[51] The State Supreme Court declared that inclusionary zoning was one affirmative measure to meet the *Mount Laurel* mandate. This declaration has spurred numerous municipalities in the state to adopt inclusionary requirements.

Local Initiatives to Produce Low-Cost Housing—Development Charges

Inclusionary zoning requires *residential builders* to contribute to the general welfare by providing lower-cost housing. Should the obligation be limited to the homebuilder as opposed to the *nonresidential* developer? Some municipalities have decided that the latter have a housing responsibility as well and are exacting requirements to fulfill this obligation. San Francisco has taken the lead in this respect. In 1981, the city created an Office/Housing Production Program (OHPP) under which developers of at least 50,000 square feet of office space must build, or cause to be built, .9 housing units (640 square feet) for every 1,000 square feet of office space:

> Developers gain "housing credits" by contributing directly to a housing trust fund, building the housing themselves, or aiding other residential developers to build or rehabilitate housing units.

> By late last year (1983), the program had produced 2,600 dwelling units and exacted $19 million in contributions from 27 office developers. Of this amount, $4.88 million was contributed into the program's Home Mortgage Assistance Trust Fund, which has subsidized the mortgages of 76 low- and moderate-income families buying existing homes. Funds from the trust also will help finance the construction of new condominium and cooperative units and subsidize mortgage payments for their low- to moderate-income buyers.[52]

Other cities are considering similar provisions. A proposed Boston "Linkage Program" would require developers of over 100,000 square feet of office space to contribute a "neighborhood impact excise" of $5 a square foot over a 12-year period to a neighborhood housing trust.[53] New York City is evaluating a similar approach which would combine developer contribution with a potpourri of other funds in order to capitalize a housing financing pool:

Their proposal calls for office developers to contribute directly to the housing fund. Residential developers have the option of setting aside units for lower-income tenants. Twenty-five percent of the cash contributions would be used within the same neighborhood, even more in poorer areas.

What's particularly interesting about this proposal is that the $200 million trust fund would come not from one but over a dozen sources: developer contributions ($30 to $60 million a year); the city's share of state mortgage recording fees ($22 million); repayments of UDAG and CDBG loans and sale of city-owned property ($17.5 million); higher building permit fees ($5 million); registration fees for real estate syndications and interest earned on escrow accounts set up to hold security deposits ($17.5 million); filing fees by newly formed cooperatives and condominiums ($7.5 million); revenues generated by taxes on major real estate transfers ($15 million); the city's capital budget appropriations ($20 million); state budget appropriations ($20 million); inclusionary zoning payments made in lieu of providing on-site units ($20 million); annual repayment of loans made by the housing trust fund ($11 million).[54]

It is important to place the inclusionary requirements and development charges in perspective. Neither fully compensates for the reductions in federal financing and provision of low-cost housing. Yet in their compensatory thrust they manifest the genius of the federal system. A change in the direction at one level of government—in this case federal support for housing—is somewhat offset by recommitment at other levels of government—state and local. Such "compensation" is evident in other ways. A reduction in federal aid in the form of revenue sharing and the like is met by state and city initiatives to expand their taxable resources and burden. To paraphrase the Bible, municipalities are in the position of attempting to make bricks without federal straw. Those that have strong development demand may succeed in doing so by increasing taxes in the process—and earmarking the results for housing. In the long run we would question the economic and political viability of this process. Thus, while for most of this century the federal government dominated the provision of lower-cost and subsidized housing, for the current and likely future the housing cast of characters is much broader and includes federal, state and local players.

Return to the National Scene:
Has Housing Lost Its Political Clout?

A thesis–antithesis may also be evident at the national level. Is the current turning away from a strong national housing commitment a temporary disfavor or a more long-lasting loss of affection? The present administration came into power with some of its principal brain trusters on record with statements which at one time would have been political anathema: that overinvestment in housing had been a crucial input in relative underinvestment in plant and equipment; that much of America's industrial lag was a function of overconsumption in this domain, which in turn would have to be cut back in order to favor a supply-side orientation. We stress here that at one time—and not too long in the past—this would have been a set of attitudes which would have been the equivalent of political suicide.

Their grudging acceptance was evidenced, despite verbal retractions to the contrary, by a turning away from new housing initiatives as a tool with which to fight the Depression of the early 1980s. Again, it is important to point out that, despite some face-saving rhetoric to the contrary, this tended to be a bipartisan cessation of the old love affair.

But Americans have not turned away from housing. Instead, they are willing to spend unparalleled portions of their income to support interest rates which are now tossed on the high, stormy seas of a homogenized financial market; of operating costs severely marked up by energy, insurance, and all the other inflationary realities. The current level of housing starts in the face of "unfavorable" ratios of income and cost-realities attests to this. Much less is heard of the crowding-out phenomenon as an indictment against the shelter industry—though its reality may threaten the future.

We would suggest in this context that—subject to the demographic realities reviewed below—if there were to be a long-term reduction in the level of housing starts caused by a downturn in the economy (or by any of the other vagaries which are all too obviously at hand, i.e., a financial crunch of substance or the equivalent), the halls of Congress would once again find the importance of housing as a major political federal reality, front and center.

The passage of the 1983 Housing Act and the preservation of public housing in the face of, at best, nominal administration support, indicate the baseline residual. On top of this is still an American belief in housing, not only as shelter but as the best possible investment for the broad spectrum of the middle class; and the vast bulk of present homebuyers of modest facilities look forward to trading up.

Such baseline residual support may be both strengthened and weakened by underlying demographic trends.

The New Demographic Reality

While the long-wave impact of demographics has been recognized in the housing arena certainly for a century, the importance of its role is highlighted as we view the future. Within the limitations of this paper, we would stress two points:

(1) *The baby-bust generation.* The same phenomenon that has emptied grammar schools throughout the nation, impacted high schools, and now is giving colleges and universities cause for alarm will soon move to household formation and with it lessened demand for additional housing units. The baby boom generation crested in the latter 1950s and was curtailed very sharply by 1962. As housing programs are planned, which in bricks-and-mortar must last thirty or forty or more years in order to make sense—witnessed perhaps more salubriously by the decline in labor force accession rates—the dearth of new households (at least in the intermediate future) and conceivably with it (difficult as it may be to believe at this writing) of demand for units per se, must be kept in mind. We now are close to the height of effective demand for homeownership based on the crest of the baby boom; the trough, however, is not that far into the future.

(2) *The increasing role of minority-group households.* While fewer households may fall into those cohorts suggesting strong housing demand, a greater share of those that do may vocally demand heightened government involvement in and support for housing. One out of 11 Americans is black; roughly one out of seven teenagers is, also; and somewhere on the order of one out of five or six children under the age of five. Americans have made a beginning toward integrated housing—but the numerical pressures of the future are evident, their impact on housing programs far from clear at this moment. The dialectic, however, of racism on the one hand and the growing political awareness of minority groups on the other, has yet to be resolved—and this is to say nothing of the increasingly important role of Hispanic Americans.

Nearly a third of America's total population increase now is represented by immigration. This, coupled with greater minority-group presence, may serve as a future demographic flywheel invigorating housing's national political clout.

Notes

1. U.S. Department of Commerce, Bureau of the Census, *Historical Statistics of the United States: Colonial Times to 1970* (Washington, D.C.: U.S. Government Printing Office, 1975). House Document #93-78, 93rd Congress, 1st Session.

2. See, for example, Lawrence M. Friedman and Michael Spector, "Tenement House Legislation in Wisconsin: Reform and Reaction," *American Journal of Legal History*, Vol. 9 (1975), p. 41; Law N.Y. 1867, Chapter 908; James Ford et al., *Slums and Housing* (Cambridge, MA: Harvard University Press, 1936); Roy Lubove, *The Progressive and the Slums: Tenement House Reform in New York City*, 1890–1917 (Pittsburgh, PA: University of Pittsburgh Press, 1963); Lawrence Veiller, *Housing Reform* (New York, NY: Russell Sage Foundation, 1910).

3. Quoted in Lawrence M. Friedman, *Government and Slum Housing—A Century of Frustration* (Chicago, IL: Rand McNally & Co., 1968), p. 28.

4. Jacob Riis, *The Battle with the Slums* (New York, NY: Macmillan, 1895).

5. See Friedman, *Government and Slum Housing;* see also *National Commission on National Problems, Building the American City*—Report of the National Commission on Urban Problems (New York, NY: Praeger Publishers, 1969).

6. Lincoln Steffens, *Autobiography* (New York, NY: Harcourt Brace Jovanovich, Inc., 1968).

7. See Barry G. Jacobs, et al., *Guide to Federal Housing Programs* (Washington, D.C.: Bureau of National Affairs, 1982), p. 3.

8. *Ibid.*

9. See Committee on Banking, Currency and Housing, House of Representatives, Subcommittee on Housing and Community Development, *Evolution of Role of the Federal Government on Housing and Community Development—A Chronology of Legislative and Selective Executive Actions, 1892 to 1974* (Washington, D.C.: U.S. Government Printing Office, 1975), p. 1.

10. *Ibid.*

11. See David Listokin, *Housing Receivership and Self-Help Neighborhood Revitalization* (New Brunswick, NJ: Rutgers University, Center for Urban Policy Research, 1985).

12. See Milton P. Semer et al., "Evolution of Federal Legislative Policy in

Housing: Housing Credits," in U.S. Department of Housing and Urban Development, *Housing in the Seventies, Working Paper 1* (Washington, D.C.: U.S. Government Printing Office, 1976), p. 3; Milton P. Semer et al., "A Review of Federal Subsidized Housing Programs," in U.S. Department of Housing and Urban Development, *Housing in the Seventies, Working Paper 1,* p. 82; *see also* Mel Scott, *American City Planning Since 1980* (Berkeley, CA: University of California Press, 1971), p. 316.

13. See *Proceedings and Report of the President's Commission on Homebuilding and Homeownership,* December 19, 1931.

14. See Scott, *American City Planning Since 1890,* pp. 194–195.

15. Public Law 72-302, July 21, 1932; see also Scott, *American City Planning Since 1890,* p. 318.

16. Public Law 73-67, June 16, 1933.

17. Public Law 73-43, June 13, 1933; Public Law 73-479, June 27, 1934.

18. Cited in Semer et al., "Evolution of Federal Legislative Policy in Housing: Housing Credits," p 9.

19. Public Law 75-412, September 1, 1937.

20. Public Law 77-59, May 26, 1942.

21. Public Law 77-421, January 30, 1942.

22. Public Law 78-346, June 22, 1944.

23. Housing Act of 1949, Public Law 81-171, July 15, 1949.

24. Martin Meyerson and Edward G. Banfield, *Politics, Planning, and the Public Interest* (New York, NY: The Free Press, 1955).

25. Quoted in Semer, "A Review of Federal Subsidized Housing Programs," p. 114.

26. Housing Act of 1954, Public Law 83-560, August 2, 1954.

27. Housing Act of 1961, Public Law 70-87, June 30, 1961.

28. Demonstration Cities and Metropolitan Development Act of 1966, Public Law 89-754, November 4, 1966; Housing and Urban Development Act of 1968, Public Law 90-448, August 1, 1968.

29. Housing and Urban Development Act of 1970, Public Law 91-609, December 31, 1970.

30. Housing and Community Development Act of 1974, Public Law 93-383, August 22, 1974.

31. See U.S. Department of Housing and Urban Development, *The Experimental Housing Allowance Program: Conclusions, the 1980 Report* (Washington, D.C.: U.S. Government Printing Office, 1980); David B. Carlson and John D. Heinberg, *How Housing Allowances Work: Integrated Findings from the Experimental Allowance Program* (Washington, D.C.: Urban Institute, 1978); Abt Associates, *Experimental Design and Analysis Plan of the Demand Experiment* (Cambridge, MA: Abt Associates, 1973); James L. McDowell, *Housing Allowances and Housing Improvement: Early Findings* (Santa Monica, CA: The Rand Corp., September 1979) Rand Report—N-1198-HUD; Jean E. Goedert, *Generalizing from the Experi-*

mental Housing Allowance Program: An Assessment of Site Characteristics (Washington, D.C.: Urban Institute, 1978).

32. Katharine Bradbury and Anthony Downs, *Do Housing Allowances Work?* (Washington, D.C.: The Brookings Institution, 1981).

33. Nathan Glazer, "Housing Problems and Housing Policies," *Public Interest*, No. 7 (Spring 1967).

34. See the National Commission on Urban Problems, *Building the American City*.

35. See David Listokin, *Housing Rehabilitation: Economic, Social and Policy Perspectives* (New Brunswick, NJ: Rutgers University, Center for Urban Policy Research, 1983), p. 15.

36. U.S. Advisory Commission on Intergovernmental Relations, *Significant Features of Fiscal Federalism 1981-82* (Washington, D.C.: U.S. Government Printing Office, 1982).

37. State of Connecticut, Department of Housing, *Housing and Land Use: Community Options for Lowering Housing Costs* (Hartford, CT: Department of Housing, 1974), p. 9.

38. In some cases, its purview has been broader. For instance, the California Coastal Commission required a hotel developer in Marina del Rey to provide a youth hostel, moderate-cost coffee shop, and special weekend discount rates for low/moderate income families. Robert C. Ellickson, "The Irony of Inclusionary Zoning," *Southern California Law Review*, Vol. 54, No. 6 (September 1981), p. 1172. *See also* "Density Bonus Zoning to Provide Low- and Moderate-Cost Housing," *Hastings Constitutional Law Journal*, Vol. 3, No. 4 (Fall 1976), p. 1015 +; and Herbert M. Franklin et al., *In-Zoning—A Guide for Policymakers on Inclusionary Land Use Programs* (Washington, D.C.: The Potomac Institute, 1974).

39. Fairfax County, Va. Code Ch. 30 (1961) as amended by Amendment 156 (1971), cited in *Hastings Constitutional Law Journal*, Vol. 3, No. 4 (Fall 1976), p. 1053.

40. Arlington County, Va. Resolution on Developer Provision of Moderate-Income Housing (February 22, 1972).

41. Montgomery County Council Bill 372, Montgomery County, Md. Code 25A (1974).

42. *Board of Supervisors v. DeGroff Enterprises*, 214, Va. 235, 198, S.E. 2d 600 (1973).

43. Fairfax County, Va. Code Ch. 30 (1961), as amended by Amendment 249 (1975).

44. Lakewood, Colorado Planning Commission Policy, No. 15 (1973).

45. Boulder, Colorado City Council Resolution 115 (1977).

46. California Government Code, Section 65302(c). Cited in Seymour I. Schwartz and Robert A. Johnston, "Inclusionary Housing Programs,"

Journal of the American Planning Association, Vol. 49, No. 1 (Winter 1983), p. 20.

47. *Ibid.*
48. Los Angeles, CA. Municipal Code §§12.03, 12.39, 13.04 as amended by Ordinance No. 145.927 (1974).
49. Schwartz and Johnston, "Inclusionary Housing Programs," p. 13.
50. *Southern Burlington County NAACP v. The Township of Mount Laurel*, 67 N.J. 151, 336 A. 2d 713, Appeal Dismissed and Cert. Denied, 423 U.S. 808 (1975) (Mount Laurel I); *Southern Burlington County NAACP v. The Township of Mount Laurel*, 92 N.J. 158, 456 A. 2d 390 (1983) (Mount Laurel II).
51. Jerold S. Kayden and Leonard A. Zan, "*Mount Laurel II:* Landmark Decision in Zoning and Low Income Housing Holds Lessons for Nation," *Zoning and Planning Law Report*, Vol. 6, No. 3 (September 1983).
52. Joel Werth, "Tapping Developers," *Planning*, Vol. 50, No. 1 (January 1984), p. 22.
53. *Ibid.*, p. 23.
54. Citizens Housing and Planning Council, "Memorandum" (1984).

4

The Housing Cycle Locomotive and the Demographic Caboose

George Sternlieb and James W. Hughes

Introduction

Persons need jobs and incomes before they can consider forming separate households. Before households can be formed, housing units must be available. And new housing units do not start with holes in the ground. America's demographics and housing markets are presently being shaped by these apparently simple, but often neglected, realities.

Conceptual revolutions come slowly and meet grudging acceptance. Conventional wisdom suggests that household formation and life-style shifts instigate housing demand, and in turn generate housing starts with remorseless ease. However, there is increasing awareness of more complex linkages: the availability of affordable residential accommodations may not merely reflect, but also shape the profiles of demand—and household formation rates. Moreover, the connections may be neither linear nor tidy, and are simultaneously conditioned by the nation's volatile economic and financial cycles.

As these elements interact during the 1980s, an understanding of housing-market dynamics is necessary in order to sift through alternative demographic futures. The potency of the conceptual inversion of

Reprinted with permission from *American Demographics*, © March 1984, Ithaca, New York.

household formation and housing production deserves particular consideration by demographers and market researchers alike. Casual assumptions of explosive household growth during this decade, based on the patterns of the 1970s, are inadequate to meet the test of recent experience. Whether one is attempting to project the future sales of carpets or lighting fixtures, household and housing forecasts must now be considered in much greater detail than seemingly held true in the last decade. Claims of "soon-to-be unleashed pent-up demand" may stand as failures to acknowledge fundamental market shifts.

Housing and the Broad Economic Cycle

Arching over the demographic–housing connection are the broad economic cycles afflicting America and the world. Increasingly immune to "fine-tuning" over the past decade, the business cycle has returned to prominence in both the academic and popular media. Indeed, the present attention granted the weekly money-supply growth would simply bewilder an observer of a decade ago. Interest rates casually vary more in one week than they previously changed over several years. Housing production too is increasingly volatile; the enormous variations in annual housing starts are the crest of the wave, the accelerated reflection of the broad cycles of economic activity as measured by gross national product (GNP).

As shown in Exhibit 1, the recessionary years of 1970, 1974–1975, and 1980–1982 were accompanied by dramatic plunges in new housing construction. In contrast, in periods such as 1971–1973 and 1977–1979, when the national economy surged under expansionist monetary policies and the cheap money which they unleashed, new housing starts were initiated at a torrential pace.

The business cycle, as measured by GNP, shows relatively minor declines during troubled economic periods. Housing, however, often experiences a virtual halving in new starts. Similarly, all the industries which expand or contract in housing's wake tend to bear the same boom–bust stigmata. Given the historical linkages, at the very least, it is evident that we cannot anticipate significant levels of housing activity in the balance of the 1980s unless there is a strong national economy. And there is every possibility that the housing cycle per se will become more extreme in the wake of a deregulated financial environment. This, in turn, will exert pressures on the nation's demographics.

The accentuated cycle in housing is a reflection of its extreme vulnerability to mortgage interest rates. As shown in Exhibit 2, conventional mortgage terms to maturity, i.e., their nominal lifetime, have shown very little variation from the latter 1970s to date. And similarly, loan-to-price ratios have remained remarkably constant. What is evident, however, are sharp changes in contract interest rates, steady increments in initial fees and charges (the nominal point discounts which are charged as "service" fees on securing the mortgage), and large increases in the absolute value of loan amounts. With debt service, i.e., the product of interest rates and loan amounts, the single largest element in the consumer's housing budget, the impact of these

EXHIBIT 1

**Gross National Product and Privately Owned Housing Units Started,
U.S. Total: 1964 to 1982**

Year	Gross National Product (In Constant 1972 Dollars) (In Billions of Dollars)	Privately Owned Housing Units Started (Number in Thousands)
1964	$ 876	1,529
1965	929	1,473
1966	985	1,165
1967	1,011	1,292
1968	1,058	1,508
1969	1,088	1,467
1970	1,086	1,434
1971	1,122	2,052
1972	1,186	2,356
1973	1,254	2,045
1974	1,246	1,338
1975	1,232	1,160
1976	1,298	1,538
1977	1,370	1,987
1978	1,439	2,020
1979	1,479	1,745
1980	1,474	1,292
1981	1,503[1]	1,084
1982	1,476	1,062

Notes: [1] Two negative-growth quarters during year

Source: U.S. Department of Commerce, Bureau of Economic Analysis, *Survey of Current Business*, Volume 62, Number 10, October 1982; U.S. Department of Commerce, Bureau of the Census, *Construction Reports*, "Housing Starts," C-20 (Washington, D.C.: U.S. Government Printing Office, Monthly).

72

EXHIBIT 2

Conventional Home Mortgage Loan Terms, National Averages for All Major Types of Lenders[1]

Year	Contract Interest Rate	Initial Fees and Charges	Effective Interest Rate[2]	Term to Maturity	Loan Amount	Purchase Price	Loan-to-Price Ratio
1976	8.88%	1.23%	9.08%	25.1 years	$31,700	$44,000	73.9%
1977	8.82	1.22	9.02	26.2	36,200	49,500	75.0
1978	9.37	1.30	9.59	26.7	41,400	57,100	74.6
1979	10.59	1.50	10.85	27.4	48,200	67,700	73.5
1980	12.46	1.97	12.84	27.2	51,700	73,400	72.9
1981	14.39	2.39	14.91	26.4	53,700	76,300	73.1
1982 (July)	15.00	2.73	15.60	26.1	55,200	78,600	72.6
1982 (September)	14.63	2.73	15.21	26.1	56,200	78,900	74.0
1982 (November)	13.62	2.66	14.17	25.8	57,300	79,300	74.9
1983 (February)	12.84	2.66	13.36	25.9	58,100	81,200	73.7

Notes: [1]Savings and loan associations, mortgage bankers, commercial banks, and mutual savings banks.

[2]Contract rate plus initial fees and charges amortized over 10 years, the assumed average life of a conventional mortgage.

Source: Federal Home Loan Bank Board Journal, monthly.

shifts is evident. The level of affordability and its complement, the number of potential homebuyers, has moved very radically. The level of housing starts in the years of unquestioned demand has essentially reflected the levels of affordability. While factors such as the levels of inflation, tax deductibility, and future confidence play major roles in the intimate vagaries of the housing cycle, the broad theme of interest rates clearly is dominant. Thus the housing cycle has a pattern which at least in the short run is relatively independent of demographics. When we view the *details* of housing dynamics, however, the interplay between demographics and changes in the realities of housing have a much more intimate relationship.

The New Economy of Shelter

Given the slightest inkling of potential consumer interest—and the financial wherewithal to initiate housing activity—builders build. While in the long run the product must be absorbed by household growth, in the short run it may be buffered by increases in inventory. Thus nominal housing-start figures may or may not be indicative of immediate sales and occupancies. And it is with the latter that purchases of furniture, appliances and related household goods are associated.

Within this context, it is useful to review household growth patterns. From 1960 to 1970, the annual average increase in households in the United States just barely topped the 1-million mark (1,043,000). From 1970 to 1980, the average soared by more than two-thirds to 1.7 million annually. And it was the latter spree that set the basic expectation for the 1980s, since it provided the historic baseline data for most projection models. At a minimum, the present decade was to experience an additional 1.7 million households per year. The reality, however, has been much more sparse. From March 1980 through March 1981, 1.6 million additional households were secured. The following year, as the recession deepened, a household "shortfall" become apparent—the net household gain totaled only 1,159,000. And for the year ending March 1983, the nation's household ranks grew by just 1 million.

Thus, while lower interest rates can yield more housing, they are not necessarily paralleled by household formation. The downward pressures on formations can be reflective of an uncertain economy and high unemployment levels. A weak economy particularly impacts the newcomers to the labor force—even those who in terms of formal education at one time would have been automatically recruited into the entry-level ranks of the upscale market, i.e., the June 1983 college graduates. Given the dearth of jobs available to such upscale aspirants, there was not the full pressure on the housing inventory that might once have been anticipated. The great, if sad, story—reflected more in anecdote than in statistics, but nevertheless a dominant theme of 1983—was the new college graduate returning to the parental hearth rather than forming a new household. This has been to the dismay not only of the graduates and their parents but marketers as well.

The economic segmentation of the 1980s, with an upscale market increasing sharply in income and wealth but leaving behind many other elements of our society, has simply precluded using trended historic headship rates as guides to the future. The early optimism of the late 1970s and early 1980s—expressed by projections of 26 million new housing starts for the 1980s—reflected the then-prevailing wisdom, not the chastening experience of the last several years. *At a time of economic certainty, the availability of housing may generate more households. At a time of economic scarcity, however, household formation may be so inhibited by non-housing constraints as to imperil the very longevity of the housing boom itself.*

The housing "boomlet" of 1983—1.7 million starts—has been modest relative to earlier powerhouse years (see Exhibit 1) as well as to most of the earlier projections for the decade. Thus it reflects all of the preceding concerns. Lower interest rates have produced more starts and permitted renters to become owners. They have not, however, encouraged household formations, which have been constrained by 10 percent unemployment and uncertainity.

Thus, the last stage of the baby boom generation has been making its housing impact felt, but at a level lower than conventionally predicted—and mainly for modest accommodations. Their housing buying power—defining the quantity and quality of housing that they can support—is far less than their older baby boom predecessors, who boarded the housing train earlier. Changing economic parameters have sharply segmented the baby boom generation and the housing market.

The New Housing Supply

Further complicating the mutual feedback among demographics, housing, and the economy is the fundamental shift in the process of housing-unit growth. "Components of change" is as fundamental a concept in housing analysis as it is with population analysis, although it has been much obscured to date. Housing growth can be disaggregated into new construction (births), removals from the inventory (deaths), and net conversions (a rough analog to net migration). And it has been the latter component—termed by the federal Department of Housing and Urban Development (HUD) as "additions from sources other than new construction"—which has been thrust into increasing prominence.

Rich societies throw away goods and amenities which would be treasured by their less fortunate peers. In turn, in the face of an uncertain economy, a reexamination of extant facilities, an extension of their longevity, and not uncommonly their much more intensive use, begin to take hold. Nowhere is this more evident than in the changing patterns in meeting housing requirements. Exhibit 3 details some evidence of the changes through 1980 as they have evolved over the past three decades. An increasing proportion of housing need has been met by sources other than new construction since the oil crunch of 1973 (which not coincidentally marked the end of the long-upward sweep of real median household incomes in America). Prior to this date, typically only 10 percent of the total number of housing units required by Americans were furnished from this source (conversions of one-family homes to two-family units, accessory apartments over the garage, and the creation of residential spaces in heretofore industrial parcels, etc.). Over the past decade, however, non-conventional sources have captured a larger and larger share of the market. In the seven-year period from 1973 to 1980, conversions represented more than a quarter (27.7 percent) of the total housing requirements in the U.S. Studies currently underway at the Center for Urban Policy Research and other housing institutes indicate that if anything, this pattern is accelerating as declines in real housing buying power—and perhaps equally important, declines in the security of employment in the future—are met by an increasingly intensive use and reuse of extant facilities. Thus new construction estimates will have to be tempered by this potential inhibitor, as well as by the reality of demographic "shortfalls." The ramifications for many sectors of the housing industry will not be trivial.

A healthy housing market requires households to absorb its product—otherwise the inevitable result is a housing bust with the carrying costs of inventory overwhelming the resources of the industry. Similarly, household formation rates are dependent upon the availability of housing units, but these households in turn must have the

EXHIBIT 3

Satisfaction of Basic Housing Requirements in the United States
1950 to 1979
(In Thousands of Units)

	Requirements Arising from				Annual Average Change — Requirements Met by		
	Net Change In Occupied Housing Units	Net Change In Vacant Housing Units	Losses	Total Requirements	New Construction	Conversions: Additions From Sources Other Than New Construction	Percent of Requirements Met by Non-New Construction Additions
4/1/50–12/31/59	1,046	204	465	1,715	1,524	191	11.1%
4/1/60–4/1/70	1,133	53	672	1,858	1,662	196	10.5
4/1/70–10/31/73	1,392	223	674	2,289	2,233	56	2.4
10/31/73–10/31/80	1,534	215	682	2,430	1,758	672	27.7

Source: Duane T. McGough, Additions to the Housing Supply by Means Other than New Construction. Department of Housing and Urban Development, Office of Policy Development and Research, Washington, D.C., December 1982.

resources to support independent housing. If the latter are not forth-coming, the response increasingly is to utilize hitherto non-conventional physical accommodations of one kind or another—as well as to inhibit the actual household formation rate itself.

Household formation and housing development are mutually captive. The market researcher must view them collectively, as well as individually. Failure to do so may lead to reckless optimism—or pointless pessimism. But certainly, both elements can function effectively only within an overall economy of growth in jobs—and stability in interest rates.

PART II

The Central City

Traveling abroad tends to generate insight on affairs at home. The complacency generated by familiarity and the acceptance of the known environment as inevitable can be shaken loose when viewed in a broader context. Certainly, that is my own personal experience when faced with the reality of the development of giant cities, particularly in the third world.

The contrast of the expansion of third-world cities, still faced with migration off the land, to urban development in the United States—with barely three percent of our population still in agricultural pursuits—is enormously telling. Our older central cities have peaked; theirs are the cities of turn-of-the-century-America—when the core areas of the Lower East Side of New York were packed to a density equalled today only by Calcutta, or perhaps Shanghai.

But the American transition was borne, if painfully, by an enormous expansion of manufacturing employment in its key cities. There was a massive symbiotic relationship between the flow off the land into the urban centers and the vigor of the latter. Cheap labor was the key to manufacturing success. At its peak, New York had more than a million people in that one sphere of activity; now it has barely a third that level. Our successful cities are moving from manufacturing to services; the cities of the third world are still seeking some economic reason for being which can be sustained by—and provide sustenance for—unskilled labor. Even the new cities of the Southwest, skipping by the manufacturing era, have added office concentration to their historic roles as trading points. This is not an adequate resolution for the world's growth cities, and at best is rarely available.

The third-world cities focus on expansion of infrastructure—ours much more on the maintenance of the old. Our urban issues frequently revolve around the mismatch between the new urban job bases that are evolving and the extant resident population. The problems of the third world are crises of human function. At worst, we have the resources for coping with basic human needs, if sometimes faltering in will. Third-world resources are overwhelmed by the incredible stampede from the hinterland.

Fertility rates in the United States, in common with western Europe, are at or below the zero-population-growth level. Many of the third-world countries still have populations which, at present rates of expansion, will double by the end of the first decade of the twenty-first century. By that time, the United States, given present demographic trends, will be drastically labor-short: The third-world cities still will face the necessity of finding some means of making a living for most of their populations.

This is far from suggesting that urban reshaping is easy in the United States. The process is a particularly painful one for the people who are stranded between the old city and the new one. And the end of the story is far from determined.

Giving a speech is a much freer form of exercise—and certainly a lot more fun—than writing a formal paper. Typically, as in the effort which follows, I work from a listing of five or ten topics as the formal preparation. Sometimes the results show this from both a positive and a negative point of view. Being forced to think on one's feet before an audience, though, provides an adrenaline—at its best sometimes a level of forced inspiration—that is all too rarely achieved in the drudgery of preparing a more formal written effort.

The first article presented here, "Cities: Fantasy and Reality," from the *Journal of Architectural and Planning Research* has had a few footnotes added to it but is essentially the same as a speech given shortly before at a plenary meeting of the American Institute of Architects. It followed a splendid presentation by John Naisbett which provided a very positive view of a new world to come—his vision of a "touchy/feely" society. Perhaps too much jaundice on my part is evident in the response. I am afraid, however, that the basic drives and themes presented here are still those which I believe will dominate the future. Principal among them is the coming of age of suburbia—and indeed the rise of exurbia—combining to yield a critical mass fully competent to compete with the central city.

The next section, "The City in a National Economic Context," is a more structured effort to place the cities' changing economic role within a national context. The thesis raised is that the cities' share of the national market, in classic, core forms of economic activity, is declining rapidly, leaving in its wake, particularly in the older industrial areas, a virtual vacuum. The concept that cities in the United States would lose manufacturing has been largely accepted by the planning community for a half-century. The countervailing trend coupled with it, however, is a continued dominance in the service industries, in those forms of economic activity requiring face-to-face contact, and the like. My coauthors, Robert Burchell, Charles Wilhelm, and I suggest that this has been far from the case. Rather, with a few exceptions, the older industrial cities in particular have been largely bypassed.

Within this context, we have clearly rejected the decline of central city as a function of a sagging national economy. The data on total employment at least certainly do not bear out the latter. Instead, what we see is an enormous shift in the way Americans make their livings—and this increasingly outside the areal limits of the municipality. The city's share of market has turned down so rapidly that even enormous levels of national employment growth leave it vulnerable to the next general downturn. The glitter of the new downtowns obscures more than it forecasts.

Since the presentation of this latter paper was made to the American Collegiate Schools of Planning, it closes with a call—about which I feel very strongly—for planners to place much more attention toward what is to be done rather than theorizing as to how we got there in the first place. While the latter is a worthwhile activity, we cannot obscure the necessity of coping—not with some idealized alternative world, but with making do with the real cards on the table.

The third essay of this section on the central city is "The Uncertain Future of the Central City," written for *Urban Affairs Quarterly*. This article, authored by James Hughes and myself, focuses on a number of themes which in retrospect run through this work as a whole. Primary among them is the concept of the city-within-the-city phenomenon: the city of the rich—or, at the very least, the upwardly mobile—living in physical proximity, but psychic isolation, from the

city of the poor. The emphasis here is on the demographic characteristics of the shifts between central city, suburban, and nonmetropolitan populations, in terms of both number—and equally
potent—income levels. The political complexity arising from the
differing aspiration levels of the rich and the poor toward the municipal entities which they occupy is detailed.

At the time of this writing, for example, the development of the
Hudson River waterfront has been shadowed by mayoralty elections
in Hoboken and Jersey City, New Jersey, with the incumbents
defeated by insurgents flying the flag of "Down with those who are
too friendly to development." There are equivalent political tides at
work in Boston and San Francisco. Even in Dallas and Houston, long
governed by business elites with a general pro-development consensus, increasing questions are now being raised.

I would suggest that these issues of the perceived interests of
present residents versus the potential of future development—with the
vision of attendant dislocation that it may bring in its wake—will not
go away. Resolutions involving creative synthesis have yet to become
established in the market. And yet, the central city cannot turn back
to the past. Indeed, maintaining its vigor in terms of the provision of
social services may be much more important to the poor, in the
absence of transfer payments for social purposes. With the faltering of
federal programming, social spending by the municipality depends, as
never before in the last half-century, on local economic reinvigoration
through new businesses and new people. The issues are defined reasonably easily—their resolution is much more difficult.

The fourth essay, "New York City: The Trauma of Emergence
into the Post-Industrial Era," was put together by James Hughes and
myself in response to a request by the organizers of a 1985 conference on the problems of major cities. The attendees came from a
broad range of geographic areas, from Lagos to Moscow; from a Mex-
ico City forecast to reach a population in excess of 20,000,000 to
Brazil's San Paolo with a population currently half that, but growing
even more rapidly. The essay focuses on an economy which was practically written off in terms of its future barely a dozen years ago. At
the time of the fiscal crunch, there were few forecasters who could
envision the resurgence of the "Big Apple." Manufacturing was disappearing and there seemed little in the way of new activity which could
support the city's tax base or its needy population. It was an era symbolized at its beginning by the so-called fiscal crunch—municipal
bankruptcy in all but word. But even at this low ebb, Olympia &

York, a major Canadian-based real estate firm, was buying nearly 10,000,000 square feet of prime office space for a total sum which is now nearly equalled by the annual rent roll of the same properties. The latter have increased in value by roughly eight to ten times in the space of as many years. The Empire City of New York, its nineteenth-century title, has given way to "World City."

Yet, the glitter of Manhattan, with its concentrations of unparalleled wealth, makes the contrast with the areas that have not partaken of this new economic exuberance all the more painful. A quarter of New York's population is below the poverty level. One out of seven of its residents is dependent upon welfare, and these traumas could be continued in even more painful detail.

Perhaps most telling of all is the declining competence of the city to prepare its youth for employment. Reduced labor participation, as well as the massive youth unemployment levels in current New York, highlight this shift from the city of yesterday. The latter had much less in the way of amenity, probably much less in the way of infrastructure. What it did have, however, was a much more positive relationship between the relatively unskilled and untutored, and its economy.

But this is the city of the past; what of the future? Within the boundaries of the five boroughs is a third-world city living uneasily with the city of the twenty-first century. The political resolution and mediation between these elements and the issues of economic development are challenges which test our capacities. They are exemplified in the housing arena.

The fifth paper in this section on New York, "Housing in New York City: Matrix and Microcosm," was prepared for one of the few institutional remnants of the fiscal crunch—the biennial meeting of academics and others involved in New York City's affairs, calling *Setting Municipal Priorities*. The results of these meetings are reported in a set of volumes under the same title, which provides a matchless profile of the city—though sometimes a very controversial one.

Dr. Listokin's (and my own) responsibility was to look at New York City's housing within the light of its changing economic functions. Our conclusions are that if New York City does not provide housing for the new technocracy and middle managers of the new office tenantry, they will leave—and this process will have a negative dynamic impact upon the city's economic base.

The cost of this is not merely to real estate holders, but to the poor as well, dependent as they are on New York's almost uniquely

self-funded provision of social amenity. The political problems of sub-
sidizing the affluent in the midst of the poor's lack of necessities,
however, are evident. Their resolution depends on political leadership
and strength.

The vast congeries of property interest, using the term in the
broad, expand with age and lead to immobility. The future has few
votes; the present and the past tend to dominate the political calculus
except at times of drastic turbulence.

There are few windows of opportunity for reform, for casting off
the institutional arrangements that have grown in previous years and
are treasured to the present—but encumber the future. In my opinion,
the city's failure to rationalize its land use, particularly in the housing
domain, during the period of the fiscal crunch when drastic reforms
were politically feasible, now severely limits its potential for adapting
to new challenges.

The old partnership between the workplaces of Manhattan and
the residence places of the outer boroughs and the inner suburbs, is
challenged by the changing demographic needs of the economic
dynamo. But this could be overcome were it not for the increasing
transportation frictions. The city's commuter lines and mass-transit
system suffer from the pangs of age. Maintenance is labor-intensive,
and we seem to have considerable difficulty in continuing the viability
of the capital investments of the past. The temptation is to reinvent
them elsewhere. Building the new is more salable than tending the
old.

In a city with less potent pulling power than New York, the
answer would be an abandonment of the inner core. What we see in
its place, however, is an enormous demand for living space reasonably
close to workplace, i.e., Manhattan and a very few of its colonies.

The failure to provide housing for all but the young, who are willing to forego quality of life, or the very affluent, suggests a pattern of
continuing dependence upon a suburban commuter labor force. This
is reinforced by the changing demographics of the workplace. The
baby-boom generation in its youth may well be willing to compromise
on housing quality—but as it ages, there is some issue as to whether it
can be maintained within the city.

In my own judgment, ultimately new jobs follow the work force,
and that may well lead much more to suburbia and indeed exurbia
than even the potency of New York City can prevent. Thus, housing
must be viewed within the context of economic development rather

than a sphere unto itself. As yet, the city is still grasping for mechanisms to assure its residential future.

Within this light, it is interesting to speculate on other cities. I would suggest that the relative failure of Denver and Houston to maintain consistently vigorous retailing establishments is a reflection of the limited success with which they have been able to lure downtown housing, and with it resident buying potential. New York City has the pulling power. It still remains to be seen whether it has the administrative competence and the political potency to optimize its current economic vigor.

But just as in the third world, where there is a belated understanding of the system implications of a failure to maintain quality of life in the hinterland—and the ultimate impact of inadequate agricultural policy on urban disaster, so in the United States the multiplier of urban housing and resident buying power is coming to the fore. While New York City in the days of its past glory toyed with the title of the fifty-first state, in this context, it provides useful insight into the reevaluation of urban dynamics elsewhere.

5

Cities: Fantasy and Reality

George Sternlieb

We have suffered in this country in our planning and, to a certain degree, in our architectural work from areal lag. We worried about getting mayors to fly right and to pave the streets in black areas when the real issue in many central cities was the flight to suburbia. Then we discovered suburbia and metropolitan government. (Does anybody anymore remember Secretary of Housing and Urban Development, George Romney, when he talked about real city? When he talked about the lion of the suburbs lying down with the lamb of the central city? I may have gotten the animals reversed, but you remember those days.) And that took place when the true areal problem and issue was regional shift. We all began to use the vocabulary of the Sunbelt and the Frostbelt, when the issue increasingly and strikingly was a whole new world, a world in which we have homogenized space and time and expertise and, most particularly, labor force. The issue of our time is not equity but, increasingly, at least in the psyches of most Americans, it is rather preservation. Within this context, the primary question that Americans periodically get up in the middle of the night and start asking themselves is "What is it that we do so uniquely well as to justify our standard of living?" And the answer that comes back is "I'm not sure."

Reprinted by permission of the publisher from *Journal of Architectural and Planning Research*, Vol. 1, No. 3. Copyright 1984 by Elsevier Science Publishing Co., Inc.

Our cities have largely been forgotten. They are remembered in academe—academe always has a flywheel relating to the past. They are remembered by academic practitioners who have been instilled with certain graces by their teachers. Increasingly, however, the older cities become the realm of "could be," "should be," "would be"—those three phrases used by losers everywhere in the world.

In the national picture, there are three numbers on median family income that you must remember. In the decade of the 1950s, median family income rose in real terms, by 38%. (That is with inflation taken out.) In the decade of the 60s, it rose by 33%, and this was real money, real buying power, real housing money, real shopping-center money. This pattern continued into the early 70s. Whether it was because of the coincidental oil crunch or not, from 1973 to present, real median income in the United States has gone down by about 9% (Sternlieb and Hughes, 1982).

What you have as a result of all this is much more in the way of an I–me society—if you want to be a bit more pretentious, call it the trauma of mid-life crisis or crisis of future expectations. Now, when you're rich and you're secure, you're charitable, you can at least dream of equity, talk about it. When you're poor, you know that life is very hard and you try to be charitable. When you're rich and you're fearful of becoming poor, you are not charitable. When you're rich and you're fearful of becoming poor, you are not charitable at all.

The temptation within the United States right now is to optimize the short run and to go with the winners. Within this context, most of our older cities, and particularly our industrial cities, are viewed as losers. Money put into them is viewed as lost money and the result of this is, at best, a leveling off of support programs.

What is the problem? Is it merely tired blood? You take a patent medicine that you all know and maybe things get better. Is it a long-run trauma? The decline and fall of the West? Maybe it's taking place. To some, it is the issue of labor. But the role of unions in the United States has been declining quite sharply. To others, it is the ineptitude of management. Before U.S. Steel bought into the oil business, you could have bought all of U.S. Steel, forgetting for the moment its major lumber holdings, it coal holdings, its tremendous chemical industries and the like, for $50.00 a ton worth of steel-making capacity. In other words, the total equity value on the market of U.S. Steel divided by its tonnage capacity was worth fifty bucks a ton. That's what the market said U. S. Steel, historically a backbone element of the American economy, was worth. In response, we have a flight into fantasy and, again, we must understand this flight in order to understand our cities.

One of the elements of this flight into fantasy is the creation of a marvelous new mythology. It's capsulized in a single utterance: "What can you expect of me? I'm a poor Caucasian faced with the Japanese super mensch!" And, as you know, the best-sellers of our time incorporate what to do about one's corpulence, cheek by jowl (hip to thigh, more commonly) with examining Japanese management, the secret of X-factor in management, etc.

We have a second thesis, and, to some degree a perhaps even more pernicious one. This thesis holds essentially that the United States is a super country, something that most of us would agree with. It has super people; most of us when we look in the mirror, at least, would agree with that. All right. Now, we're not doing very well. We could not have been defeated by lesser folk. We could not be impacted by lesser countries. We had to be stabbed in the back by other Americans. This may sound somewhat familiar to those of you knowledgeable in German history: Germany lost the first World War, they couldn't have lost it to those inferior people, they had to have been stabbed in the back by bad Germans. Who are the bad Americans? It's youth not willing to work hard enough. It's old age demanding too much. It is the labor unions, featherbedding. It's the unemployed. It's the welfare recipients. It's government itself. And you heap paranoia on the paranoid and you get some of the politics of our time. But notice that within this context, there is no outside world. There are only interior barnacles. There is no decline in education. There is no issue of research and development. There is no external competition. There are no national requirements other than liberation because the only problem is what Americans have done to America and to their fellow Americans. Remove the barnacles, all will be well. Now, that is a very attractive thesis.

At this point, a brief view of the economic role of cities in America is worthwhile. One, and a very big one, is that big American cities are not the same as their equivalent in Europe. Our cities, for better or worse, at least our big ones, are the cities of business, not of government. You only have to reflect on our state capitals: Albany in New York, Springfield in Illinois, or whatever its name is in Pennsylvania, and the like. Government was a very small enterprise in this country. Cities were the cities of commercial activity and, in very, very large numbers, we called big industrial conurbations "cities," whether the reality justified that broad a title or not. Now we must face the deindustrialization of the United States. The absolute number of jobs in manufacturing in the United States has been constant for the last twenty years, plus or minus one million at the twenty million mark. That has not deviated in a generation. The absolute number of jobs in manufacturing in Japan has been nearly static for fifteen years. It is now declining slightly. The virtues of a strong back and a willing, if weak, mind are at an all-time low (Sternlieb and Hughes, 1984).

What we have used our central cities for, very largely, is essentially as repositories for those people who not only may have fallen off the train but perhaps have never gotten on it and never will get on it. With the decline of manufacturing in the United States in terms of its absolute importance, with its shift from the older areas into the newer ones, with the running away from structure and unionization to lack of structure and nonunionization, the older industrial cities are dying. You do not have to invent their future, all you have to do is look at the current reality with a cold, cold eye. There is nobody who can figure out what to do with a used smokestack city—whether it is a Buffalo or a Youngstown—and there are lots of them.

The City Within The City

Within a number of our cities, a very limited number, we are evolving a city within the city. This is the city that the urbanologist visits; this is the city of the tourist. It is a relatively small city. It strikes the eye, it bemuses the mind, it gives the illusion that we are recreating the cities of yesterday in a new format. It is much smaller. To a certain degree, it is much more sophisticated and to a very large degree, it has no relationship to the old functions or, for that matter, in many cases to the people who remain housed within the older city. If you go to a Philadelphia, for example, you see possibly one of the most charming urban environments in the world. You step two or three blocks out of the charmed zone and you are in the middle of the jungle. You have a labor union meeting in one of our principal cities and you have the leadership of the union being chastised because leaflets are given out telling the attendees, "Fellows, here are the appropriate streets—don't walk anywhere else at night." And we keep thinking of these elements as noise rather than the basic message.

In very large part, what we have are people in our larger cities by default of choice. These are cities of transfer payments, not cities of an organic economic meaningfulness. They live or die based upon the transfer of payments from the county, from the state, from the Federal government, and the basic rule of those payments is try to keep the occupants unrebellious, though perhaps sullen (Burchell et al., 1984). Within the cities there are new jobs, but the old jobs are fading away. Again, let me turn to Philadelphia where I have done some work. When the city of Philadelphia, which is a major manufacturing city, loses a hundred manufacturing jobs, seventy of those are held by municipal residents. When the city gains one hundred office jobs, only thirty are held by central city residents—thus the mismatch function.

A good deal is currently being made of the gentrification phenomenon. For the moment at least, with the exception of just a few places in the United States, this is much more an anecdotal reality than a statistical reality. An anecdotal reality is that everybody knows somebody who has brownstoned somewhere, with marvelous tales of profits made, plumbers lost, or whatever the case may be. Statistical reality is when you go out and you do your head counting—you can't find them. When you try to revive downtown retailing, you can't find them. It doesn't mean that it is going to be a minimal phenomenon but, for the moment, it is a very small one.

Now, when you're rich, you throw away many things that the poor treasure. My students, not uncommonly, tell me that it is still possible to go to the dump at any affluent suburb and, in a good weekend, furnish an apartment. But it is getting less possible because when you're rich, you throw away things that poor folk find very useful. When you get a little bit poorer, the definition of an antique becomes younger and younger, furnishing becomes "eclectic" rather than a clutter of used furniture, and you no longer throw away used cities with quite the contempt and abandon that we had in the past.

The only way we will have a return to the city as a mass phenomenon is not out of love, not out of some great font of economic rationalism, but rather because we can't afford the alternative. That's what took place in the Depression. Many planners have had experience with premature subdivisions out in suburbia that were undertaken in the 20's. We turned out as many automobiles in the United States in 1929 as we turned out domestically in 1982. Think about that. We went from 900,000 housing starts in the late 20's to less than 100,000, and we reinvented the central city. There are long-term cycles in our behavior, and sometimes in the exigencies of the moment we tend to forget them.

The allure, the glamour of the city within the city sometimes creates a feeling that all is well; it is not well. Let me take New York City, for example. No. Pardon me, let me amend, the city of Manhattan: The city of Manhattan right now is the hottest real estate market in the United States. Now, that's not saying a hell of a lot because we don't have too many hot central city real estate markets. But, within that fabric, it is the best. Cadillac-Fairview may have reneged on a piece of land at $1900 a square foot—it will get sold for $1400 or $1500 a square foot.

Check by jowl with this new super-world city is a sad fact—in public housing, there are now seventeen thousand units in which doubling up has taken place by count (and then they stopped counting because it is illegal). You have a very uneasy existence of the increasingly impoverished on the one hand and the affluent on the other. The incongruity—any of you who have been in downtown Atlanta after five o'clock at night know this—is all too evident. You really don't have to invent the future. Let me repeat to you, it is here. The jobs that will come into the central city will not be jobs that fit the present characteristics of the occupants thereof.

Let me turn, more specifically, to the city as a whole. The mass generation, the mass market, the center of the pork chop for the builder of yesterday, that immediate post-World War II generation, obviously, has aged. Its successor, the baby-boom group, is splintering. The relative ease with which marketers and builders could ride that baby boom, from the teeny bopper generation to the Gap stores and the branded blue jeans for the older sister's derriere and the like, that was relatively easy, but it has come to an end. We have market segmentation and within each of those several markets, you have critical mass. In New York City, for example, in the last two years, there have been more housing units generated out of the recycling of hitherto nonresidential facilities than were created from scratch. The research center with which I am affiliated did a study of 500 loft convertees (and that is not a study to be taken lightly because the lofts were all illegal and getting into those buildings was an act of genius on our part) and you have in New York—remember, in New York, not elsewhere, necessarily—the answer to the urbanologist's dream: median income well over $30,000; 40% self-employed; very few children; little use of municipal services (Ford, 1979). You can't find a loft in New York; the market, basically, has moved up so very, very rapidly.

The demand for differentiation has never been so strong or so broad. Within this market segmentation, we have reinvented history as a marketing tool. In more cynical moments, you can say that history is the psychological refuge of losers—before we were Romans and now we are Greeks—before we disregarded history, we were vandals, we built from scratch, we desecrated the old, we disregarded the old. But John Wayne is dead. Now we revere the past. We merchandise it, and the intriguing thing is that we are grudgingly beginning to discover that history sells just as well (and the plumbing is infinitely better), if you create new history rather than utilizing true artifacts of the past. So, we have both the true and the make-believe now as mechandising tools.

We are all selling the same merchandise. The issue is how do we package it, whether it's Victoriana, whether it's colonial, whether it's the land of make-believe. We have the triumph of Disney World and Disneyland and it is an appropriate triumph because when you charge $15.00 a day per head, you screen out the unruly. It is history and it is fantasy with charm and plenty of toilets. What could be better! We have the creation of new pulling power for, let's call it the affluent top third of the market. Left outside the wall are those who can't afford the $15.00, and that is a good thing because the rich love the poor but they really don't like playing with them. The poor are very unruly and may not wash frequently enough and, besides, they don't have any money. When you contrast the level of housekeeping within the new synthetic artifact versus the public predecessor artifact, the contrast can bring tears to anybody raised in Prospect Park, as I was. No bashed-in benches, no broken and shattered comfort stations; it is safe, sound, sanitary, and it sells.

What we are going through is an effort of product differentiation, not by changing the product but, essentially, by changing the container. There was a time when I was firmly convinced that all the French restaurants in Washington were connected by an underground pneumatic tube system to one central kitchen. There is no such tube system—it is hot and cold running messengers. Be that as it may, if you go to Ghirardelli Square, if you go to any of the Rouse development, you, in effect, go to Disney World; you go anywhere, it is the same garbage. The only interest is the design of the shopping bag. That's where you come in. This process, which I would have to call the Ghirardelli Squaring of America, and the issue of how many unique and different seaport museums we are going to have, is most intriguing. Just an aside on the seaport museums—we have, in New York, a new one called the South Street Seaport; much to the consternation of the historic preservationists, the developer really would like to take down all those old, dirty buildings and build new, synthetically aged structures.

Within this changing shape of the central city, we have the new drive for defensible space, not in the Oscar Newman "How do I protect some little piece of public housing?" (1973) sense so much as "How do I protect my suburban commuter who I have to bring in town in order to service the buildings which I have created peripheral to the jungle of the cities?" There are recent articles in the *Journal of the American Planning Association* which look at the fortress towers of San Gimignano as the new urban alternative to come (Greenberg and Robe, 1978). So you see, for example, the Prudential Center in Newark with its aerial walkway that links you with the commuter train that goes directly into New York City. If you are reasonably careful, you do not have to breathe the air of the central city. That's very important because that air is not very good. We have the enormous, incredible fiasco of the Renaissance Center in Detroit because, after a while, if you provide enough in the way of security, the consumer says instead of this being a safety blanket, "I'm strangling. And besides, if they offer so much security, maybe I should be scared. I won't go there any more."

Now, let me return to yesteryear. One of the great sort of leitmotifs of the American psyche is represented by the longevity and the popularity, reinvented for every generation, of books such as *Robinson Crusoe* and *Swiss Family Robinson*. There is a marvelous atavistic allure to the concept of "Here is the island, I am master of my fate, I accumulate, I build, I hunt, I fish, I raise food, I am independent of the outside world. I have stopped the world, I have gotten off." I would suggest to you that this is an enormously potent psychopolitical reality. It accounts, in part, for those silly people who scamper around in the California hills preparing to turn away the invaders and the like. We've got lots of them.

We mourn for a lost world or a world that never was. It's a world of neighborhoods, it's a world of closeness, it's a world of self-sufficiency. Some of these elements are self-contradictory, but they are all there. It's a world in which the family unit and/or the individual by himself or herself is essentially independent of the outside environment. Regardless of its validity or lack of validity at any time in the past, there is some substantial question as to its value as a personal guideline for the future. The hope, however, that this is an adequate resolution for the realities of the new world is the most foolish of all fantasies.

The United States is very similar, from an industrial point of view, to the Italian city-states of the fifteenth and sixteenth centuries. And, to remind you they were far advanced from the rest of near-barbarian Europe in terms of industry, commerce, and culture. But the rest of Europe, particularly France and Spain, was pulling itself together in terms of national states, crude and vulgar though they were, and the national states, by the very reason of their organizational capacity, ate up the city-states.

The path to the future, painful as it may be, requires more in the way of national direction and less in the way of "Go do it yourself and somehow or other the invisible hand will bring it all together." That is the painful reality. Within the United States, we do have enormous opportunities, but we will probably not be able to invent or reinvent our central cities at the scale and with the functions of yesterday. There is no yesterday, there is only tomorrow. Within that tomorrow, the central cities will be smaller, but, hopefully, they will have provision for the populations that occupy them. There will be very few world cities and/or fun-and-game cities, that have enough vigor to generate real growth and real forward mobility.

What is going to be required is a much broader revitalization of the implicit social compact that keeps this country glued together. That social compact, basically stated, is the following: "You have a safety net for the poor; you make it possible through specialized institutions for the middle class and the working classes to buy housing and, in return, both groups may envy the rich but they will not kidnap or shoot them."

We are in the process of doing away with that social compact at the very same time that we have to test it with the rise of a new economic function and nationalism in the best sense of the word, not a denigration of the people outside, not a screaming to mama, "They're treating me unfairly. When they choose up games, I end up with the outfield position," but, rather, a reconcentration on what we do well. We do a hell of a lot of things economically, socially, institutionally, very well. We will not become the England of the 1990s—we are infinitely richer. It takes enormous incompetence to raise the shadow of paucity in the future in the United States and to raise it meaningfully. You have to do a hell of a lot of things badly and we have. The issue, in very large part, is how do you cope with a time of transition? How do you pour off or decant population that finds the city, once the land of opportunity, now strictly the land of handout?

References

Burchell, Robert W. et al. (1984). *The New Reality of Municipal Finance: The Rise and Fall of the Intergovernmental City.* New Brunswick, NJ: Center for Urban Policy Research.

Ford, Kristina (1979). *Housing Policy and the Urban Middle Class.* New Brunswick, NJ: Center for Urban Policy Research.

Greenberg, W. and W.M. Robe (1978). "Neighborhood." *Journal of the American Planning Association* 48 (Winter 1984).

Newman, Oscar (1973). *Defensible Space.* New York, NY: Macmillan.

Sternlieb, G. and J. Hughes (1982). *Demographic Trends and Economic Reality.* New Brunswick, NJ: Center for Urban Policy Research.

Sternlieb, G. and J. Hughes (1984). *Income and Jobs: USA.* New Brunswick, NJ: Center for Urban Policy Research.

Sternlieb, G. et al. *Philadelphia's Fiscal Crisis* (unpublished manuscript).

6

The City in a
National Economic Context

George Sternlieb, Robert W. Burchell and Charles M. Wilhelm

The apocalypse is always popular. Whether the Old Testament's Jeremiah, or the millenarian, there is a human leitmotiv which tends to relish the thought of the sky falling. A modest counterpart in our own time has been the new cult of gloom-and-doom extended to the comparative economic competitiveness and confidence in the future of the United States. Thus, there are figures, at both ends of the political spectrum, who have projected with considerable public acclaim a decline and potential fall of the American economy. While both their prescriptions and their diagnoses of the underlying disease may vary, the somber vision is remarkably constant.

In turn, this Gotterdamerung serves as a springboard for a variety of nostrums. Thus, to the right, the United States is slowly being dragged down by self-inflicted wounds: of slackers, of welfare waste, by a failure of the work effort and its concomitant, the hedonistic, unmoral society. Government itself is seen as a reflection and, indeed, an amplifier of these trends; their proposals, in turn, involve a return to the stoic virtues of yesteryear, an unleashing of the forces of free enterprise which "made the country great"—and the severe limitation, or the very dissolution, of the governmental role. The older cities are seen as the epitome of economic/social/political misdoing: focal points of transfer payments rather than production, burdened by overwhelming social costs whose very presence ousts business and enterprise.

To the New Left, the projected twilight comes as a pleasing confirmation of the long sought-for decline of capitalism, confirming the nineteenth century's leading Nostradamus—Karl Marx. Capitalism lacks the legitimacy to withstand the vast changes which are taking place in technology, and the sacrifices and adjustments which will be necessitated by its needs. Indeed, the latter are so formidable as to require a commensurate revolution in social and business organization. The woes of our society, whether among welfare recipients, the unemployed former industrial elite of the steel mills, or automobile workers—indeed, the very decline of our cities—are viewed as cracks in the structure, foretelling its near-term dissolution.

The pressures of an increasingly homogenized worldwide labor force and expertise are seen as semi-phantasies invoked by union busters. They are not part of the right-wing counter revolt against the remnants of the New Deal—and the social revolution which inevitably must come. The cities' plight has been deliberately augmented if not invented by the new conservatives, rather than being a reflection of new technological reality. In turn, a new romantic yearning is brought to life among some critics: Think small; work in personalized units; worker control of shrinking markets and obsolete processes. Scramble in a little isolationism, and you can hold the world—and time—at bay.

Scurrying in the middle of this battlefield of woeful visions are the meliorists, desperately shouting slogans such as "Reindustrialization before it is too late," "10-5-3," "high-tech," or "Look what I did in New York," and a variety of other magic bullets peddled by one or another of the new generation of media economists.

It is the thesis of this article that many of the somewhat casually treated assertations cited above may have substantial validity in the future. It is our further thesis, however, that there is little in the way of statistical support in the immediate past which endorses them. They do indicate in our view, however, even bleaker tomorrows for our central cities.

Contrary to much present wisdom, our assertion is that the country has enjoyed relative economic vigor in the last decade, with unparalleled job growth—and much of it in categories long viewed as urban. The cities' failure to be rejuvenated in this context forecasts continued decline. What did *not happen* in central cities in the course of the 1980s, it seems to us, provides a very telling commentary and strong predictor of their growing obsolescence in the future. This has been cloaked by the thin veneer of UDAG- and EDA-stimulated convention centers and core office structures. The "Rouseian" boutique retail developments are few in potential sites, and at best can not replace the pulling vitality of the giant downtown department stores of yesteryear.

The basic hypothesis of this article is that the trend lines in employment in the United States since 1970 (1) have shown enormous vigor, and (2) have been skewed toward those facets of employment which traditionally are viewed as particularly conducive to central city occupancy. Indeed, forecasts that go back as far as those in the 1920s by the Regional Plan Association, and its work in the classic Vernon/Hoover study in terms of the shape of the new high employment nodes, have come true.[1] Unfortunately, the second part of this prediction, i.e., that the vision of the information economy would tend to be focused physically within central cities, has not. The true test of the future economic viability of cities in the United States—a test which in our estimation they are in the process of failing—lies in the incongruity between the growth of service employment (particularly production services) at unparalleled rates, and the central cities' share of the new dynamic. The latter clearly is inadequate to provide full economic regeneration.

The material which follows serves merely to underline this harsh reality.

Basic Trends in Employment

Exhibit 1 provides a simplified data base reflecting two facets of employment in America from 1940 to 1982. The first is for total employment; the second provides some insight into manufacturing activity. When total non-agricultural employment is viewed, the sheer vitality of the post-World War II economy becomes evident. Those who scoffed at Henry Wallace's call for 60,000,000 jobs, under the fear of a return to the Depression years with the end of World War II, saw 70,000,000 employed in 1970. Even this figure was eclipsed in the decade from 1970 to 1980, with a total job growth of nearly 20 million. And while certainly this has suffered in the downturn of 1982/1983, the absolute decline is relatively trivial.

Within this context, it is evident that manufacturing employment has been relatively stagnant. Indeed, in the last 20 years, manufacturing employment in total has essentially been static at roughly the 20-million mark plus or minus a few percent. A further division of this activity between durable goods and non-durable goods employment does not indicate a particular bias in either direction.

EXHIBIT 1

Trends in Manufacturing, Durable and Non-Durable Goods Employment
United States 1940–1982

Year	Total Non-Agricultural Employment (000)	Manufacturing Employment (000)	Percent	Durable Goods Employment (000)	Percent	Non-Durable Goods Employment (000)	Percent
1940	32,361	10,985	33.9	5,363	16.6	5,622	17.4
1945	40,374	15,524	38.4	9,074	22.5	6,450	16.0
1950	45,197	15,241	33.7	8,094	17.9	7,147	15.8
1955	50,641	16,882	33.3	9,541	18.8	7,341	14.5
1960	54,189	16,796	31.0	9,459	17.4	7,337	13.5
1965	60,765	18,062	29.7	10,405	17.1	7,656	12.6
1970	70,880	19,367	27.3	11,208	15.8	8,158	11.5
1975	76,945	18,323	23.8	10,688	13.9	7,635	9.9
1980	90,405	20,285	22.4	12,187	13.5	8,098	9.0
1981	91,105	20,173	22.1	12,117	13.3	8,056	8.8
1982	89,630	18,848	21.0	11,112	12.4	7,736	8.6

Sources: U.S. Department of Labor, Bureau of Labor Statistics, *Employment and Earnings, United States, 1909–1978* (Bulletin 13 12-11), Washington, D.C., U.S. Government Printing Office, 1979. U.S. Department of Labor, Bureau of Labor Statistics, *Supplement to Employment and Earnings, Revised Establishment Data.* Washington, D.C., U.S. Government Printing Office, 1982. U.S. Department of Labor, Bureau of Labor Statistics, "Employment and Earnings," Vol. 30, No. 3. Washington, D.C.: U.S. Government Printing Office, March 1983. [Based on data from Establishment Reports. Includes all full-time and part-time employees who worked during or received pay for any part of the pay period reported. Excludes proprietors, the self-employed, farmworkers, unpaid family workers, domestic servants, and armed forces.]

The two basic observations embodied in this table are both of great importance to cities. First is near-stagnancy in manufacturing; this is not a new phenomenon, but rather a relatively long-term one. Whether one is turning to the millions of square feet of vacant mill building in Philadelphia, or the depopulated area of Hough in Cleveland, the results are the same: Those cities that have depended upon manufacturing employment growth have indeed been leaning on a very weak reed. Moreover, by the turn of the century, current forecasts suggest a near halving of national manufacturing employment. This is particularly important as we painfully turn to the industrial conurbations which we have in this country labeled as "cities." In Wilbur Thompson's formulation, "We did not, for the most part, build great cities in this country; manufacturing firms agglomerated in tight industrial complexes and formed labor pools of half a million work-ers. . . . There was Detroit . . . the biggest factory town on earth."[2]

Given no-growth in manufacturing, as a whole, coupled with the rise of new areas within the United States to which much manufactur-ing has moved, the decline of the Youngstowns, Clevelands, and all the other older smokestack areas becomes evident. But equally evi-dent is the enormously virile growth of total employment which since 1965 has expanded by approximately 30 million. While the first data may explain the virtual abandonment of Hough and the other blue-collar areas of cities like Cleveland and the equivalent phenomenon in a Gary, or the industrial areas and the housing accompanying them in Philadelphia, the latter should have provided the wherewithal for the new post-industrial cities to flourish with very great vigor indeed.This should have been further fortified by the fact that even within the manufacturing segment, there has been some shift of employment from production to non-production personnel as shown in Exhibit 2. And this group similarly would have been envisioned, a generation or two ago, as fitting quite comfortably within the central cities—while more noxious "elements" might be relegated to the hinterlands.

Similar nominally salubrious trends for cities are evident as the distribution of employment is further analyzed. Exhibit 3, for exam-ple, provides trends in wholesale and retail trade, services and govern-ment employment. The first of these, wholesale and retail trade, was long the premier possession of the central city, and while certainly one of the keynotes of the last generation has been the rise of subur-ban shopping centers and the like, the sheer vitality of total employ-ment within this sector should have been supportive of central city vigor. From 1970 to 1980, for example, there was a growth of abso-lute jobs in this sector in excess of 5 million.

Even more striking is the rapid jump in service employment with a near doubling from 1970 to 1982. By the latter date there were 19 million employed in this sector from a baseline of only 11½ million. And clearly, despite protestations to the contrary, government employment as a percent of total has remained remarkably constant in the face of a variety of efforts and statements to lower it. These were the two premier areas envisioned for the face-to-face contact which dominated the conceptual projections of the Vernon/Hoover group and other thinkers and prognosticators on the future of the central cities.

While government employment may be viewed as a relatively passive secondary derivative of basic population and employment shifts (subject to some programmatic vagaries and policy interventions), service employment was viewed as the locomotive activity which truly would sustain central cities. Even the very distribution of service employment, as sketched out in Exhibits 4 and 5, clearly has little within it which, at least within the classic vision, could not have been housed within central cities.

EXHIBIT 2

Production Workers in the U.S. Economy 1940-1982

Year	All Employees (000)	Production Employees (000)	Percent Production Employees	All Employees (000)	Production Employees (000)	Percent Production Employees
	Total Non-Agricultural Employment			Manufacturing Employment		
1940	32,361	N/A		10,985	8,940	81.4
1945	40,374	N/A		15,524	13,009	83.8
1950	45,197	34,349	76.0	15,241	12,523	82.2
1955	50,641	37,500	74.0	16,882	13,288	78.7
1960	54,189	38,516	71.1	16,796	12,586	74.9
1965	60,765	42,278	69.6	18,062	13,434	74.4
1970	70,880	48,156	67.9	19,367	14,044	72.5
1975	76,945	50,991	66.3	18,323	13,043	71.2
1980	90,406	60,331	66.7	20,285	14,214	70.1
1981	91,105	60,881	66.8	20,173	14,021	69.5
1982	89,630	59,587	66.5	18,848	12,782	67.8
	Durable Goods Employment			Non-Durable Goods Employment		
1940	5,363	4,477	83.5	5,622	4,463	79.4
1945	9,074	7,541	83.1	6,459	5,468	84.8
1950	8,094	6,705	82.8	7,147	5,817	81.4
1955	9,541	7,548	79.1	7,341	5,740	78.2
1960	9,459	7,028	74.3	7,337	5,558	75.8
1965	10,405	7,715	74.1	7,656	5,719	74.7
1970	11,208	8,055	71.9	8,158	5,989	73.4
1975	10,688	7,557	70.7	7,635	5,485	71.8
1980	12,187	8,492	69.7	8,098	5,772	71.3
1981	12,117	8,301	68.5	8,056	5,721	71.0
1982	11,112	7,364	66.3	7,736	5,418	70.0

Sources: U.S. Department of Labor, Bureau of Labor Statistics, Employment and Earnings, United States, 1909-1978 (Bulletin 13 12-11), Washington, D.C., U.S. Government Printing Office, 1979. U.S. Department of Labor, Bureau of Labor Statistics, Supplement to Employment and Earnings, Revised Establishment Data. Washington, D.C.: U.S. Government Printing Office, 1982. U.S. Department of Labor, Bureau of Labor Statistics, "Employment and Earnings," Vol. 30, No. 3. Washington, D.C.: U.S. Government Printing Office, March 1983. [Based on data from Establishment Reports. Includes all full-time and part-time employees who worked during or received pay for any part of the pay period reported. Excludes proprietors, the self-employed, farmworkers, unpaid family workers, domestic servants, and armed forces.]

EXHIBIT 3

Trends in Wholesale and Retail Trade, Services and Government Employment
1940–1982

Year	Total Non-Agricultural Employees (000)	Wholesale and Retail Trade Employment (000)	Percent	Service Employment (000)	Percent	Government Employment (000)	Percent
1940	32,361	6,750	20.8	3,665	11.3	4,202	13.0
1945	40,374	7,314	18.1	4,222	10.4	5,944	14.7
1950	45,197	9,386	20.8	5,357	11.8	6,026	13.3
1955	50,641	10,535	20.8	6,240	12.3	6,914	13.6
1960	54,189	11,391	21.0	7,378	13.6	8,353	15.4
1965	60,765	12,716	20.9	9,036	14.9	10,074	16.6
1970	70,880	15,040	21.2	11,548	16.3	12,554	17.7
1975	76,945	17,060	22.2	13,892	18.0	14,686	19.1
1980	90,406	20,310	22.5	17,890	19.8	16,241	18.0
1981	91,105	20,551	22.6	18,592	20.4	16,024	17.6
1982	89,630	20,551	22.9	19,001	21.2	15,788	17.6

Sources: U.S. Department of Labor, Bureau of Labor Statistics, *Employment and Earnings, United States, 1909-1978* (Bulletin 13 12-11), Washington, D.C., U.S. Government Printing Office, 1979. U.S. Department of Labor, Bureau of Labor Statistics, *Supplement to Employment and Earnings, Revised Establishment Data.* Washington, D.C., U.S. Government Printing Office, 1982. U.S. Department of Labor, Bureau of Labor Statistics, "Employment and Earnings," Vol. 30, No. 3. Washington, D.C.: U.S. Government Printing Office, March 1983.

The incredible growth of health services employment from 1970's barely 3 million to 1982's nearly 6 million, has certainly been enjoyed by central cities. As a function of government-funding efforts—Medicare, Medicaid, SSI, and the like—one sees in central cities the sudden rise of health-services employment as one of the few growth industries, whether in New York or Philadelphia or their midwest equivalent.

Educational services on the other hand, at least at the lower levels, have been relatively static—a victim of the baby bust generation. The initial reinvigoration of central cities through a combination of urban renewal and urban campuses has pretty much come to an end. The limitations of municipal budgets in the light of a shrinking population base, even when fortified by increased levels of transfer payments, suggest a diminution in the future.

Much more sanguine, however, has been the growth of production-service employment—the classic accounting firms, law firms, advertising firms, consultants, etc. This arena has seen a dou-

EXHIBIT 4

Trends in Service Employment 1960–1982

Year	Total Service Employment (000)	Personal Service[1] Employment (000)	Percent	Business Services[2] Employment (000)	Percent	Health Services Employment (000)	Percent	Educational Services Employment (000)	Percent	Membership Organization Employment (000)	Percent	All Other Services[3] Employment (000)	Percent
1960	7,378	894.2	12.1	777.7	10.5	1,547.6	20.0	616.1	8.4	N/A	N/A	3,542.4	48.0
1965	9,036	985.4	10.9	1,138.9	12.6	2,079.5	23.0	772.1	8.5	N/A	N/A	4,060.1	44.9
1970	11,548	989.0	8.6	1,675.5	14.5	3,052.5	26.4	939.6	8.1	N/A	N/A	4,891.4	42.4
1975	13,892	860.9	6.2	2,041.9	14.7	4,133.8	29.8	1,000.9	7.2	1,452.3	10.4	4,402.2	31.7
1980	17,890	900.7	5.0	3,092.0	17.3	5,278.0	29.5	1,138.2	6.4	1,539.3	8.6	5,941.8	33.2
1981	18,592	913.9	4.9	3,255.0	17.5	5,555.1	29.9	1,173.2	6.3	1,529.0	8.2	6,165.8	33.2
1982	19,001	924.5	4.9	3,298.2	17.4	5,776.5	30.4	1,180.5	6.2	1,534.8	8.1	6,286.5	33.1

[1] Personal services includes laundry, cleaning, beauty shops and funeral services.

[2] Business services includes advertising, credit reporting and collection, mailing, reproduction, etc., building services, and computer and data processing services.

[3] "All other services" includes hotels, motels, auto repair services, miscellaneous repair services, motion pictures, amusement and recreation services, engineering and architectural services, and accounting, auditing and bookkeeping services.

Sources: U.S. Department of Labor, Bureau of Labor Statistics, Employment and Earnings, United States, 1909–1978 (Bulletin 13 12-11), Washington, D.C., U.S. Government Printing Office, 1979. U.S. Department of Labor, Bureau of Labor Statistics, Supplement to Employment and Earnings, Revised Establishment Data. Washington, D.C., U.S. Government Printing Office, 1982. U.S. Department of Labor, Bureau of Labor Statistics, "Employment and Earnings," Vol. 30, No. 3. Washington, D.C.: U.S. Government Printing Office, March, 1983.

EXHIBIT 5

**Trends in All Other Services Employment as a Percent of Total Employment
1960–1982**

Year	(000)	Percent Of Total	(000)	Percent Of Total	(000)	Percent Of Total	(000)	Percent Of Total
	Hotels and Other Lodging Places		*Auto Repair Services and Garages*		*Miscellaneous Repair Services*		*Motion Pictures*	
1960	N/A		N/A		N/A		189.6	2.6
1965	N/A		N/A		155.0	1.7	185.1	2.0
1970	N/A		N/A		188.7	1.6	204.1	1.8
1975	898.4	6.4	438.8	3.2	217.5	1.6	205.7	1.5
1980	1,075.8	6.0	570.9	3.2	288.8	1.6	216.9	1.2
1981	1,118.6	6.0	572.3	3.1	296.2	1.6	217.0	1.2
1982	1,099.2	5.8	579.5	3.0	294.3	1.5	211.8	1.1
	Amusement and Recreation		*Legal Services*		*Social Services*		*Miscellaneous*	
1960	N/A		144.0	2.0	N/A		N/A	
1965	N/A		181.5	2.0	N/A		N/A	
1970	N/A		236.0	2.0	N/A		N/A	
1975	396.8	4.3	340.3	2.4	689.9	5.0	723.5	5.2
1980	763.5	4.3	497.7	2.8	1,134.3	6.3	977.4	5.6
1981	772.6	4.2	532.4	2.9	1,156.6	6.2	1,044.7	5.6
1982	837.1	4.4	566.4	3.0	1,183.2	6.2	1,061.3	5.6

Sources: U.S. Department of Labor, Bureau of Labor Statistics, *Employment and Earnings, United States, 1909–1978* (Bulletin 13 12-11), Washington, D.C., U.S. Government Printing Office, 1979. U.S. Department of Labor, Bureau of Labor Statistics, *Supplement to Employment and Earnings, Revised Establishment Data.* Washington, D.C., U.S. Government Printing Office, 1982. U.S. Department of Labor, Bureau of Labor Statistics, "Employment and Earnings," Vol. 30, No. 3. Washington, D.C.: U.S. Government Printing Office, March 1983.

bling since 1970. Certainly when one looks at the tenant list in many of the new central city skyscrapers, this is the group which is most heavily represented. And yet, despite its growth, it has been insufficient to maintain the total job base of our largest central cities. Moreover, in the future, there is very clear evidence of a growing tendency toward dispersion as the campus-office park in suburbia and indeed exurbia begins to become a major presence.

In Exhibit 5 we have broken out other services by major category. While the time series are insufficient in some cases to give a long perspective, they do provide support for the basic thesis, i.e., a considerable vigor in the growth within job categories which historically have been viewed as central-city prerogatives.

While there are some deviations in the basic trend lines of employment change from 1960 to 1970, and 1970 to 1980, once again the basic thesis is supported. If central cities could not maintain their economic vigor within the context of this redefinition of national job profile, their future as major job hubs must be seriously questioned as labor growth contracts in the 1990s, courtesy of the baby bust generation.

Conclusions

The long era of national economic vigor has essentially bypassed the major central cities of the nation. If they could not stabilize within prosperity, can they survive the increasing stress on cost/benefit analysis of our own relatively low-growth time? Despite a job base "pie" which classic analysis envisioned as uniquely conducive to central city growth, there has been no general reinvigoration. For the first time in history there is more office building outside of America's central cities than with them—and this *before* the full tide of decentralization-facilitating technology is on the scene. *Central city economic decline is not a mere accompaniment of general national job lethargy but rather, at least in major part, independent of it. The pleas for redress, whether of the right or the left, face an enormously potent degenerative inertia which will not easily be corrected.*

Efforts at political steering, of legislating central-city location, such as those promulgated in the dying days of the Carter administration and epitomized by the Community Conservation Guidelines, could not mobilize a real constituency. While lip service may be given to their reinstitution in the future, there is little to be hoped for.

Yet in the face of this harsh reality the planning community as a whole has made and is making little positive contribution. Too many of its most talented members have fallen prey to the temptation to be villain hunters: "Who killed Cock Robin?" This is a worthwhile effort for historians but scarcely worthy of a mass effort.

Much more pertinent is to turn from "would have been, could have been, should have been" to a consideration of what is and will be. There is far less glamour to coping with decline than vigor, more psychic joy perhaps in looking for the past turning point and isolating the lines of force that led to the downward road, than in coping with reality. But the latter is the planners' professional responsibility.

Notes

1. R. Vernon and E.M. Hoover, *Anatomy of a Metropolis* (New York, NY: Doubleday, 1959).
2. George Sternlieb and James W. Hughes, *Post-Industrial America: Metropolitan Decline and Interregional Job Shifts* (New Brunswick, NJ: Center for Urban Policy Research, 1975).

7

The Uncertain Future of the Central City

George Sternlieb and James W. Hughes

The major central cities of the United States no longer are the key growth nodes of society. The demographic trend lines of the past decade raise to new heights the crisis of function of the American city. Its major historic role in this country had been as recipient of successive waves of immigrants, which provided a unique focal point for the agglomeration of manufacturing operations. It was the only place that could supply masses of workers for the emergence of mass production after the Civil War. For virtually a century thereafter, the city provided entrepreneurs with a source of cheap labor; and for the migrant to it, the city offered employment at levels of skill he could meet.

But the last generation has seen the end of this historic linkage of manufacturing activity and urban location. A worldwide revolution has occurred in the technologies of goods production, information processing, and communications. Automation and technological change have rationalized labor-intensive industries, undermining the traditional economic foundations of America's cities. While adaptations to a new industrial order have been made, the demographics of the 1970s bear witness to the harsh realities of the transformation.

From *Urban Affairs Quarterly*, Vol. 18, No. 4, June 1983, pp. 455–472. Copyright © 1983 by Sage Publications, Inc. Reprinted by permission of Sage Publications, Inc.

Although population trends are far from all-encompassing criteria of the phenomena, they do provide a major focal point, the full implications of which sometimes are overlooked.[1] During the decade of the 1970s, for example, central cities in total for the first time experienced absolute population losses. As shown in Exhibit 1, their faltering is evident. While the population of the United States as a whole was rising by an estimated 11.5 percent, central cities (as defined in 1970) actually lost population. By the end of the decade, the nonmetropolitan head count of the nation exceeded that within central cities by over 11 million people. The urban history of the United States was characterized by the concentration of development initially in central cities and then within their close-in suburban areas. This process clearly has aborted.

The very loose definition of central cities in the aggregate cloaks the demographic withdrawals which have overtaken the aging industrial cores of America. The scale of population contraction afflicting the once-dominant urban giants has been monumental. As shown in Exhibit 2, nine of America's major cities have lost more than a quarter of their population base in the past 30 years; leading the sad procession of losers are St. Louis (−47.1 percent), Buffalo (−38.3 percent), Pittsburgh (−37.4 percent), Cleveland (−37.3 percent), and Detroit (−34.9 percent). And it is apparent from the data in Exhibit 2 that the process of population shrinkage accelerated over the decade of the 1970s.

EXHIBIT 1

Metropolitan and Nonmetropolitan Population, 1970 to 1980, U.S. Total
(Numbers in Millions)

	1970	1980	Average Annual Percent Change
Total SMSAs	139.4	151.8	0.9%
Central Cities	63.8	63.1	−0.1
Outside Central Cities	75.6	88.7	1.7
Nonmetropolitan Areas	63.8	74.7	1.7
Total U.S.	203.2	226.5	1.1

Notes: Covers 243 SMSAs as defined in 1970 census publications

Source: U.S. Department of Commerce, Bureau of the Census, *Census of Population, 1970 and 1980*

EXHIBIT 2

Population Change, Selected Cities
1950 to 1980

City	1950[1]	1970[2]	1980[3]	Change: 1950–1980		Change: 1970–1980	
				Number	Percent	Number	Percent
Boston	801,444	641,071	562,994	−238,450	−29.8	−78,077	−12.2
Buffalo	580,132	462,768	357,870	−222,262	−38.3	−104,898	−22.7
Chicago	3,620,962	3,369,357	3,005,072	−615,890	−17.0	−364,285	−10.8
Cincinnati	503,998	453,514	385,457	−118,541	−23.5	−68,057	−15.0
Cleveland	914,808	750,879	573,822	−340,986	−37.3	−177,057	−23.6
Detroit	1,849,568	1,514,063	1,203,339	−646,229	−34.9	−310,724	−20.5
Minneapolis	521,718	434,400	370,951	−150,767	−28.9	−63,449	−14.6
New York City	7,891,957	7,895,563	7,071,030	−820,927	−10.4	−824,533	−10.4
Newark	438,776	381,930	329,248	−109,528	−25.0	−52,682	−13.8
Philadelphia	2,071,605	1,949,996	1,688,210	−383,395	−18.5	−261,786	−13.4
Pittsburgh	676,806	520,089	423,938	−252,868	−37.4	−96,151	−18.5
St. Louis	856,796	622,236	453,085	−403,711	−47.1	−169,151	−27.2

Notes: [1] April 1, 1950 Census.
[2] April 1, 1970 Census.
[3] April 1, 1980 Census.

Sources: U.S. Bureau of the Census, *County and City Data Book, 1956* (A Statistical Abstract Supplement), U.S. Government Printing Office, Washington, D.C., 1957; and U.S. Bureau of the Census, *Commerce News*, "Three Cities of 100,000 or More At Least Doubled Population Between 1970 and 1980, Census Bureau Reports," CB81-92, Public Information Office, Washington, D.C., June 3, 1981

As a result, the maintenance of infrastructure becomes increasingly difficult as the user base recedes, self-raised revenues depart with population, and near vacuums begin to be generated in hitherto-viable areas. There would be no national focus on the trauma of the South Bronx if New York City's population had expanded beyond the peak of slightly under 8 million people which was achieved during the 1960s. Similarly, the thousands of abandoned homes of Detroit, though often viewed as a tribute to the ineptitude of federal housing programs, clearly had their demand base swept away by the disastrous shift of population away from the city. From mass-transit ridership to the viability of shoe-shine parlors on Main Street, the thinning out of the central city reduces the motor power of the metropolis.

The shifts of American population that presently are occurring clearly are much broader than those of the classic suburban growth highlighted in the immediate post-World War II era. Suburbanites, if nothing more, were by definition within calling distance of core services, retailing, cultural activities, and the like. The evolution presently taking place is to areas external even to the new ring city, which has been established on the circumferential highways—the last monuments to the National Highway Program. This is often at radii twenty miles or more from the traditional urban core. The critical mass of services that has been established on the ring, not least among them the enclosed suburban shopping mall, provides an alternative to "downtown." Perhaps even more harmful is the flow of regional population shifts which has thinned out the regions within which our older industrial cities are concentrated.

The combination of these elements is measured by the demographic disaster which has overtaken the major northeastern/midwestern cities detailed in Exhibit 2; it is far from exclusive to them, however. Subject to statistical distortion as a function of annexation, clearly it is intruding on some of the newer high-growth southwestern cities as well.

Migration

The vast migrational trek of Americans is illustrated in the data of Exhibit 3. In the period from 1965 to 1970, migration into and out of metropolitan areas was nearly in balance, with only a slight leakage to nonmetropolitan areas. But a decade later the latter had become a substantial flow, with a net outmigration from the metropolitan areas—long viewed as the most vibrant growth sectors of American society—well in excess of a million individuals for each five-year tabulation. It is the central city which highlights this process, with net outmigration from 1970 to 1980 of more than 13-million persons. While the suburbs continued to expand, it was at a faltering rate, far outweighed by the losses of the core. And it is most striking to note that the outflow from the central city has been joined in by blacks as well as whites, with net outmigration as shown in Exhibit 3 accelerating very sharply in the latter half of the decade.

The Decline of Resident Income and Buying Power

The differential migration flows into and out of the central city are evidenced not only in number, but also in income, as shown in Exhibit 4. There is a very clear linkage: The higher the family income

EXHIBIT 3

Migration Patterns
(Numbers in Thousands of Persons)

Metropolitan and Nonmetropolitan Migration:
1965-70, 1970-75, and 1975-80

	1965-70	*1970-75*	*1975-80*
Metropolitan:			
Inmigrants	5,457	5,127	5,993
Outmigrants	5,809	6,721	7,337
Net migration	−352	−1,594	−1,344
Nonmetropolitan:			
Inmigrants	5,809	6,721	7,337
Outmigrants	5,457	5,127	5,993
Net migration	+352	+1,594	+1,344

Central-City and Suburban Migration:
1970-75 and 1975-80

	1970-75	*1975-80*
Central cities:		
Inmigrants	5,987	6,891
Outmigrants	13,005	13,237
Net migration	−7,018	−6,346
Suburbs:		
Inmigrants	12,732	13,628
Outmigrants	7,309	8,627
Net migration	+5,423	+5,001

Central-City and Suburban Migration of Blacks:
1970-75 and 1975-80

	1970-75	*1975-80*
Central cities:		
Inmigrants	737	724
Outmigrants	980	1,163
Net migration	−243	−439
Suburbs:		
Inmigrants	827	1,123
Outmigrants	446	567
Net migration	+381	+556

Source: U.S. Bureau of the Census, Current Population Reports, Series P-20, No. 368, *Geographical Mobility, March 1975 to March 1980*, U.S. Government Printing Office, Washington, D.C., 1981.

EXHIBIT 4

Central City Migration by Families: 1975 to 1980[1]
(Numbers in Thousands)

	Movers from:		Ratio of Suburb Movers to Central-City Movers
Family Income[2]	Central City to Suburbs	Suburbs to Central City	
Under $5,000	20	21	0.95
$5,001 to $9,999	133	68	1.66
$10,000 to $14,999	244	100	2.44
$15,000 to $24,999	744	262	2.84
$25,000 and over	1,020	313	3.26
Total	2,161	764	2.83

Note: [1]Married couple (husband–wife) families with householder (head) 14 to 54 years of age

[2]Income in 1979

Source: U.S. Bureau of the Census, Current Population Reports, Series P-20, No. 368, Geographical Mobility: March 1975 to March 1980, U.S. Government Printing Office, Washington, D.C., 1981.

level, the greater the propensity for the direction of migration to be from central city to suburb; conversely, the lower the income level, the greater the propensity for suburb to central city migration. For example, for families with incomes under $5,000, the absolute flows were roughly equal; for those with incomes of $25,000 and over, the ratio of suburban movers to central city movers was at the 3.26 mark. To restate this crucial factor, for every three families with incomes of $25,000 and over that moved from the central city to the suburbs in the period from 1975 to 1980, only one moved from the suburbs to the central city.

This is merely to highlight the crest of the wave of comparative decline in central city incomes. Exhibit 5, for example, provides data on median family incomes by geographic area from 1975 to 1980. Families living inside central cities or major (1,000,000 or more persons) metropolitan areas—the category which encompasses our aging, industrial concentrations—had the smallest income increments of any of the groups isolated here in absolute dollars. Indeed, by 1980, they had the lowest absolute incomes of any of the geographic partitions shown, except those living outside metropolitan areas. (The latter case is deflated by the pockets of rural poverty which still dot much of America, particularly in the South and Northeast.) By 1980, the

EXHIBIT 5

Median Family Income
1975 to 1980[1]

Residence by Metropolitan Area Size	1975	1980	Change: 1975 to 1980	
			Number	Percent
Inside Metropolitan Areas	$14,909	$22,590	$7,681	51.5%
1,000,000 Persons or More	15,550	23,825	8,275	53.2
Inside Central Cities	12,957	18,908	5,951	45.9
Outside Central Cities	17,156	26,339	9,183	53.5
Under 1,000,000 Persons	14,139	21,317	7,178	50.8
Inside Central Cities	13,031	19,817	6,786	52.1
Outside Central Cities	14,859	22,393	7,534	50.7
Outside Metropolitan Areas	11,600	18,069	6,469	55.8
U.S. Total (All Families)	13,719	21,023	7,304	53.2

Note: [1] Income during calendar years 1975 and 1980

Source: U.S. Bureau of the Census, Current Population Reports, Series P-60, No. 127, *Money Income and Poverty Status of Families and Persons in the United States: 1980 (Advance Data from the March 1981 Current Population Survey)*, U.S. Government Printing Office, Washington, D.C., 1981. U.S. Bureau of the Census, Current Population Reports, Series P-60, No. 105, *Money Income in 1975 of Families and Persons in the United States*, U.S. Government Printing Office, Washington, D.C., 1977.

suburbanites of our major metropolitan areas had incomes nearly half again as high as those within the same areas' central cities.

The discrepancy is far more muted as we consider smaller metropolitan areas, those with under one-million persons. Here, central city incomes are under the $20,000 mark, with their equivalent suburbanites slightly in excess of $22,000—a far-from-trivial discrepancy of 10 percent. But this category is bolstered by the newer smaller cities located in the burgeoning national "sunbelt."

As a consequence of lagging central city income, and a general growth in the nation's poverty population in the past decade, increasingly the central city has become a refuge for those unable to migrate from it. By 1980, as shown in Exhibit 6, more than one-in-six persons (17.2 percent) residing in central cities fell below the poverty level. The equivalent figure for the suburbs (outside central cities) was less than one in twelve (8.2 percent). And this is a gap which had widened over the course of the 1970 to 1980 decade.

The nation's statistical ledgers document a faltering central city, characterized by heavy outmigration (particularly by the more affluent), absolute population losses, lagging incomes, and growing

EXHIBIT 6

Persons Below Poverty Level
(Numbers in Thousands)

	1970		1980	
	Number	Percent	Number	Percent
Total	24,877	12.3	29,272	13.0
Inside Metropolitan Areas	15,348	10.8	18,021	11.9
Inside Central Cities	9,090	15.0	10,644	17.2
Outside Central Cities	6,259	7.6	7,377	8.2
Outside Metropolitan Areas	10,529	15.4	11,251	15.4

Source: U.S. Bureau of the Census, Current Population Reports, Series P-60, No. 127, *Money Income and Poverty Status of Families and Persons in the United States: 1980 (Advance Data from the March 1981 Current Population Survey)*, U.S. Government Printing Office, Washington, D.C., 1981. U.S. Bureau of the Census, Current Population Reports, Series P-60, No. 105, *Money Income in 1975 of Families and Persons in the United States*, U.S. Government Printing Office, Washington, D.C., 1977.

concentrations of poverty. This statistical reality stands in marked contrast to visible stirrings of a more positive note—of an urban resurgence, of areas revitalized through brownstoning, of new office buildings on the city skyline, of new hotel and convention complexes, and of new playgrounds and consumption spaces of the affluent (or at least the business person on an expense account). While less susceptible to quantification (and perhaps dwarfed in scale by the demographics depicted above), this rebirth remarkably co-exists with the phenomenon of increasing central city impoverishment.

The Two Cities

Thus, the vision of the city becomes strikingly bipolar: on the one hand the city of the poor with anywhere from one-quarter (Boston) to one-seventh (New York) of the population on welfare; of crime rates that stagger the imagination even when appropriate allowance is made for their vagaries; and of truancy levels vastly understated by official reporting techniques, which make a mockery of the traditional role of public education as a homogenizing influence and ladder upward for the urban proletariat.

Separate and distinct from this—though frequently in physical proximity, it is psychologically and fiscally at a vast distance—is the city of the elite. Varying in scale from a very few select blocks in some municipalities to substantial and growing population thresholds in others is the city whose inhabitants are matched to the new post-manufacturing job base, peopled by groups who do not require or utilize the impacted local service base.

Typically, they are either childless or sending their children to select private schools, never to be found in the overcrowded municipal hospitals, and certainly not dependent on the welfare provisions of the city. While their actual numbers may be relatively few, they inhabit the city of the tourist and the visitor. Since they are relatively novel, as distinct from the overstudied masses, they attract perhaps more attention than their numbers warrant from observers both amateur and learned. Indeed, so vigorous are the numbers of studies of such individuals as to magnify their importance and in turn to generate the new buzzword of "gentrification."

The functional reality of new cities is easily summarized: There are a select number of non-smokestack cities which bear the visible signs of compatibility with a post-industrial economy. This is evidenced by the dominance of major service-production facilities—the massive office buildings which characterize the new downtowns. Their tight clusterings attain even more visible mass with the appearance of the increasingly vigorous central city hotel–convention phenomenon. But this represents only in part an increase in accommodations; rather more strikingly, it also reflects a replacement of old, no-longer-adequate facilities—geared for lower-income groups—with new, highly visible structures whose patronage is divided between serving as an accessory to production services and information processing on the one hand, and the city as elite consumption hub on the other.

In select cities, complementary residential appendages have arisen, paralleling this economic growth. Again, in turn, these represent more of a recompaction of the more affluent central city strata from crumbling neighborhoods than they do net inmigration.

However, in the very act of bringing these groups together, a critical mass of appeal is generated which in turn fosters a greater pulling power of the center city as alternative life-style. It is this phenomenon which has given birth to the image of urban revitalization, with the imperial city of Washington, D.C., given its unparalleled job base in the van, with New York City certainly, and Philadelphia, if less so, showing remarkable vigor.

But the dimensions of this vitality should not be exaggerated. The demographic trend lines provide little evidence indicative of a widespread process of gentrification. Indeed, they are sufficiently somber to dim the potential of the new "vibrant kernels."

In terms of employment, the passing of the age of manufacturing has not been fully compensated by the rise of in-city service industry replacements.[2] The recent development of automation within the office sector—of the rationalization of labor-intensive, white-collar activities—is perhaps even more striking than its predecessors in manufacturing. The absolute scale of central city employment, with few exceptions, is at best constant—and much more commonly shrinking. The gap between the skills, work habits, and acceptance accorded the poor (particularly the minority poor) and the requirements of the new occupations has resulted in a mismatch between the bulk of central city residents and the jobs proximate to their homes. Thus, one finds very high levels of unemployment cheek by jowl with basic shortages of skilled clerical personnel. And on a more mundane level, the savage attrition which has taken place in central city resident incomes as a function of selective migration has reduced the opportunities for small-scale service operations. In this context, the potential for resident services provided by fledgling entrepreneurs must endure a most hostile incubator.

The existence of the two-cities phenomenon, and the extreme disparity between the human elements that characterize the segments, are shown in Exhibit 7. This provides data on a variety of parameters for the universe of New York City renters compared with the new elite inhabiting the much-publicized converted buildings and new private structures constructed under recent tax incentive provisions. The new elite are characterized by their relative youthfulness, high incomes, and concentration in the new prestige occupations (including the burgeoning artistic professions) as compared to the overall city renter profile.

Reconciliation

Is there a potential reconciliation between these two elements? Are we doomed to have a city of Manhattan—and a city of the rest of New York? A city of North Michigan Avenue—and a city of the rest of Chicago? Indeed, are there possibilities of a political as well as functional split?

The real necessities which we believe will emerge are very simple—at least in our more socially advanced areas. Much of the ser-

EXHIBIT 7

**Occupant Characteristics of New Residential
Structures, New York City, 1977**

Category	New York City Total[1]	New Structures (Tax Incentives)	Converted Buildings	
			Apartments	Lofts
Household Income	$8,395	$26,302	$21,479	$22,253
Occupation				
Professional/ Technical	13.6%	41.7%	38.2%	33.2%
Manager/ Administrator	7.8	26.0	21.3	18.7
Artist	2.1	8.8	15.7	35.0
Clerical	27.1	4.4	3.7	2.3
Craftsman/ Operative	25.2	1.4	1.1	2.3
Median Age	44.4 years	33.6 years	29.6 years	34.0 years

Note: [1]1975 data.

Source: Kristina Ford, *Housing Policy and the Urban Middle Class* (New Brunswick, N.J.: Rutgers University, Center for Urban Policy Research, 1978).

vices upon which the poor are dependent are linked to the fiscal vigor of the city which is called on to provide them. From this point of view each new downtown ratable, rather than being at best unimportant—at worst a potential threat to the poor—is rather a triumph. Cities can provide adequate social services within our political environment only if they are cities of economic vigor. There is no flow of transfer payments from state or federal governments, at least currently on the horizon, which will obviate this basic reality. Bankrupt cities reduce services first. The lessons of municipal cutbacks are all too clear-cut in this regard. National funding is an inadequate surrogate given local variance in standards and the increasing voter predominance of relatively socially conservative regions.

If cities are to be reconstructed, what is going to be required is a reconciliation between the two warring parties. *The poor need the rich.* If nothing more, the history of the last twenty years indicates that if the cities become wards of the state, the latter is far less generous and the quality of social services is far more limited.

The poor need the city of resource. In order for cities to flourish, however, they must secure flexibility of land use, a capacity to entice truly significant levels of the affluent to stay—and hopefully even to return to them. The myth of gentrification as a large-scale phenomenon has created alarm well in advance of any commensurate reality. The "two cities" are increasingly dominated by the poor yet there are potentials for positive rebirth. These may well abort. The cooperation of the bulk of the extant population is essential. America's urban future requires many inputs—but certainly not least among them is forestalling the adversary relationship which is evolving between the "two cities."

Notes

1. There are a limited number of economic measuring sticks available for the central city. To a certain degree, their very scarcity indicates some of the priorities of our society. For example, nearly a decade and a half after the urban riots, data on central city employment is still limited essentially to those cities coterminous with counties. For reasons lost in history, metropolitan labor markets reflect society's interests of generations ago in providing labor availability data for the growth of business.

    Thus the vigor of cities per se in this crucial parameter is difficult to ascertain. The latter are left to the varying interests of states, some of whom collect material by municipality under their state-covered employment programs. Even with these latter, however, there is a lack of standardization, which makes generalizations more than inadequate. Reviews undertaken at the Center for Urban Policy Research indicate a general urban decline in market share at best—and in absolute level in all too many cases. In both situations this is complicated by the misfit of the central city's current population's training and education to the post-industrial functions which dominate its job base growth.

2. The three poles of central city business and service demand have historically been divided into, first, resident population (the data presented previously documents the attrition which has taken place); second, the daytime population—the commuters who work in the city—but given the folkways of our society, these are increasingly users of suburban services as well; and third, and the most difficult to weigh—those who are brought to the city from areas external to it by its unique pulling power—its unique competence to provide services and/or experiences which are exceptional. There are very few places that have this quality.

Once one leaves the immediacies of a New York, a San Francisco, a Boston and perhaps a half dozen others, this most important of all central city facets clearly has waned most substantially.

The sum of these developments is reflected by the changing role of central city retailing, particularly the old monolithic department store of yesteryear. Sited at the very nexus of the city's transportation web, it catered to all socioeconomic elements within a very substantial reach. Its new equivalent tends to be a much more highly specialized operation, and typically not much more than one-fifth its size. A splendid case in point is the decline of the historic department store giants of the Chicago Loop in favor of the relatively small emporia of the North Michigan Avenue area, or the dissolution of the old retailing palaces that dominated Philadelphia in favor of the relatively compact Galleria, and the like. These reflect the city-within-the-city theme—but may have little relevance, little meaning, and sometimes deliberately, little appeal to the external city.

8

New York City:
The Trauma of Emergence
Into the Post-Industrial Era

George Sternlieb and James W. Hughes

Introduction

New York City always has been an amalgam of the rich and the poor,
straddling an uneasy middle class, separate and distinct from each of
them. The stresses between the several groups were never trivial and
frequently bubbled to the surface; as witness stands a long history of
urban riots and labor warfare. But within this context, there was a
logic and economic rationale which tended to provide common
denominators.

An evolving post-industrial world has shattered that balance.
New York is coping with the necessity of putting together a new realpolitik consonant with both the limitations and new potentials of its
economy. The process is hindered by a failure to comprehend the
irrevocable changes both in demographics and economic functions
which must be accepted for a successful shaping of the future. The city
as we have known it, and the forms of social and economic organization which have characterized it, are simply irrecoverable. From the
viewpoint of the poor, the city of goods production, of large-scale rela-

From *The Metropolis Era*, ed. by Mattei Dogan and John D. Kasarda, Beverly Hills,
CA: Sage, Inc., 1986. Reprinted with permission.

tively unskilled employment, has become the city of redistribution—of transfer payments and welfare. For the elite there is a city—far from new, but increasingly vigorous—of information processing and economic facilitation, of consumption rather than production. Lost between these two poles and fast disappearing are the middle groups. They find both the lifestyles and economic opportunities of suburbia (and increasingly exurbia) affordable and much more fulfilling.

Unlike the cities of the Third World, the pressures of population growth per se have subsided. In contrast with the older industrial hubs of the West, a successful new economy is emerging. The real crisis of New York is not embodied in the care of the poor, the cleaning of its streets, or even in crime rates, potent though these factors may be. It is rather the socio-political difficulties involved in the shifts of function. Can the city adapt to its post-industrial future? Or will it be submerged by the pressures of the past?

There is an enormous difference in goal structures between the two groups—the poor and the elite—who increasingly dominate the urban political arena. It has many aspects but is perhaps most easily characterized in terms of attitudes toward housing and municipal expenditures. In the former regard, the poor seek inexpensive shelter. They look toward the city either to provide housing directly, or to manage the private market so as to assure low rents and minimal increments in shelter costs. Indeed the extreme difference with the elite is captured by the stress on housing as shelter. To the elite caught up in a post-shelter society, housing increasingly is viewed as a form of investment. To them, the goal is capital enhancement through increase in housing value. They have the resources for housing purchase either in fee-simple, or condominium/cooperative forms of ownership. They have the tax status that practically demands housing ownership. Thus to the affluent group, housing as shelter from the elements is far less important than housing as a tax shelter. While the poor are victimized by housing cost/price increases, to the affluent they are the justification for investment.

Municipal politics increasingly has as one of its irritants the rival housing demands of the two groups: the one seeking neighborhood improvement, enhanced values and ownership; the other fearful that any change will increase their rents, that changes for the benefit of the affluent might endanger their own facilities. While the situation sketched here is far from perfectly defined—as witness the love affair of affluent renters with rent control—the schism is becoming increasingly evident.

The variants in housing policy goals are paralleled by attitudes toward the municipal budget. To the poor, municipal expenditures on health, education and welfare are among the few rays of light in an otherwise dismal environment. To the new elite groups in the cities, these are extraneous. In their place are rather environment-enhancing—and real estate price-increasing—investments in parks, recreational facilities, libraries and the like. The yin-yang of this conflict dominates budget meetings in every major city in America.

But these are merely two facets of a struggle which is increasingly securing definition: the rival roles of the city as the port of last resort for those who have fallen off, or who were never able to secure passage on, the economic train versus the city as an entity whose care and enhancement, by very definition, require a restructuring in order to recapture the affluent. The common interest is often obscured. Social expenditures are increasingly dependent on locally raised revenues. This requires the provision of a variety of incentives for land use activities which will generate more in the way of revenues than costs. However, the process conflicts with the provision of amenities and necessities for the poor and, perhaps even more strikingly, with their sense of priorities. Fear leads to immobility. And this in turn may endanger the city's future.

Organization

This paper is organized into four major sections, starting with overviews of the broader economic and demographic context. The details of New York's new economic base, and its demographic mismatch, are then presented.

International and National Economic Framework

Employment trends and industrial structures of the United States and five industrialized nations are compared, and New York City's employment profile is set in the context of that of the United States.

Population: The Broader Context

Population growth rates of the U.S. and OECD nations are reviewed, and the major distributional shifts within the U.S. are presented, including regional, metropolitan and central city trends.

New York City's New Economy

> The 1970s' economic turnaround in New York is examined, the emerging employment structure detailed, and future economic opportunities and threats suggested.

The Demographic Dilemma

> The shifting composition of the city's population is analyzed and the mismatch to the new economy evaluated. Income and housing cost parameters are also reviewed.

International and National Economic Framework

Cities in the United States, particularly within the aging industrial heartland, have been struggling to adapt to a changing worldwide economic environment. The great manufacturing metropolitan areas are lagging, their long-term regenerative capacity severely tested. Before delving into the immediacies of New York City, and its response to the new imperatives, a broader economic perspective is required. This section will briefly highlight the changing employment patterns and industrial structures of the United States and five industrialized nations, and provide a preliminary overview of New York City's employment matrix in the context of that of the United States.

Employment and Industrial Structure: International

Broad economic cycles have always set a challenge for national economies and their cities. This has been particularly the case in the post-1973 period, when the energy revolution brought sharp changes to the industrialized world. A decade of economic shocks hastened the process of economic evolution; nowhere is this more evident than in the United States.

The gross parameters of civilian employment in the United States compared to some of the major developed nations provide insight into the phenomena at work. The absolute and relative growth of U.S. employment from 1970 to 1982 has little parallel in the four major western European countries, nor for that matter in Japan. The total employment increase in the U.S. was very comparable to the *total* employment base of France or Italy, and barely lagged the *total* number of jobs extant in Great Britain or Germany. While the U.S.

job increase was more than a quarter (26.5 percent), the pattern was actually negative for the four European countries combined, with a net reduction of 0.4 percent. Germany and Great Britain each lost more than one million jobs over the 12-year period, with total civilian employment declining by 3.9 percent and 5.6 percent, respectively. Japan, in contrast, represents a far more salubrious picture. Its absolute employment growth approached 6 million jobs, or 11.6 percent. This rate of increase, however, is less than 40 percent of the U.S. equivalent; in absolute job growth it represents less than 30 percent of the gain of the United States.

While the use of 1982—the recession trough—as a terminal year in this data sweep may introduce some distortions, it is apparent that the American economy has been a job-generating machine. In the broad, then, its cities are not constrained by total national job-creation stagnation. It is the changing mix of employment—and its ultimate geographic loci—which provide the challenge.

Comparisons with the same set of major industrial nations underscore the disparate sectoral growth patterns. The basic picture is a relatively static one in the goods-producing sectors for *all* of the countries. The United States from 1970 to 1982 experienced minor growth; the several European countries collectively were stagnant at best, while Japan's gain in goods-producing employment, though slightly larger than that of the United States, was still modest. (It should be noted that Japan includes utilities in its definition, unlike the United States.)

It is not surprising that the service-producing sector demonstrated absolute growth in all the nations. What is startling is the unique level and scale of the expansion in the United States. Thus while the pattern of services enlargement is international, the United States leads the procession with an absolute increase of 20,000,000 jobs in this sector alone. This is nearly twice the total in France, Germany, Italy, Great Britain, and Japan combined. And, as the United States faces a future in which labor-intensive, goods-producing employment increasingly is seen as the province of the newly industrializing nations, it is the service sector which must compensate. To the degree that this statement has validity, the United States has progressed much further (has less adjustment to make) than its peers.

It is of interest to note the pattern in agriculture. The United States, with the exception of Great Britain, has the smallest proportion of its labor force involved in this sector. And the absolute level is declining. Again, with the exception of Great Britain, the problems of

agriculture displacement, as opportunities in this domain shrink, may
be much more substantial for the other major industrial nations. But
in the U.S. a potential source of new urban recruits has been virtually
depleted. The great era of the rise of the city as an industrial mecca,
strengthened by agricultural displacees, is at an end in the more
mature industrial nations, unlike the situation in the Third World.

The National Transformation and New York

A preliminary overview of New York City's changes within this
broader transformation is provided in Exhibit 1 and emphasizes the
changes that have taken place. Despite substantial national total
growth, New York's employment base has experienced long-term contraction. As will be noted in a later section, decline actually halted in
1976, with modest growth occurring subsequent to that point.
Nonetheless, the 1983 employment level was still 10 percent below
that of 1969. In the aggregate, the city did not reflect the overall
national job surge.

New York City did experience expansion in two of the fastest-
growing national industrial sectors—finance, insurance and real estate,
and services—and remained virtually stable in the broader service-
producing sector. But in the goods-producing arena, the city faltered
markedly, losing almost one-half (47.7 percent) of its manufacturing
employment. Within the national and international economic transformations, New York City has been hit by harsh dislocations to its
economic base. While analyses presented subsequently will show that
the city has adapted much more positively in a shorter-term time
frame, it is clear that mass employment growth has been captured by
other geographic regions. This is illustrated by shifts in population,
the subject of the following section.

Population: The Broader Context

The changing population and demographics of New York City do not
exist in a vacuum; they tend to reflect broader processes operating
nationally, and internationally as well. Before examining the dominant
United States phenomena, it is useful to view total population growth
within the context of selected OECD nations.

EXHIBIT 1

Nonfarm Payroll Employment, United States and New York City:
1969 to 1983
(Numbers in Thousands)

Industry	United States Total				New York City			
			Change: 1969 to 1983				Change: 1969 to 1983	
	1969	1983	Number	Percent	1969	1983	Number	Percent
Total	70,384	89,978	19,594	27.8%	3,797.7	3,344.2	-453.5	-11.9%
Goods-Producing	24,361	23,646	-715	-2.9	932.3	521.0	-411.3	-44.1
Mining	619	1,021	402	64.9	2.0	1.7	-0.3	-15.0
Construction	3,575	3,947	372	10.4	104.5	87.2	-17.3	-16.6
Manufacturing	20,167	18,678	-1,489	-7.4	825.8	432.1	-393.7	-47.7
Service Producing	46,023	66,332	20,309	44.1	2,865.4	2,823.2	-42.2	-1.5
Transportation and Public Utilities	4,442	4,941	499	11.2	323.9	236.0	-87.9	-27.1
Wholesale and Retail Trade	14,705	20,513	5,808	39.5	749.1	608.1	-141.0	-18.8
Finance Insurance and Real Estate	3,512	5,454	1,942	55.3	465.6	493.8	28.2	6.1
Services	11,169	19,680	8,511	76.2	779.8	966.8	187.0	24.0
Government	12,195	15,744	3,549	29.1	547.0	518.5	-28.5	-5.2

Source: U.S. Department of Labor, Bureau of Labor Statistics, *Employment and Earnings,* monthly.

Total Population: United States vs. OECD Nations

In the absence of national population growth, city shrinkage would not be an unexpected occurrence. While the *rate* of population growth in the United States has decelerated the past 30 years, it still remains at the leading growth edge of the major industrialized nations. With the exception of Canada, only Japan exceeded the United States's increase of 12.3 percent from 1969 to 1980 among major OECD nations. The population levels of Germany, Switzerland, the United Kingdom, and Belgium were essentially stable, with growth increments hovering around the two-percent mark.

The rate of growth of the United States was more than 50 percent greater than that of OECD Europe, and more than 150 percent greater than that of the European Economic Community (EEC). Thus population expansion in the United States is such that the pool of *potential* city residents could stabilize despite redistributional forces. But this has not been the case. Regional and metropolitan shifts have more than offset overall growth, and have worked to the detriment of the older industrial cities as well as New York.

Regional Population Shifts

Within the overall context of population growth in the United States, there has been a shift in broad regional settlement patterns. Differential regional population growth is one dimension of the forces impacting New York City.

The Longer-Term Patterns

As a backdrop to present concerns, it is useful to examine the patterns of regional change for the two decades prior to 1970, the baseline of the present transformation on a regional and divisional base. Between 1950 and 1960, the United States as a whole experienced a rate of growth of 18.5 percent and an absolute increase of 28 million people. The growth was relatively evenly shared (in total numbers) among the major regional clusters (between 7.2 million and 7.9 million) with the exception of the Northeast, which expanded by only 5.2 million people. Those areas trailing the national growth *rate* most severely were the industrialized Northeast (13.2 percent) and the agricultural states of the West North Central (9.5 percent) and East South Central (5.0 percent) divisions. In contrast, the West was the fastest-growing area of the nation, increasing in population by 38.9 percent.

Between 1960 and 1970, regional disparities began to sharpen, with the Northeast and North Central regions lagging in both absolute growth and percentage change. In the face of a shrinking national growth increment (24 million people), the South's net gain in population (7.9 million) was greater than that of the previous decade. It was the only region to experience an increasing level of absolute growth, despite the continued dissolution of its labor-intensive farming.

The Recent Acceleration

The trends evident in the two decades prior to 1970 foreshadowed the general pattern of events that were to take place in the 1970s, but not their scale and magnitude. A gradual evolution rapidly accelerated. The 1970 to 1980 growth rates of the South (20.0 percent) and West (23.9 percent) were more than a hundred times greater than that of the Northeast (0.2 percent) and over five times greater than the North Central region (4.0 percent). Lagging most severely were the highly industrialized states of the Middle Atlantic and East North Central divisions, the historic manufacturing belt of America stretching from New York to Chicago.

The improved relative performance of the West South Central and East South Central divisions gives some indication that the phenomenon of rural agricultural displacement has ended; the latter is no longer available to bolster the sagging populations of the northern industrial cities. The post-industrial era marches on the heels of agricultural displacement in the United States. The results are mirrored in central city decline, completely unlike the evolution currently taking place in much of the Third World. Secondly, the former farm states "unloaded" their redundant agricultural populations, setting the stage for improved growth performance.

The energy and natural-resources crises of the 1970s improved the economic status of those states which serve as exporters of these vital commodities. Not only is this reflected in the southern divisions cited above, but also in the Mountain states—whose growth rate (37.1 percent) was the highest in the nation. For the first time it eclipsed that of the Pacific division (19.8 percent)—and the oil- and natural-gas-rich territories of the West South Central division.

Thus, the rise of the Sunbelt and the stagnation of the Northeast and North Central states represent significant changes in America's population disposition. The data emphasize one of the hazards of forecasting: that of being right in direction but wrong in time and scale. While earlier trends made apparent the shifts in regional growth (at least in hindsight), the future actually arrived much faster than was anticipated. The bulk of the national population growth from 1970 to 1980 was the province of the South (54.0 percent) and West (36.9 percent), while the Middle Atlantic region, which encompasses New York, showed a net resident loss of 1.8 percent.

Thus, New York City is set in a regional population context of slow growth. At the same time, another basic force influences the city: metropolitan stabilization.

Metropolitan-Nonmetropolitan Shifts

For the past half-century, the major growth nodes of American society were its metropolitan centers. Large metropolitan agglomerations (as defined in 1981) were the nation's dominant growth loci during the 1960-to-1970 era. Their average annual population increase (1.7 percent) exceeded that of the United States (1.3 percent), and far outdistanced nonmetropolitan territories (−0.2 percent). Yet even this convention was challenged in the 1970s.

Despite the energy crises of the decade, from 1970 to 1980, large metropolitan areas were transformed into settings of slow growth, with an average annual rate of population increase of 0.6 percent. At the same time, smaller (other) metropolitan areas experienced growth rates of 1.4 percent. Even the latter were challenged by the revolutionary surge of nonmetropolitan growth, in which population increases also averaged 1.4 percent annually. Some of this shift undoubtedly signifies the drive toward exurbia and can be attributed to the lagging pace of metropolitan definition. However, the latter may be only a secondary explanation for the phenomenon.

It is the large metropolitan complexes of the Northeast that dominate the post-1970 experience of metropolitan decline with a loss of 4.4 percent. Also exhibiting similar symptoms, although not yet shrinking, are their equivalents in the North Central states. In sharp contrast is the status of large metropolitan areas in the South and West, with a sustained pattern of growth through the decade of the 1970s.

The major focal points of growth in the Northeast and North Central states are nonmetropolitan areas, which exceeded even the positive growth performances of the smaller metropolitan areas. In the South and West, the largest increments of population growth on an absolute basis accrued to small metropolitan settings. The linkage of regional and metropolitan growth patterns becomes apparent when it is realized that the Northeast has nearly three-fifths of its total population concentrated in four large metropolitan areas. The virtual national halt in large metropolitan growth therefore had a much greater effect in the Northeast than the South, where only one-fifth of the population resides in large metropolitan settings. Similarly, the revitalization of the nonmetropolitan sector has negligible positive effects in the Northeast, where only one-seventh of the population is nonmetropolitan; in contrast, in the South, one-third of the population is nonmetropolitan.

The South and West have the advantage of maturing late; the older areas of the country are frozen in the patterns of yesteryear. Avoiding the question of which shift—regional or metropolitan—is the primary causal factor, we can be certain that their connection has been a major force and has had major impact on New York City. Post-1980 data is still fragmentary. There is some indication of recentralization—but the demographic scene is still dominated by the previous decade.

New York in Context

When the data for the twenty largest metropolitan areas (as defined in 1981) are further dissected, the losses appear alarming. As shown in Exhibit 2, seven out of ten major metropolises in the Northeast and North Central regions experienced population losses from 1970 to 1980. Yet in the South, only Washington, D.C., and Baltimore reflect slow growth. More than compensating for the latters' performance has been the phenomenal growth of Houston, Miami, Atlanta, and Dallas, indexed by decade growth rates exceeding 25 percent.

As expected, the West exhibits a pattern similar to the South. Indeed, the San Diego SMSA experienced a growth rate of 37.1 percent, partially reflecting its attractiveness as a magnet for military retirees.

And the rates of population decline of the older regions' metropolises are far from trivial. In New York, for example, 5.4 percent of

EXHIBIT 2

Population for the Twenty Largest Metropolitan Agglomerations:[1] 1960 to 1980
(Numbers in Thousands)

Region and Area	Population			Change: 1960-1970		Change: 1970-1980	
	1960	1970	1980	Number	Percent	Number	Percent
Northeast Region							
New York SCSA	15,405	17,035	16,120	1,630	10.6	-915	-5.4
Philadelphia SCSA	5,024	5,628	5,549	604	12.0	-79	-1.4
Boston SCSA	3,193	3,526	3,448	333	10.4	-78	-2.2
Pittsburgh SMSA	2,405	2,401	2,264	-4	-0.2	-137	-5.7
North Central Region							
Chicago SCSA	6,794	7,726	7,868	932	13.7	142	1.8
Detroit SCSA	4,122	4,669	4,618	547	13.3	-51	-1.1
Cleveland SCSA	2,732	3,000	2,834	268	9.8	-166	-5.5
St. Louis SMSA	2,144	2,411	2,355	267	12.5	-56	-2.3
Minneapolis–St. Paul SMSA	1,598	1,965	2,114	367	23.0	149	7.6
Cincinnati SCSA	1,468	1,613	1,660	145	9.9	47	2.9
South Region							
Washington, D.C. SMSA	2,097	2,910	3,060	813	38.8	150	5.2
Dallas–Ft. Worth SMSA	1,738	2,378	2,975	640	36.8	597	25.1
Houston SCSA	1,571	2,169	3,101	598	38.1	932	43.0
Miami SCSA	1,269	1,888	2,640	619	48.8	752	39.8
Baltimore SMSA	1,804	2,071	2,174	267	14.8	103	5.0
Atlanta SMSA	1,169	1,596	2,030	427	36.5	434	27.2
West Region							
Los Angeles SCSA	7,752	9,981	11,496	2,229	28.8	1,515	15.2
San Francisco SCSA	3,492	4,631	5,182	1,139	32.6	551	11.9
Seattle, SCSA	1,429	1,837	2,092	408	28.6	255	13.9
San Diego SMSA	1,033	1,358	1,862	325	31.5	504	37.1

Note: [1] Standard consolidated statistical areas (SCSAs) and standard metropolitan statistical areas (SMSAs) defined by Office of Management and Budget as of June 30, 1981.

Sources: U.S. Bureau of the Census, *Commerce News,* "Major Metropolitan Complexes Show Slower Overall Population Growth During 1970s, 1980 Census Analysis Reveals," CB81-61, Public Information Office, Washington, D.C., April 8, 1981; and U.S. Bureau of the Census, 1980 Census of Population, *Supplementary Reports,* "Standard Metropolitan Statistical Areas and Standard Consolidated Statistical Areas: 1980," PC80-S1-5, U.S. Government Printing Office, Washington, D.C., 1981.

its 1970 population was lost, with similar rates afflicting the Pittsburgh (−5.7 percent) and Cleveland (−5.5 percent) metropolitan areas. Even the nondeclining metropolitan areas of the Northeast and North Central states (excluding Minneapolis–St. Paul) are growing at a rate far slower than all of the southern and western metropolises.

Historically, it was the sheer growth in population, particularly through migration, which generated much of the social and economic stress of older urban centers. This pattern has changed very markedly, providing both hope and new challenge. The problems of coping with increased housing demand, overcrowded schools, and overstressed physical facilities may be somewhat alleviated by the new conditions of population stability and decline; but in their place is the question of fiscal balance—of the economic wherewithal within older metropolitan settings to service the remaining population and to support overly massive infrastructure. These questions take on even more significance as equally important patterns of change surface inside metropolitan areas.

Intra-Metropolitan Shifts

The history of America's major cities is one of meeting—and surmounting—the problems of growth and change. But for the first time, the nation's central cities in total are losing population, and doing so quite markedly, while their corresponding suburban rings expand considerably. But even the latter positive pattern does not strictly hold for the nation's large, aging metropolitan areas in the Northeast and North Central regions. As detailed in Exhibit 3, the large central cities of the "Frostbelt," while afflicted with substantial population losses, often fail to account for all of the decline of their metropolitan areas. For example, between 1970 and 1980, New York City and Pittsburgh lost 825,000 and 96,000 people, respectively. However, the New York metropolitan area lost 915,000 people while the Pittsburgh SMSA lost 137,000, totals in excess of their central city losses. Thus, suburban decline is beginning to appear in select metropolitan settings (although the presence of smaller, aging sub-cities within this context plays a significant role).

The actual magnitude of some central city declines is remarkable when viewed over a longer time frame (Exhibit 3). From 1950 to 1980, St. Louis lost 47 percent of its population, Buffalo 38 percent,

EXHIBIT 3
Population Change, Selected Cities
1950 to 1980

City	1950[1]	1970[2]	1980[3]	Change: 1950–1980		Change: 1970–1980	
				Number	Percent	Number	Percent
Boston	801,444	641,071	562,994	−238,450	−29.8	−78,077	−12.2
Buffalo	580,132	462,768	357,870	−222,262	−38.3	−104,898	−22.7
Chicago	3,620,962	3,369,357	3,005,072	−615,890	−17.0	−364,285	−10.8
Cincinnati	503,998	453,514	385,457	−118,541	−23.5	−68,057	−15.0
Cleveland	914,808	750,879	573,822	−340,986	−37.3	−177,057	−23.6
Detroit	1,849,568	1,514,063	1,203,339	−646,229	−34.9	−310,724	−20.5
Minneapolis	521,718	434,400	370,951	−150,767	−28.9	−63,449	−14.6
New York City	7,891,957	7,895,563	7,071,030	−820,927	−10.4	−824,533	−10.4
Newark	438,776	381,930	329,248	−109,528	−25.0	−52,682	−13.8
Philadelphia	2,071,605	1,949,996	1,688,210	−383,395	−18.5	−261,786	−13.4
Pittsburgh	676,806	520,089	423,938	−252,868	−37.4	−96,151	−18.5
St. Louis	856,796	622,236	453,085	−403,711	−47.1	−169,151	−27.2

Notes: [1] April 1, 1950 Census
[2] April 1, 1970 Census
[3] April 1, 1980 Census

Sources: U.S. Bureau of the Census, *County and City Data Book, 1956* (A Statistical Abstract Supplement), U.S. Government Printing Office, Washington, D.C., 1957; and U.S. Bureau of the Census, *Commerce News*, "Three Cities of 100,000 or More At Least Doubled Population Between 1970 and 1980," Census Bureau Reports, CB81-92, Public Information Office, Washington, D.C., June 3, 1981.

and Pittsburgh and Cleveland 37 percent—with the largest proportion of the declines attributable to the 1970-to-1980 period.

Cities in the United States, particularly those born in the industrial era, are experiencing the painful adjustments of shrinkage. New York City's population losses are significant in this context, but its economic fortunes have taken a different course. It is the "new" economy now emerging that is analyzed in the following section.

New York City's New Economy

The changing economic functions of the central city in the United States are epitomized by New York. Absolute employment declines in the goods-producing sector and declining relative shares in service-producing employment have characterized virtually all cities. But New York, from an economic point of view, may be the most successful adaptor to the new American imperatives. The changes in its form and function are briefly outlined below.

The Economic Turnaround

One of the best measures of economic vitality is changes in payroll employment. As shown in Figure 1, the first half of the decade of the 1970s was marked by precipitous employment losses, with annual declines averaging close to 100,000 jobs between 1969 and 1976. But just as the city was an advanced indicator of the adjustment pattern of the national economy in terms of decline, so was its position in the expansion which started in 1976. Though interrupted by the harsh recession of 1981–82, the resurgence has yielded increments of growth averaging 30,000 to 40,000 jobs per year between 1976 and 1983 (see Figure 2).

The sheer vitality of the New York metropolitan area is emphasized when we compare it with Los Angeles—typically viewed as the premier "new" configuration—where, from December 1979 to 1983, there was a loss of 55,000 jobs (Figure 3). The case is made even stronger when we turn to an exemplar of the old American industrial hegemony, the Chicago–Gary metropolitan area, which in the same period lost 263,000 jobs. In contrast, the New York–Northeastern New Jersey metropolitan area secured nearly a quarter-of-a-million new jobs. Indeed, as shown in Exhibit 4, New York had

FIGURE 1

Changes in Payroll Employment, New York City, December 1969-76

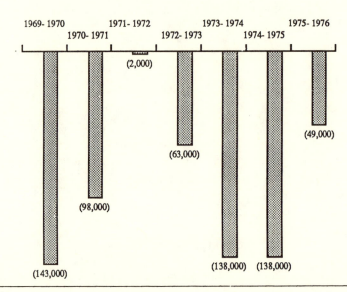

Source: New York Regional Office, Bureau of Labor Statistics, U.S. Department of Labor, 1984.

the highest absolute employment growth of all the U.S. metropolitan areas, with over a million jobs between 1982 and 1983. A city that had lost 631,000 jobs from 1969 to 1976 (Figure 1) suddenly became the focal point of America's greatest metropolitan growth. While Houston was actually losing employment between 1982 and 1983, and the torchbearers of the Southwest, such as Dallas–Fort Worth, were recording relatively modest gains, the dominance of the New York metropolitan area was restored.

The Emerging Economic Structure

But this growth was achieved only through radical shifts in employment structure—shifts which in turn have rendered obsolete portions of the city's population. America's older cities, unlike many of their

FIGURE 2

Changes in Payroll Employment, New York City, December 1976-83

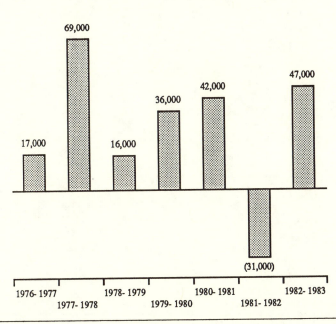

Source: New York Regional Office, Bureau of Labor Statistics, U.S. Department of Labor, 1984.

European equivalents, have been much more the creation of the business activity, particularly manufacturing, rather than administrative or governmental function.

The synergism between flows of immigrants—both domestically, off the farm, and from abroad—and the manufacturing opportunities available in the earlier industrial city, created the massive "smoke-stack" concentrations which for so very long dominated the image of urban America. They were predicated on agglomerations of productive power, massed population, and industrial technology. New York shared in the sheer energy generated by the new industrial era in combination with the essential raw material of cheap labor.

But this is an era that is rapidly contracting in America—and in few places more dramatically than in New York City. As shown in

FIGURE 3

Changes in Payroll Employment Among the Nation's Three Largest Areas, December 1979-83

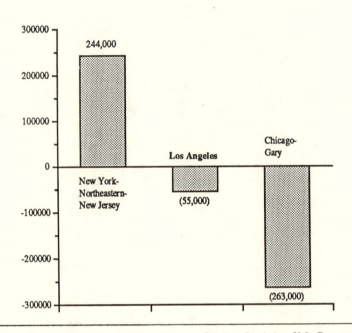

Source: New York Regional Office, Bureau of Labor Statistics, U.S. Department of Labor, 1984.

Figure 4, manufacturing employment in New York in 1950 was well in excess of one million. By the mid-1980s, barely 400,000 manufacturing jobs remained. Sharp declines are evident across virtually the entire manufacturing profile—and these have continued to the present date. Only publishing, of the twenty major industrial employment industries, has held its own.

The chief loser has been non-durable goods. The city's dominance in apparel manufacturing initially shifted to cheaper labor markets within overnight trucking distance, then moved to the deep South, and finally dispersed in a worldwide stream. It is Korea, Taiwan, Brazil, Hong Kong, and other non-United States locations that now dominate this sector. Local manufacturers—and with them local manufac-

EXHIBIT 4

Payroll Employment Change for Metropolitan Areas With Over a Million Jobs, December 1979–83
(Numbers in Thousands)

Area	Employment December 1983	Number change			Percent change		
		1979–82	1982–83	1979–83	1979–82	1982–83	1979–83
Atlanta	1,093.9	61.7	65.4	127.1	6.4	6.4	13.1
Dallas–Ft. Worth	1,621.7	113.8	73.9	187.7	7.9	4.8	13.1
Houston	1,512.6	120.5	–27.0	93.5	8.5	–1.8	6.6
Washington	1,675.1	37.2	52.3	89.5	2.3	3.2	5.6
District of Columbia	598.5	–20.3	5.3	–15.0	–3.3	0.9	–2.4
Boston	1,543.2	23.0	38.8	61.8	1.6	2.6	4.2
New York–Northeastern New Jersey	6,988.9	101.7	142.7	244.4	1.5	2.1	3.6
New York City	3,408.0	46.5	46.9	93.4	1.4	1.4	2.8
Rest of area	3,580.9	55.2	95.8	151.0	1.6	2.7	4.4
Nassau–Suffolk	1,002.3	45.7	33.8	79.5	5.0	3.5	8.6
San Francisco–Oakland	1,585.0	–5.1	19.0	13.9	–0.3	1.2	0.9
Philadelphia	1,967.8	–24.1	40.2	16.1	–1.2	2.1	0.8
City of Philadelphia	759.5	–42.0	2.6	–39.4	–5.3	0.3	–4.9
Minneapolis–St. Paul	1,106.6	–43.3	43.4	0.1	–3.9	4.1	—
Los Angeles–Long Beach	3,619.5	–140.4	85.1	–55.3	–3.8	2.4	–1.5
Chicago–Gary SCA	3,250.6	–238.9	–23.6	–262.5	–6.8	–0.7	–7.5
Chicago	3,037.3	–228.0	3.2	–224.8	–7.0	0.1	–6.9
Detroit	1,581.6	–252.3	47.3	–205.0	–14.1	3.1	–11.5

Source: New York Regional Office, Bureau of Labor Statistics, U.S. Department of Labor, 1984.

FIGURE 4

Manufacturing Employment, New York City, 1950-83

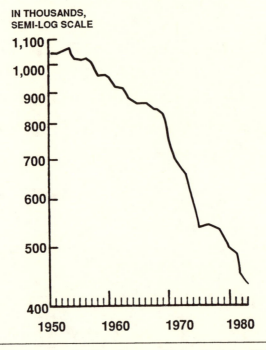

IN THOUSANDS,
SEMI-LOG SCALE

Source: New York Regional Office, Bureau of Labor Statistics, U.S. Department of Labor, 1984.

turing jobs for the relatively unskilled—have been and are departing. In their place is a new economy.

The Rise of the Service Economy

As indicated earlier, 1976 was New York City's pivotal point, the year in which the rise of new activities more than overcame the loss of the old. Figure 5 summarizes the shifts which have taken place from December 1976 through 1983. The loss of more than 100,000 manufacturing jobs, together with shrinkage in wholesale and retail trade as well as transportation and public utilities (both of them

FIGURE 5

Changes in Payroll Employment, New York City
December 1976-83

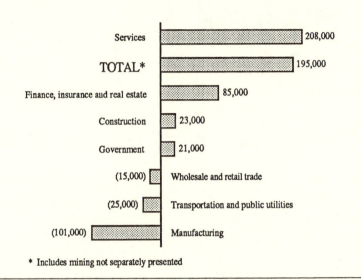

Services — 208,000
TOTAL* — 195,000
Finance, insurance and real estate — 85,000
Construction — 23,000
Government — 21,000
(15,000) — Wholesale and retail trade
(25,000) — Transportation and public utilities
(101,000) — Manufacturing

* Includes mining not separately presented

Source: New York Regional Office, Bureau of Labor Statistics, U.S. Department of Labor, 1984.

perhaps victims in whole or in part of the declining population base), was more than made up by an increment in service employment in excess of 200,000.

The new leitmotiv of the city is its increased role as a world headquarters, symbolized by a growth of 85,000 jobs in finance, insurance, and real estate. America's involvement in international trade was expanding—and New York City was increasingly its center.

Figure 6 graphically portrays the abrupt nature of the changes in New York City's economic raison d'être. By 1980, employment in finance and business services together passed that of manufacturing within the city. The subsequent years indicate an enormous broadening of the gap. A whole new economy became increasingly ill-matched to the resident masses of the city.

New York City's new profile is one in which private sector employment provides nearly six times as many jobs as that of government, and nearly six out of seven of the private sector jobs are

FIGURE 6

Payroll Employment in Manufacturing and Finance and Business Services, New York City, 1977-1983

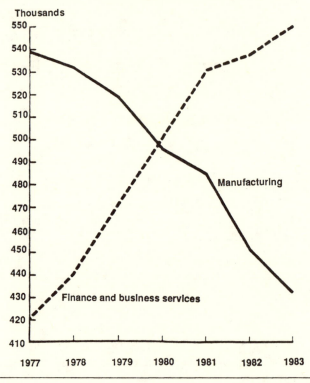

Source: New York Regional Office, Bureau of Labor Statistics, U.S. Department of Labor, 1984.

service-producing. Indeed, all goods-producing employment now has been reduced to the scale of government employment.

If we view data on New York City's share of metropolitan area employment, the new areal job calculus becomes evident. New York City accounts for 49 percent of all private sector employment, but only 37 percent of goods-producing jobs. Its leadership in finance, insurance and real estate is evident, with 71 percent of the regional jobs located within the core city. Indeed, in the "securities" area, the proportion is 92 percent.

It is significant that of all the service-producing sectors, New York's share is greatest in social services. It is the clash of the social-services imperatives (and needs of the resident population) versus the rise of the new post-industrial opportunities which will be detailed in a later section of this paper.

The changing role of cities versus their suburban areas, even in municipalities as vigorous as New York, is evident. More than two-thirds of the total job growth in the metropolitan area from 1977 to 1983 took place *outside* of the city. It is only in the finance sector that New York continued its dominance. Once again, this was equalled only by the provision of social services. This latter sector enjoyed a job growth of over 51,000 in the metropolitan area; New York secured four out of five (or 40,000) of the increment.

While both the city and the metropolitan area lost jobs in the goods-producing arena, New York City's losses were in excess of 83,000; in the rest of the area, barely 13,000. Thus, while New York had 37 percent of the goods-producing jobs in 1983, it accounted for 86 percent of the job loss in that sector in the preceding six years (1977 to 1983). Goods-producing has been relegated to suburbia, exurbia, other regions of the U.S., and most significantly, to other nations. Yet, there is substantial indication of a successful transition, at least from a macro-perspective, of New York City's economy from one dominated by industrial opportunity to the new post-industrial/information-based era.

The city's job base is towering, but highly specialized—and there is little in the dynamics of change which would seem to alter this pattern as we look into the future. This is the case even when analysis is undertaken by employment in high-technology industries, often viewed as having a potential for reversing the outflow of goods-producing activities. Regardless of which of the several definitions of high-tech is employed, there is little indication of factors which will radically add to employment within the city. And in the more dynamic service-information economy, high-technology gains have been relatively small. As we look to the future, technological shift may even have a negative impact.

Future Economic Opportunities and Threats

Radical as have been the changes in New York City's job base, they may not yet reflect the impact of future technology. There is a progression as a function of technological competence and information technology which suggests that certain common elements of back-office work may be shifted, relatively easily, from high-cost core areas. The back-office operations in New York City's large commercial banks—Chemical, Chase, Manufacturers Hanover—have long been located in Long Island, while Citicorp has back-office facilities in South Dakota and Florida, as well as in New York City and Long Island. As banks, brokerage firms, and insurance companies become national operations, the location of their back-office functions may increasingly be dispersed across the country rather than being based in New York City or the surrounding region.

The equivalent of the sewing machine operator or leather-goods finisher of yesterday's labor market in New York City may well be the basic clerk, stenographer, or keypunch operator of today. The skills and orientations of the latter are different from the former, but even they may be disappearing as well. An analogy to the evolution of New York City's apparel industry is foreseeable within the information-processing sector. The shift of back-office (information processing) activities to areas of cheaper rents and better labor-force characteristics—places less subject to the disruptions of the central city in general—is reminiscent of the apparel industry of a generation ago. The front office may remain, but the bulk of the support activities, as a function of improved communications and transportation, can be situated elsewhere.

The skill requirements for these activities become even more rarified than presently is the case. The mismatch between present needs and present city residents is evident; in the future the incongruity may prove to be even more substantial. It is the suburbs that have college-educated women seeking part- and full-time employment—and at a great remove from the threat of unionization as well. Cities, by very definition, impose a very high level of support costs as a function of their relative complexity and infrastructure, to say nothing of their age and social support problems. Much of this can be avoided in the flight to suburbia and less-developed areas.

In the midst of its incredibly successful turnaround—at a time when the New York City realty market may be the most expensive in the entire world and when the vision of a world city has replaced that of regional equivalents—the potential for economic thinning of the service sector should not be overlooked. The city will have to compete even harder to stay in place, much less expand. This requires a government with the credibility to turn to an electorate which is poor and needy, and ask for programs and indeed even subsidies with which to attract and retain the skilled and rich. This, in turn, involves a level of legitimacy which seems to be evading present political leadership. If New York City cannot maintain its "export" jobs, the negative multiplier potential is enormously evident.

Within this context, the distance between *the city of tomorrow* and *the residents of yesterday* requires exploration. The post-industrial economy has bypassed the residuals of an industrial population sector. A dispersed information-based economy will further widen the gap in the future. An *urban economy* can shift much more rapidly than the capacities of an *urban population;* and it is this growing incongruity which is described in the following section.

The Demographic Dilemma

The American city of the post-industrial era is very different in capacity and need from its predecessor. The march off the land into the urban centers of the last century provided the key raw material for urban industrial development. Cities had little in the way of public services but they did have jobs. In many cases these were brutal, poor-paying occupations. The very desperation of the agrarian displacees, however, caused them to view these in a positive light. The U.S. city had not only a unique scale of labor force concentration, but very cheap labor as well. Cities grew in potency and industrial hegemony in concert with population growth.

In the United States—and we would suggest possibly in other developed economies—these are reinforcing patterns which have now aborted. New York City, as perhaps the most visible focal point of post-industrial activity, yields insight into the dynamics at work.

The Long-Term Pattern of Population

In Exhibit 5 data is presented on United States population, the New York metropolitan region, and New York City from 1820 through 1980. The broad sweep of time indicates the early dominance of the city, with percentage increments in population exceeding that of the nation until the mid-1880s. While city and nation were roughly matched through the 1940s, the decade of World War II is clearly the turnover point. The rest of the New York metropolitan region which had achieved parity in growth with the core at the turn of the century suddenly became the expansion area, sweeping past the city. The

latter, for the first time in its history, lost population on a decennial
base in the decade of the 1950s. But even New York's suburbs began
to show their age in the 1970s, with a population loss of three percent. While the population of the United States still expanded by 11
percent, New York City's declined by an equal percentage. Even its
hinterland—the metropolitan region outside the city—began to suffer
from the same erosion. The era of dominance of the giant industrial
conurbations of the industrial era was coming to an end.

Racial and Ethnic Shifts

New York City from its very inception has been a melting pot of all
nations. Much of U.S. history has been practically unique in terms of

EXHIBIT 5

Population of U.S. and New York Metropolitan Region: 1820–1980

Census Year	Population (in thousands)				Percentage Change from Preceding Census			
	U.S.	Total NYMR	N.Y.C.	Rest of NYMR	U.S.	Total NYMR	N.Y.C.	Rest of NYMR
1820	9,638	364	152	212				
1830	12,866	484	242	242	33	33	59	14
1840	17,069	681	391	290	33	41	62	20
1850	23,192	1,072	696	376	36	57	78	30
1860	31,443	1,755	1,175	580	36	64	69	54
1870	39,818	2,274	1,478	796	27	30	26	37
1880	50,156	2,907	1,912	995	26	28	29	25
1890	62,948	3,807	2,507	1,300	26	31	31	31
1900	75,995	5,191	3,437	1,754	21	36	37	35
1910	91,972	7,208	4,767	2,441	21	39	39	39
1920	105,711	8,660	5,620	3,040	15	20	18	25
1930	122,775	11,021	6,930	4,091	16	27	23	35
1940	131,669	11,839	7,455	4,384	7	7	8	7
1950	150,697	13,154	7,892	5,262	14	11	6	20
1960	178,464	15,125	7,782	7,343	18	15	−1	40
1970	203,212	16,694	7,895	8,799	13	10	1	20
1980	226,505	15,571	7,015	8,557	11	−7	−11	−3

Note: The region includes the five counties of New York City; the New Jersey counties of Bergen, Essex, Hudson, Middlesex, Monmouth, Morris, Passaic, Somerset, and Union; and Nassau, Putnam, Rockland, Suffolk, and Westchester counties in New York State.

Sources: U.S. Bureau of the Census, *Census of Population*, decennial editions. Emanuel Tobier, "Population," in Charles Brecher and Raymond D. Horton (eds.), *Setting Municipal Priorities 1982* (New York: Russell Sage Foundation, 1982).

the ease of inmigration. (While this process was sharply contracted in the early 1920s, it should be noted that current net legal inmigration nationally is still on the order of one-half-million persons per year.)

Each and every ethnic group that came into New York has been viewed as a threat and danger to the status quo with persistent questions raised on their assimilative capacity as well as doubts on their contribution to the economy as a whole. More affluent immigrants could afford the trek to the farmlands. Those who had less in the way of resources tended to terminate their journey—not uncommonly near-penniless—in the central city. And of all central cities, New York was the most potent in this regard as the chief port of entry.

A major function of the Industrial City–USA of yore was to take unskilled immigrants, harness them to industry, and provide an infrastructure adequate in its scale both to sustain the first generation—and to tutor its successors. The definition of success was for the immigrant to look on new "greenhorns" with the same disdain as had been exhibited to his own generation. This was an enormously potent process. The graduation ceremony typically was a shift, either in the first or second generation, to a suburban residential location—making way for new groups. Ethnic groups varied in the pace of adaptation, and certainly even the most successful left their less fortunate brethren behind. But the demographic/economic "fit" was there.

The issue at hand is whether the current inheritors of the city will find it an equally positive springboard. The answer to this issue is not at hand. Certainly, however, its successful resolution is dogged not only by the changing role of the central city—the new job structure earlier described—but also by race.

In the years from 1920 through the last decade, the most important segment of migration was the internal flow of population. This is evident as we view the proportion of blacks within New York City, shown in Exhibit 6. As late as the turn of the century they represented less than two percent of the population. The shift off the land, particularly marked in the 1920s and 1930s, combined with substantial birthrates, as well as wartime-generated job opportunities, produced a massive swelling. By 1950 nearly 10 percent of the city's population was black; currently it is estimated to be over 25 percent.

One of the metaphysical issues of urban analysis is the question of whether, if there had not been a racial shift, America's cities would have been very different in their residential roles—or indeed their economic functions, as well—regardless of the underlying motivations. Exhibit 7 indicates the massive shifts which are still taking place in the

EXHIBIT 6

Total and Black Population, New York City: 1900 to 1980

Year	Total Population	Black
1980	7,071,639	1,788,377
1970	7,894,851	1,668,115
1960	7,781,984	1,084,862
1950	7,891,957	749,080
1940	7,454,995	458,444
1930	6,930,446	327,706
1920	5,620,040	152,467
1910	4,766,883	91,709
1900	3,437,202	60,666

Source: New York City, Department of City Planning.

EXHIBIT 7

Shifts in Racial/Ethnic Composition: New York City, 1978–1984

Changes in the Racial and Ethnic Composition of New York City, 1978–1984

	1978	1981	1984	Percent Change 1978–1981	Percent Change 1981–1984	Percent Change 1978–1984
Total	6,947,986	6,872,294	6,949,895	− 1.1%	+ 1.1%	0%
White	3,804,861	3,642,487	3,477,784	− 4.3	− 4.5	− 8.6
Black	1,547,468	1,526,718	1,683,980	− 1.3	+10.3	+ 8.8
Puerto Rican	804,084	764,634	773,700	− 4.9	+ 1.2	− 3.8
Other	336,147	429,692	634,445	+27.8	+47.7	+88.7
Not Reported	445,425	508,763	379,986	N.A.	N.A.	N.A.

Racial/Ethnic Composition of the Population, New York City: 1978, 1981, 1984

	1978	1981	1984
Total	100.0%	100.0%	100.0%
White	58.5	57.2	52.9
Black	23.8	24.0	25.6
Puerto Rican	12.4	12.0	11.8
Other	5.2	6.8	9.7

Note: The data in this exhibit are from the New York City Housing and Vacancy Survey conducted every three years. The data in Exhibit 6 are from the decennial censuses. There are minor deviations in result.

Source: Michael A. Stegman, Housing in New York City, 1984 (New Brunswick, NJ: Center for Urban Policy Research, 1985).

city's ethnic composition. New York will shortly become majority–minority. Hispanics are rapidly challenging blacks in absolute number and have passed them in growth. While other ethnic groups, particularly a very substantial inmigration of Asians, are expanding, their numbers are still relatively small, but their upward mobility is already evident.

Other newcomers to the city who do not possess skills commensurate with its new economy find it an increasingly inhospitable place. In a city whose affluence is marked by most tourists, roughly one-quarter of the population is below the poverty level, and more than one in seven are on welfare.

Geographic Changes Within the City

None of the sub-regions of the city—which is divided into five boroughs—are unmarked by these shifts. The traditional blue-collar enclaves of the Bronx and Brooklyn have seen the greatest population losses, with the first losing fully one in five of its 1970 population in the subsequent ten-year period, and nearly half of all its whites. Even Manhattan, despite its economic resurgence in the later 1970s, still lost 7.3 percent of its population—10.9 percent of its whites, and a striking 18.6 percent of its blacks. While the newer borough of Queens and the relatively small enclave of Richmond were more stable, they too reflect the ethnic turbulence within the city.

Population, Households and Housing

Despite the absolute declines in population, New York City still suffers from a severe housing shortage. Corporate executives complain bitterly of rents in new structures in excess of $2,000 per month for an 800-square-foot, non-super-luxury accommodation. Condominium and co-operative sales within Manhattan, again outside of the super-luxury category, are averaging nearly $300 a square foot. On the other side of the spectrum is an abandonment rate of 20,000 units a year and shattered hulks occupied only by squatters. The peculiar calculus of declining population and sustained housing pressures is at work. The inconsistency was made up by a shrinkage in household size, which declined to a 1980 level of only 2.4 persons. The number of households was barely altered; fewer bodies were occupying as much or more space. Manhattan was at the forefront of this phenomenon with a 5.6 percent increase in housing units, while its population declined by 7.3 percent. And yet the pressures increased as the average household size in 1980 achieved a remarkable level of under two persons. The number of non-minority-group children in the city has declined markedly, with public schools, at both the primary and secondary levels, in total having roughly only one-quarter of their attendees white (non-Hispanics).

The City of the Poor Masquerading as the City of the Rich

Over the past 25 years, New York has changed from having a median family income above the national average to an average family income well below it; this trend holds for all racial groups. For the whole city in 1982, the median income was 82 percent of the nation's median income. In 1959, it was 11 percent above the United States.

The problem is most evident among the approximately 70 percent of all New York City households who are renters. As such they dominate not only the housing politics of the city as evidenced by strong rent control ordinances, but also non-residential development as well. The latter typically runs head on into the property interests which have grown around tenancy. Alternate use of buildings, demolition, any form of making way for the new post-industrial elite—these are very difficult to achieve within the city. The risk of development aborting is so substantial as to require very large gains to offset its hazards.

Some indication of the incongruity between the mass of New York City residents and its newly defined economic functions is indicated by the key parameters of the rental market in contrast to homeowners. In Exhibit 8 is shown median household income of renters and owners in current dollars by race and ethnic origin for the city. Even New York's white renters had income levels only half that of its more affluent owner households—and minority levels were far worse.

The pattern of decline is all too clear-cut. From 1969 to 1980 there was a reduction in constant dollar income of some 28.3 percent. Even in the years of relative prosperity from 1980 to 1983, as the city added substantially to its employment rolls, the decline among renters was still 4.4 percent. The loss has been most striking in the city's key demographic growth sectors, blacks and Hispanics, with the latter group showing an income shrinkage of nearly 40 percent in the 11 years from 1969 through 1980. While the minority of the city's households who are owners become more affluent (regardless of race), only white renters are ahead of inflation.

The erosion of real incomes for the bulk of New York's households now is a predominantly outer-borough phenomenon. In the most current years, Manhattan has moved to near stability. The City of Manhattan with its post-industrial economy now is flourishing. But despite the existence of a few enclaves in Brooklyn and Queens which are part of its economy, the other boroughs—and with them the bulk of the municipal population—show little evidence of the economic good fortune which the core has enjoyed.

EXHIBIT 8

Median Household Income by Race and Tenure, 1980 and 1983, New York City

	Current Dollars			Constant 1967 Dollars		
			Percent Change			Percent Change
	1980	1983	1980-1983	1980	1983	1980-1983
All Households	$12,687	$16,166	+27.4%	$5,349	$5,602	+4.7%
White	16,023	20,255	+26.4	6,755	7,018	+3.9
Black	10,613	13,035	+22.8	4,474	4,517	+1.0
Puerto Rican	7,171	8,596	+19.9	3,023	2,979	-1.5
Other	12,300	13,928	+13.2	5,185	4,826	-6.9
CPI*	237.2	288.6	+21.7			
All Renters	$11,001	$12,797	+16.3	$4,638	$4,434	-4.4
White	13,474	17,326	+28.6	5,680	6,003	+5.7
Black	9,142	10,957	+19.9	3,854	3,797	-1.5
Puerto Rican	6,460	7,698	+19.2	2,723	2,667	-2.1
Other	10,903	12,129	+11.2	4,597	4,203	-8.6
All Owners	$20,333	$25,183	+23.9	$8,572	$8,726	+1.8
White	21,142	26,298	+24.4	8,913	9,112	+2.2
Black	17,517	23,225	+32.6	7,385	8,047	+9.0
Puerto Rican	16,708	21,308	+27.5	7,044	7,383	+4.8
Other	21,907	26,941	+23.0	9,236	9,335	+1.1

Note: *Consumer Price Index

Source: Michael A. Stegman, *Housing in New York, 1984* (New Brunswick, NJ: Center for Urban Policy Research, 1985), p. 122.

In the face of the politics of shrinking real-dollar incomes, the city has been driven to harden its housing policies, yielding a near immobilization. The poor and the middle-income groups cannot hazard displacement—nor rent increases commensurate with the market. But the effort to control rents has been a losing struggle. The shrinkage in incomes has more than overcome the safeguards against rent increments.

Exhibit 9 provides the product of incomes and shelter costs. Median gross rent-to-income ratios are substantially above those of the nation. From 1950's 18.9 percent, they reached a high of 29.3 percent in 1984. An increasing proportion of New Yorkers simply cannot afford their rents. The long-held tradition of one-quarter of one's income going for shelter clearly has long been bypassed. As of 1984 nearly a quarter of the city's renter households were forced to make shelter payments in excess of half their incomes. While some of this may be mitigated by welfare payments, the pressures are evident. The relatively small-though-glittering locomotive of Manhattan's banking and production-service economy must pull an increasingly lengthy train of people who have little relationship to it.

EXHIBIT 9

Rent-Income Ratios, New York City

Median Gross Rent-Income Ratio	*Median Gross Rent-Income Ratio, All Renter Households New York City, Selected Years*								
	1950	*1960*	*1965*	*1968*	*1970*	*1975*	*1978*	*1981*	*1984*
	18.9%	18.7%	20.4%	21.0%	20.0%	24.7%	28.3%	28.0%	29.3%

Gross Rent-Income Ratio	*Percent of Households with Rent-Income Ratios Over Specified Levels New York City, Selected Years*								
	1950	*1960*	*1965*	*1968*	*1970*	*1975*	*1978*	*1981*	*1984*
25% or more	N.A.	N.A.	34.9%	37.2%	35.5%	49.1%	57.1%	56.6%	60.2%
30% or more	25.0%	24.0%	25.3%	27.4%	N.A.	38.1%	46.3%	45.6%	48.2%
35% or more	N.A.	19.0%	18.7%	21.2%	23.2%	30.8%	38.0%	37.1%	39.5%
40% or more	N.A.	N.A.	14.5%	16.7%	N.A.	25.2%	31.6%	30.5%	32.9%
50% or more	N.A.	N.A.	N.A.	N.A.	N.A.	N.A.	N.A.	N.A.	23.2%

Source: Michael A. Stegman, *Housing in New York, 1984* (New Brunswick, NJ: Center for Urban Policy Research, 1985).

In turn the staffing of the new towers is increasingly the role of suburbanites—non-voters in the city. Three-quarters of the job growth from 1977 to 1981 went to non-city residents. The lack of fit, of congruity between the urban economic growth sectors and its resident population—expands. The political results of this mismatch are felt presently, and may be even more compelling in the future.

Problems and the Future

New York City has renewed its magnetism to the young elite of the country. The most prestigious of the law firms vie for new graduates at starting salary levels of $50,000—a rate of income triple that of the median household. At the other end of the spectrum, there is clear evidence of new immigrant groups moving into the basic retailing/service sector. Largely isolated between them are those groups who qualify neither in skills nor in family structure/orientation to either of these growth nodes. Exhibit 10 indicates the scale of the problem. It compares labor force participation, i.e., the proportion of people (16 to 64 years of age) who are either employed or seeking jobs. This is shown in 1983 for the United States as a whole and the City of New York.

In general, labor force participation is far lower in the central city than holds true for the nation, and this is without regard to race. When we focus on the latter, however, a number of incongruities are evident. Black men have the lowest labor force participation, at 65.8 percent, of the three groups shown. While it is somewhat higher for black women than for New York's white equivalent, it is still substantially under the national equivalent.

The situation is even more strikingly incongruous as we turn to Hispanics. Much of New York's population under that rubric is from Puerto Rico; much of the national incidence outside of the Northeast region is of Mexican origin. The latter seem to partake much more vigorously in the labor market than do the former.

Even more troubling are the data on youth from 16 to 19. New York City simply is not a hospitable place for adolescent entrants into the labor force. Nationally, for example, 56.9 percent of whites 16 to 19 are in the labor force; the equivalent in New York City is only 31.1 percent. The national incidence rate for blacks is down at the 36.4 percent level; for Hispanics, intermediate. While data is lacking for black youth in the city, data for the greater New York labor

EXHIBIT 10

Employment Patterns
(1983 Averages)

	Labor Force Participation		Unemployment Rates		Employment Rates	
	United States	New York (Central City)	United States	New York (Central City)	United States	New York (Central City)
White						
Men	77.1%	68.5%	8.8%	8.4%	70.4%	62.7%
Women	52.7	40.7	7.9	7.5	48.5	37.7
Both sexes, 16 to 19 years	56.9	31.1	19.3	26.0	45.9	23.0
Black						
Men	70.6	65.8	20.3	16.9	56.3	54.7
Women	54.2	45.9	18.6	10.8	44.1	40.9
Both sexes, 16 to 19 years	36.4	25.2*	48.5	50.2*	18.7	12.5*
Hispanic						
Men	80.8	68.8	13.5	12.5	69.9	60.2
Women	48.5	32.2	13.8	12.4	41.8	28.2
Both sexes, 16 to 19 years	45.3	N.A.	28.4	N.A.	32.5	N.A.

*New York Labor Market Area. Central City data is not available.

Source: Bureau of Labor Statistics, *Geographic Profile of Employment and Unemployment*, 1983 (Government Printing Office, 1984).

market area indicates an involvement of only 25.2 percent, i.e., barely two-thirds that of the national figure for blacks, and well under the halfway mark for whites.

Incongruity in unemployment rates is even more striking. The base, 1983, was a very mixed year, with the recession bottoming out in the Spring on the national level, and substantial employment growth, particularly at the end of the year. New York's economy as a whole fared far better than that of the nation. Despite this factor, the unemployment level for black youths was an appalling 48.5 percent.

When we focus on the city, the hostility of the job market for black men versus black women is evident: the former had an unemployment level of 16.9 percent, double that of white men; the latter, at 10.8 percent, somewhat higher than white women (7.5 percent), but clearly not at the same levels of incongruity. Again, Hispanic men within the city—with an unemployment level of 12.5 percent—were nearly precisely intermediate.

While there is no separate unemployment data for Hispanic adolescents either for the city or for the U.S. labor market as a whole, data on blacks indicates an unemployment level of fully 50.2 percent. The absorptive capacity of New York's economy for this group— damned by race, age, and sadly enough, educational attainment—is at a very low point indeed.

The sum of these data indices is shown in the last two columns of the exhibit, which give the employment rates. A far-greater proportion of New Yorkers, for any of a variety of reasons, simply are not on the employment rolls when compared with the nation, regardless of race. But both nationally—and in New York, very particularly—the proportion of black men who are employed is at a very low point indeed, with only 54.7 percent of those residing in New York employed on average during the 1983 period. Hispanic men within New York do far better, at 60.2 percent, versus all whites, at 62.7 percent.

The employment levels for women are somewhat different, with black women actually leading in terms of the proportion employed, at 40.9 percent; whites are at 37.7 percent, Hispanic women at 28.2 percent. Much of this latter incongruity, however, seems to indicate the better "fit" of women to the post-industrial economy particularly for blacks, and the cultural preferences among New York's largely Puerto Rican Hispanic population.

While data is lacking for New York City's minority group adolescent employment, the product of the low labor force participation rates and unemployment data for the region suggest a relatively trivial proportion finding their way into entry-level employment. Comparisons over time are not available due to changes in definition, but a glance at what data is available over the last decade indicates a substantial subsequent degeneration of minority employment activity.

The trauma of youth in a city which no longer is hospitable to them can only be hinted at. A dreadful parameter is suggested by homicides which accounted for nearly half of all deaths in 1981 for those males 15 to 24 years of age.

There is some measure of resemblance to a series of geological strata as we view the world's cities, each of them representing a different time stream. The metropolises of high birth rates and agricultural displacement are currently beset by the problems of growth and provision of infrastructure—sewerage, water, basic shelter—in a fashion reminiscent of urbanization in the United States of the past century. The issues of fit at that time—of matching socioeconomic demographic characteristics to job base—were cruel and painful. But by and large, the process worked remarkably effectively. Past experience provides little insight, however, as we turn to the premier post-industrial city—New York.

As we have suggested before, many of the earlier urban focal points of industry have seen an erosion of their economic base—and catastrophic shrinkages of population. The latter's scale, though monumental, has still not been able to yield a reasonable relationship between residual jobs and residual populations. Thus, as we view a Newark, a Cleveland, a St. Louis, we see cities that have shrunk in head counts within the last score of years by anywhere from one-third to one-half. Yet, despite this, there is every danger of continued erosion in jobs and population.

New York City's situation is far more salubrious. There has been a remarkable thickening up of economic functions, nearly adequate in size to replenish its peak job base. The population shrinkage to date is on the order of one in eight. While this mitigates some of the problems of the more purely industrial complexes, it leads to yet other issues of accommodation. These, we have suggested, are focused on the increasing mismatch between the requirements of the new growth sectors and their resident populations. How do we reconfigure a city, much of whose voting bloc seemingly is uninvolved in its own employment base? Many of them are poor; yet the city's future demands not only a national but, increasingly, an international elite.

To the poor, support services are essential, particularly welfare and other forms of social services. The bulk of New York City's voter population is still involved in a shelter society: basic accommodations and costs are the key priorities. Increasingly, however, the city's economic base depends upon a post-shelter society. Proximity to the fun and games of the core, direct linkage to work place, and a capacity to avoid the increasingly frictional and dangerous public transit facilities are their key priorities. The affluent are concerned about taxes; they require not merely the provision of literacy for their children, but facilities competitive with those of the best of the nation. As the city's political wars grow heated, the one major common denominator is fear of crime. But even in this arena there are severe differences in approach to its constraint.

Unlike many other cities in the United States—and we would suggest elsewhere, as well—New York City has the economic vitality with which to reshape itself. The problem is the development of political consensus. The issues of reconciling not merely class elements, but those of race and ethnicity as well, are the keys to its future development.

9

Housing in New York City: Matrix and Microcosm

George Sternlieb and David Listokin

The Shelter and Post-Shelter Housing Agendas

New York City's housing supply may well define its future not only as residence place but in employment as well. While there have been ebbs and flows in the level of housing concern, they are rapidly reaching a high point. And this is in the face of a population which two decades ago had reached close to the 8-million mark—and has since diminished by fully one in eight. Thirty-five years ago the city had 2,360,000 households. Despite the population shrinkage, in 1980 that number had expanded to nearly 2.8 million. Overriding drastic levels of clearance (averaging over 100,000 units a decade), the city managed to add nearly one-half million housing units from 1950 to 1980.

Its housing success is measured by a shrinkage in household size in three decades since 1950 from an average of 3.34 persons per household to 2.54—the latter figure fully 10 percent below that of a nation as a whole. Its failures, however, are mirrored on the one hand by the unplanned wasting of the South Bronx and the devastation of East New York; on the other by a shelter stock which is rapidly grow-

ing unaffordable by or undesirable to middle management and/or tech-
nocratic recruits for its economic base.

The poor are housed badly; the mobile may leave and ultimately
take their jobs with them. Gross rent-to-income ratios in 1950 were at
a median of 18.9 percent, by 1981 were at 28 percent, and reached
up past the 29.0 percent mark in the spring of 1984, based on the
vacancy study conducted by the Census Bureau for the city.[1] While
this pattern of change is not unique to New York, the pressures of
housing shelter costs are accentuated there. It is a city of the poor
masquerading as the city of the rich. The 1984 median income of
New York's 1,900,000 renter households was $12,797. Less than
one-quarter were over the $25,000 mark. Even among owner house-
holds, barely half met that threshold figure.

There are few places in the world in which poverty and extreme
plenty exist in such areal intimacy. Hard-core slum areas are a casual
stroll away from housing whose cost is startling even by London or
Tokyo standards. The marvelous mansions near Brooklyn's Pratt Institute crumble while aged Manhattan lofts sell for more than $300 a
square foot.

New York City's housing, in the very richness of its complexity,
is a mirror of the city both past and present. The old law tenements
of Manhattan are a response to the nineteenth century's need for
worker housing near the sweatshops; the art deco remnants of the
Bronx's former grandeur reflect the capacity of the subway lines to
link the outer boroughs. This in turn made them available to a
managerial and professional class which commuted to the core. The
recent centennial of the Brooklyn Bridge serves as a reminder of the
potency of this and other equivalent transportation channels to make
an ecological unit of the city.The decline in Manhattan's population
(which dates back to the World War I era, continued for nearly
seventy years, and perhaps only now is beginning to flatten out) was
not a disaster for the urban entity called New York, but a tribute to
specialization of function. Presently, the intimate linkage of the city's
housing and economic functions is in flux, the ultimate results beyond
the forecaster's capacity.

*The city's housing is far from a passive element in its economic develop-
ment; it is rather a vital input, and most important independent factor in
and of itself. Its very availability and cost shape and define the availability of the city's most important resource—people.*

Over a period of time this feeds back on corporate decisions to
locate in the city, the kinds of business functions which take place

there, and perhaps equally important, those that do not. If, at opposite ends of the spectrum, the city is defined as residence place only for the poor who cannot afford to leave it and the rich who can insulate themselves from it, clearly the city's enterprises which require people in the middle will be dependent upon non-New York residents. Given the increasing negatives of commuting—of cost, time and uncertainty—the tendency toward a narrowing span of economic function, following the housing-limited demographic profile of workers, will ultimately take place. A balance of housing mixes and the demographic elements which they incorporate do not guarantee an equivalent range of economic enterprise, but are an essential condition.

New York's network of commuting facilities is increasingly fragile, its capacity to gather in the staff of the post-industrial economy increasingly challenged. The areas of the island of Manhattan and its selected residential colonies in Brooklyn and Queens open to development are much too small—and much too expensive—to provide an adequate work force. And this is to say nothing of the disputes over territorial clout which inhibit their full exploitation.

Can the range of the city's housing opportunities encourage a settlement pattern for a broad spectrum of workers and entrepreneurs? If the answer is less than positive, it will have as its consequence a thinning out of the city's economic functions. Reflecting this, the residential population that will be left are those who can afford proximity—and the swollen ranks of the unskilled who cannot afford to leave. The post-1980 economic euphoria cloaks the thinning of the former group. The city's share of families with more than $50,000 income in 1980 dollars fell from 66 percent of the SMSA in 1960, to 62 percent in 1970, and only 54 percent in 1980. Barely one in eight of its renter households in 1984 had incomes of over $35,000. Even among owners, the equivalent ratio was nearly one-third. And, as a critical mass of affluence moves to suburbia, it takes jobs with it.

Thus, the challenge of New York City's housing is complex. On one side there are the issues of the city of the poor: Nearly one in seven New Yorkers is on welfare. The number below the official poverty line has also increased. In 1979 approximately 1,400,000 persons qualified; the equivalent in 1981 was 1,500,000; and by 1984 it was estimated to be over 1,700,000, one in four of the total population.[2] The relatively modest levels of income for most of its residents are all too evident from the statistics, though obscured at times by the glitter of the core. And this is a problem compounded by the diminished flow of housing-subsidy mechanisms, and indeed of the priority of low-income needs on the national level. But this is the shelter society: people whose needs are the basics of adequate physical housing and adequate environment.

Affluent middle America is much more embraced by the post-shelter society; here the dwelling unit plays a far more complex role, not only of prestige and as a symbol of "making it," but increasingly important as a vehicle for capital accumulation. For the group most influenced by this last element housing becomes an investment—not a machine for living, but rather a vehicle for saving and speculation. The primary element in dwelling-unit choice for middle America is not only whether one can afford the investment in a house, but rather whether it is retrievable and then—and even more importantly—at a profit. For the younger members of this latter group, this is paralleled by an equally key housing imperative, location proximate to core areas of jobs and consumption. But will the baby boom generation age within the city? Or will it follow the suburban path if the city does not yield appropriate opportunity?

The clash between the shelter and the post-shelter societies parallels in very substantial degree the split between the old city of New York, with its industrial-worker base, and the new city of the affluent. The scale of the latter has been much exaggerated—they are the focal point of the media and serve as prototypes of the popular vision of the New Yorker. They are the gentrifiers, the loft-residents, the occupants of the new high-cost residential facilities in the city. In their youth, they are willing to compromise on absolute housing standard and increasingly are to be found doubled and tripled up in prestige neighborhoods, but for many of them the long-term goal is ownership and amenity. If this cannot be satisfied within the city, it will drive many of them outside of it—and their essential skills as well. The city's housing policy and the products which are delivered—or not—are vital inputs to the ultimate decision.

Conflict between the city of the poor and that of the affluent or aspiring affluent, is not unique to New York; but with the possible exception of Boston, San Francisco, and perhaps Washington as well, nowhere else is it as accentuated—and nowhere else is the scale of the phenomenon so consequential. The conflict is taking place against the backdrop of significant change in the vigor and composition of the city's housing production.

Housing Delivery: Past and Present

The Roller Coaster of Housing Production and Subsidy

Housing nationally is a capricious dependent of the economic cycle with boom and bust yielding varying levels of activity. Within a two-year time frame, there are peaks past the two million housing-start mark—only to be followed by a halving of that figure. New York City's housing record, as in so many sectors of its ecology, bears all of the problems of the national pattern with accentuated stigmata of its own. One of the latter is a long-term, new housing-start drought without previous parallel in the city's history. The long-term trends, unlike those of the nation, are clearly down. Thus, from the halcyon days of the early 1960s, with an average level of perhaps 65,000 new units (three to four percent of the national figure), New York was reduced to barely a third that level by the end of the decade. While there was some recovery in the peak national years of the early 1970s to a shade over the 30,000 mark, this was only one-and-one-half percent of the equivalent for the nation, indicating a market share that had gone down by half (see Exhibit 1).

Even that figure was dependent on public assistance, with nearly two-thirds of the permits granted in the early 1970s involving some form of direct assistance (see Exhibit 2). In succeeding years, the combination of the federal housing moratorium in the early days of the second Nixon administration, followed by the fiscal crisis, reduced the city to levels of housing starts whose paucity probably was unmatched in more than a century. Even in the heart of the Great Depression, there was more housing construction in New York than existed from 1975 to 1977—with an average level in the latter years of only 5,000 units. While there has been some pickup, it is still at a very modest 10,000 to 12,000 units currently.

New York City, with more than three percent of the United States's households, thus has the dubious distinction of currently generating barely half of one percent of its new housing starts. It now takes four years to create as many new units as were added to the stock in any one year of the early 1960s, while nationally current production actually exceeds those base years. Certainly the flow of new production in the state outside of the city has suffered—but the level of decline is much more modest.

EXHIBIT 1

New Housing Units Based on Building Permits Issued, by County and Building Type

	1970	1971	1972	1973	1974	1975	1976	1977	1978	1979	1980	1981	1982	1983	Total
Manhattan	3,826	8,468	15,818	7,887	10,812	424	1,707	3,106	5,983	8,464	4,406	5,275	2,830	5,487	84,448
One Family	–	–	–	–	–	–	–	1	1	–	3	11	–	4	17
2–4 Family	5	–	4	–	2	–	–	–	3	16	4	–	2	–	40
5+ Family	3,821	8,468	15,813	7,887	10,810	424	1,707	3,105	5,934	8,448	4,399	5,264	2,828	5,483	84,391
Bronx	6,282	5,369	2,759	3,390	285	322	316	983	535	486	312	873	466	731	23,109
One Family	21	32	10	33	29	3	4	5	10	8	–	44	45	112	356
2–4 Family	340	297	270	306	256	146	216	181	141	83	34	128	67	72	2,537
5+ Family	5,921	5,040	2,479	3,051	–	173	96	797	384	395	278	701	354	547	20,216
Brooklyn	5,083	4,939	7,239	4,369	1,728	595	485	723	824	1,442	680	1,674	1,631	1,524	32,936
One Family	29	45	128	1	3	5	6	10	37	13	27	19	194	463	980
2–4 Family	582	638	568	613	393	326	323	286	233	205	200	183	348	518	5,416
5+ Family	4,472	4,256	6,543	3,755	1,332	264	156	427	554	1,224	453	1,472	1,089	543	26,540
Queens	2,858	7,942	3,243	3,384	1,282	1,032	663	805	1,529	1,214	1,048	1,763	1,025	1,326	29,114
One Family	200	151	86	81	73	92	54	59	42	55	38	49	61	128	1,169
2–4 Family	1,176	1,383	1,181	908	521	762	512	349	436	457	887	1,449	456	633	11,110
5+ Family	1,482	6,408	1,976	2,395	688	178	97	397	1,051	702	123	265	508	565	16,835
Richmond	2,841	4,071	4,504	2,739	1,636	1,437	2,263	2,022	2,270	2,918	1,354	1,475	1,697	2,690	33,917
One Family	1,088	1,121	1,045	737	608	812	1,215	1,155	1,452	2,000	732	561	739	649	13,914
2–4 Family	1,106	1,586	2,350	1,580	451	489	662	664	668	695	526	587	624	1,424	13,412
5+ Family	647	1,364	1,109	422	577	136	386	203	150	223	96	327	334	617	6,591
Total NYC	20,890	30,789	33,563	21,769	15,743	3,810	5,434	7,639	11,096	14,524	7,800	11,060	7,649	11,758	203,524
One Family	1,388	1,349	1,270	852	713	912	1,279	1,230	1,542	2,076	800	684	1,039	1,352	16,436
2–4 Family	3,209	3,904	4,373	3,407	1,623	1,723	1,713	1,480	1,481	1,456	1,651	2,347	1,497	2,651	32,515
5+ Family	16,343	25,536	27,920	17,510	13,407	1,175	2,442	4,929	8,073	10,992	5,349	8,029	5,113	7,755	154,573
Total Manhattan as % of NYC	18.3	27.5	47.1	36.2	68.7	11.1	31.4	40.6	53.5	58.3	56.5	47.7	37.0	46.7	41.4

Source: New York State, Division of Housing and Community Renewal, *Construction Activity in New York State, Based on Building Permits Issued.* Annual Series, 1970–1983.

A very large part of the city's poor recent showing results from the near cutoff of publicly assisted units. At peak in 1971, there were 21,000 permitted units—accounting for two-thirds of the total—which had some form of direct public assistance. Currently it is but a small fraction of that. While the private sector in recent years shows some positive signs of increase (though barely at a fifth of its past glories of a generation ago), it is the public sector which much more dramatically accounts for the difference.

EXHIBIT 2

Number of New Housing Units (Private and Publicly Assisted) Based on Permits Issued, New York State and New York City, 1960–1981

	New York State				New York City			
Year	Total	Private	Publicly Assisted	% Publicly Assisted	Total	Private	Publicly Assisted	% Publicly Assisted
1960	92,679	82,221	10,458	11.3	46,792	37,108	9,684	20.7
1961	117,629	95,297	22,332	19.0	70,606	49,813	20,793	29.4
1962	121,758	100,739	21,019	17.3	70,686	50,681	20,005	28.3
1963	103,458	89,444	14,014	13.5	49,898	38,335	11,563	23.2
1964	75,433	67,780	7,653	10.1	20,594	14,184	6,410	31.1
1965	91,170	76,722	14,448	15.8	25,715	14,053	11,662	45.4
1966	75,420	61,578	13,842	18.4	23,142	10,750	12,392	53.5
1967	77,003	64,810	12,193	15.8	22,174	11,173	11,001	49.6
1968	80,960	64,799	16,161	20.0	22,062	9,872	12,190	55.3
1969	70,295	58,716	11,579	16.5	17,031	8,416	8,615	50.6
1970	68,831	43,190	25,641	37.3	22,365	6,959	15,406	68.9
1971	103,233	68,838	34,395	33.3	32,254	11,243	21,011	65.1
1972	111,282	80,561	30,721	27.6	36,061	17,550	18,511	51.3
1973	79,470	60,154	19,316	24.3	22,417	7,605	14,812	66.1
1974	51,637	45,926	5,711	11.1	15,743	11,386	4,357	27.7
1975	32,623	30,699	1,924	5.9	3,810	3,024	786	20.6
1976	33,370	32,231	1,139	3.4	5,434	5,235	199	3.7
1977	41,611	36,649	4,962	11.9	7,639	6,053	1,586	20.8
1978	43,751	36,606	7,145	16.3	11,096	8,462	2,634	23.7
1979	39,842	35,100	4,742	11.9	14,524	13,722	802	5.5
1980	26,804	22,368	4,436	16.5	7,800	6,493	1,307	16.8
1981	29,850	24,703	5,147	17.2	11,060	8,636	2,424	21.9
Total	1,568,109	1,279,131	288,978	18.4	558,903	350,753	208,150	37.2
1982	25,280	NA	NA	NA	7,760	NA	NA	NA
1983	36,029	NA	NA	NA	11,758	NA	NA	NA

Note: Publicly assisted housing includes federal, state, and city direct assistance programs but excludes units receiving just tax incentives.

NA = Information not available

Source: New York State Division of Housing and Community Renewal, unpublished data.

In retrospect, the increasing difficulties of New York City's delivery capacity in jobs during the early 1970s had their equivalent in housing. In the former there was at least initially little notice taken of the falling off of the private sector and its replacement by governmental or near governmental jobs. In the latter, it was the private housing sector whose levels of production fell by 60 to 80 percent with publicly assisted efforts filling in the gap. In both cases, when the capacity to fund these surrogates disappeared, the harsh realities became evident.

Certainly the tidal wave of suburban and regional demographic and job shifts accounts for part of the housing phenomenon. But equally obviously, the balance of New York State, which shares in these traumas, has been far less seriously impacted by them, at least as gauged by the delivery capacity of the private sector. In a word, while New York State's record may be weak—the city's is far worse.

Exhibit 3 contrasts the dependence of the state and the city on publicly assisted housing. With less than half of the state's population, New York City in the 1960s secured nearly three-quarters of all the public housing units, roughly half of the federal middle-income, and nearly all of the state and city middle-income efforts. These alone in the 1960s accounted for more than 80,000 starts in the city. All three elements currently have shrunk or literally disappeared. The surrogate, Section 8, found the state in a much more receptive and/or aggressive—or perhaps just plain better—qualifying role, with a total of 25,000 units by 1981 supported under this program—but less than 30 percent were in New York City.

Other data sources reveal a similar trend line of diminished new housing production in New York City and declining housing subsidy availability. The dramatic change in *completed new housing* units is illustrative. The city's peak was reached in the 1920s when over 750,000 new units were completed—almost exclusively by the private sector. The depression of the 1930s saw completions drop to roughly 210,000 housing units; the war years and difficult recovery of the early post-war period saw a further decline in the 1940s to approximately 165,000 units. Production increased to almost 325,000 completed units in the 1950s, and just shy of 350,000 units in the 1960s—decades of increased public housing assistance (see Exhibits 4 and 4a).[3] While publicly aided completions continued at the same pace, accounting for 115,000 units, the number of new housing units completed plummeted to 165,000 in the 1970s. The 1980s with

EXHIBIT 3

Publicly Assisted New Housing Units Based on Building Permits Issued, New York State and New York City, 1960–1981

Year	Total		Public Housing[1]		Federal Middle-Income[2]		State and City Middle-Income[3]		Federal Section 8[4]	
	New York State	New York City	New York State	New York City	New York State	New York City	New York State	New York City	New York State	New York City
1960–64	75,476	68,455	29,056	25,356	1,950	834	44,470	42,265	—	—
1965–69	68,223	55,860	18,312	11,864	8,287	4,286	41,624	39,710	—	—
1970–74	115,784	74,097	21,564	12,095	16,991	8,944	77,229	53,058	—	—
1975–79	19,912	6,007	2,190	873	100	0	922	830	16,700	4,304
1980	4,436	1,307	310	266	0	0	0	0	4,126	1,041
1981	5,147	2,424	1,072	600	0	0	0	0	4,075	1,824
Total	288,978	208,150	72,504	51,054	27,328	14,064	164,245	135,863	24,901	7,169

[1] Federal and state-assisted low-income public housing operated by local public housing authorities.

[2] Just federal assistance with no state involvement.

[3] State- and city-assisted middle-income housing with or without federal involvement (e.g., Section 236).

[4] Just Section 8 new construction.

Source: New York State Division of Housing and Community Renewal, unpublished data; and Charles Hogg, New York State Housing Division, Telephone, 8/27/84.

diminished public subsidy availability suggest even lower new housing production levels unless the private sector can be reenergized.

These data raise a variety of questions which are pertinent as New York views its housing priorities for the future. Was the shrinkage of the private sector for much of the last two decades a simple tribute to the incongruity between the costs of construction in New York—and a population whose housing buying power was decreasing rapidly? Or was the situation more complex? Was it a displacement phenomenon? Did various forms of government-supported efforts— typified by Mitchell-Lama housing, geared as it was to middle-income households, combining both subsidies and perhaps fast-track handling through the involved procedures that all construction endures in the city—preempt purely private efforts? Or perhaps even as a corollary of assisted elements, permit the city the false luxury of avoiding the hard issues: of restoring its privately funded housing sector through removal of encumbrances which had encompassed it over time? Certainly from a realpolitik point of view, private housing construction—or its failure—would have been a more adequate hostage in the reformulation of rent control and land use regulations if there had not been the surrogate of government-aided housing effort.

EXHIBIT 4

New Dwelling Units Completed: New York City — 1921–1982

Period	Units (in 000s)			Percentage Composition		
	Private	Public[1]	Total	Private	Public[1]	Total
1921–1930	761.4	0.9	762.3	99.9%	0.1%	100.0%
1931–1940	192.1	15.2	207.3	92.7%	7.3%	100.0%
1941–1950	127.8	37.8	165.6	77.2%	22.8%	100.0%
1951–1960	234.0	89.3	323.3	72.4%	27.6%	100.0%
1961–1970	232.6	115.4	348.0	66.8%	33.2%	100.0%
1971–1980	50.3	115.3	165.6	30.4%	69.6%	100.0%
1981	4.8	3.9	8.7	55.2%	44.8%	100.0%
1982	3.6	3.7	7.3	49.3%	50.7%	100.0%

[1] Includes public housing (units built/operated by the New York City Housing Authority) and publicly assisted housing (units insured, subsidized and in other ways aided by the municipal state/federal governments)

Source: City of New York, Department of City Planning, *Housing Database – Public and Publicly Aided Housing* (New York, NY: City Planning, August 1983); City of New York, Department of City Planning, *New Housing in New York City* 1981-1982 (New York, NY: City Planning, December 1983); City of New York, Department of City Planning, *New Dwelling Units Completed* – Annual Series (New York, NY: City Planning, Series).

EXHIBIT 4A

New Dwelling Units Completed: New York City – 1921–1982

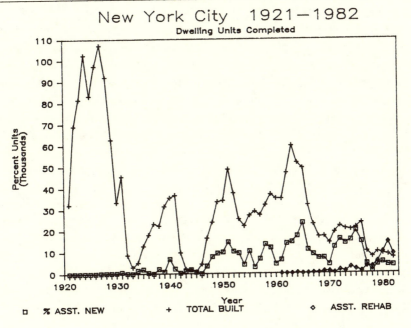

New York City   1921–1982
Dwelling Units Completed

□   % ASST. NEW   +   TOTAL BUILT   ◇   ASST. REHAB

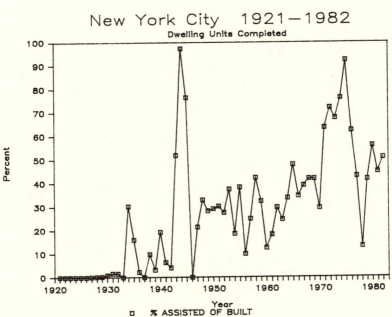

New York City   1921–1982
Dwelling Units Completed

□   % ASSISTED OF BUILT

These are questions which are of much more than historical interest. The actual level of new housing production, whether measured in terms of starts or completions, is miniscule. And this is in the face of rent levels, at least in selected areas of the city, that are the envy of housing developers everywhere else in the world. The costs of construction, despite occasional verbal exhortations, have soared out of sight. In a peculiar reifying fashion, they make it incumbent on developers, if they are to build at all, to build and construct within the winner's circle, i.e., the relatively small area which is attractive to those who can afford the enormous rents that a combination of New York's land and construction costs entail. To what degree did the city so injure the institutional fabric of its private residential housing industry in the past twenty years as to result in this phenomenon? And even if it was substantial, is it rectifiable?

While there was some slight pickup in housing starts through 1984, the level at best currently barely exceeds 10,000 units a year, well below the attrition through abandonment. *Without a re-energization of the private housing industry within the city, not only will there be an abrupt halt of the filtering process which has improved at least the physical characteristics of the city's low- and moderate-income housing stock, but also an increasing competition between middle-income groups and those less fortunately endowed.*

In essence this suggests that the sum of the housing policies of the city have failed to yield a sturdy enough base. The intimate calculus of housing availability and desirability to population retention and expansion, and, with the latter, the city's future economic functions, suggests a greater intensification of the elimination of the middle.

The linkage to the city's job base and employment future is evident. In the 1970s, six percent of Manhattan's jobs were held by New Jerseyans. But 23 percent of the borough's job growth in the 1980s is held by that state's residents.[4] And this is to say nothing of other commuters. The city's new business functions—and its future economic vitality—increasingly depend on people who do not live within it. And, given new communications capacity, ultimately jobs are following residence place. The commuter lines are jammed, the discomfort, time, and cost expand—and the employer moves to join his work force. New York does not, and seemingly cannot, provide the housing required to complement its evolving economic base. The competition is evident; it does not wait on new communications methods or other hi-tech assumptions. As shown in Exhibit 5, New

York City's share of the market in terms of the region's new housing and office production has slipped markedly.

This is particularly the case when measured against New Jersey—with the northern counties of that state generating two-and-one-half times the number of dwelling units that are being constructed within the city. And ultimately the population housed within those

EXHIBIT 5

New York Regional Housing and Office Market

	1980	1981	1982	1983	1984
Housing Market: 1980–1984* *(Annual Activity)*					
Total Units (Number)	28,883	29,801	27,447	44,965	35,000
Location (Percent)					
New York City	24%	22%	23%	24%	20%
Long Island	13	15	11	11	13
New Jersey	44	41	49	50	54
Northern Suburbs	19	22	17	15	13
Type (Percent)					
Single-Family	40%	39%	40%	45%	42%
Two-Family	4	4	4	6	5
Apartment	56	57	56	49	53
Office Market: 1980–1984* *(Annual Activity)*					
Total Construction (Millions of Square Feet)	17.8	19.5	18.7	22.5	21.0
Location of New Space (Percent)					
New York City	44%	32%	32%	30%	20%
Long Island	3	6	11	4	11
New Jersey	38	43	40	45	50
Northern Suburbs	15	19	17	21	19
Vacancy Rates (Percent) New York City					
(Annual Average)	3%	3%	4%	6%	5%
Suburbs (Range)	4–10	5–14	5–15	5–20	5–24
Lease Rates Range (Dollars per Square Foot)					
New York City	$35–$40	$40–$50	$38–$42	$38–$42	$28–$45
Suburbs	$11–$24	$25–$24	$17–$24	$18–$27	$20–$28

*Consolidated Metropolitan Statistical Area

Sources: F. W. Dodge, Inc. (1980–1983) and Landauer estimates (1984) (Housing Market Data); Landauer Associates, "New York Metropolitan Area Market" in ULI, *Development Review and Outlook* (Washington, D.C.: ULI, 1984), pp. 253, 257 (Office Market data).

dwelling units is complemented by job movement as well, at the cost
of the City of New York. Manhattan is flourishing with its new
suburbs. Left behind is the old city. And even its core may be
threatened in time.

If New York did not have the renewed economic vigor and functions that have characterized these last half-dozen years, its situation
would be similar to any of the lesser municipalities of the country,
i.e., a shrinking job base, population outflow, and an increasing problem of abandoned housing—not dying through the ravages of neighborhood environment or the arsonist's torch, but rather quietly
through lack of demand.

New York still has the capacity to reverse its population shrinkage. It is nearly unique among America's great older industrial cities in
that regard. Whether it has the will is unclear. Failure to enhance
both resident buying power and number must ultimately feed back
into the support of the city's infrastructure as well. User charges,
when applied to a shrinking base, must self-destructively increase. It
is growth which can save the city—and vital as an input in this regard
is an augmented flow of housing.

It should be pointed out that in response to severely curtailed
new housing production in New York City, the rehabilitation of the
extant stock has increased significantly. The rise in publicly assisted
rehabilitation is illustrative. In the early 1960s, the government (city,
state, and federal) aided the rehabilitation of a few hundred units
annually in New York City.[5] A decade later such rehabilitation
increased to a few thousand per year; by the late 1970s–early 1980s,
roughly 10,000 to 15,000 units were rehabilitated annually with public
assistance. Privately initiated and financed rehabilitation has also
increased in vigor in recent years.

Rehabilitation may be viewed by some as a triumph of rationality
against the waste inherent in a failure to upgrade older facilities. In
part, however, when it is by default of new construction, the result is
a lack of affordable housing choice in New York. Rehabilitation is a
necessary but insufficient part of New York's required shelter strategy.
It is essential in coping with a housing stock whose average age is
over the half-century mark. But it cannot cope with the sheer level of
total obsolescence that characterizes so much of the city—nor can it
replace the heavy levels of abandonment.

The reality of a diminished federal priority for housing subsidy
programs—evidenced by the demise of Section 8—leaves the city with
few options. It must either divert its own resources to subsidize hous-

ing, or painfully reanalyze the components of housing development inhibition. Politically, it is easier to attempt to paper over, however inadequately, institutional inadequacies than it is to remove them. The fiscal costs and failure to produce under this approach raise serious question for the future. The city's principal tool for "market housing" has been tax benefits. But this, as will be described later, is now under assault. Even with it, there was little action. Must reform wait for disaster?

The changing shape of new additions to the supply are further illustrated in Exhibit 2, which provides data by borough and by configuration for housing starts from 1970 to 1983. (It should be noted that there are slight differences in the absolute levels of starts as shown in this exhibit because of variations in recording procedures; they do not alter the import, however.) Despite all the problems of development in Manhattan, it now accounts for nearly half the city's production, the bulk of it in large-scale configurations, and nearly all south of 96th Street. Roughly another quarter of the total starts are developed in Staten Island, typically in smaller buildings. Practically left out of the calculus are the other three boroughs. *In 1983, for example, the sum of all the housing permits in the Bronx, Brooklyn, and Queens, was barely half the total a dozen years before in any one of them alone.* What is cause and what is effect? Is the shrinkage of population in these boroughs a passive reflection of a lethargic building market guided by inexorable demographic forces? Or could (and should?) the comparative vigor of Manhattan be diverted to them? As yet, the city has not been able to develop a steering mechanism adequate to the challenge. Municipal efforts have been much more punitive than positive: reducing the building potential of Manhattan rather than enhancing the ease of development, *in scale* of the balance of the city.

New York's housing configurations are quite unlike those of the nation. One-family permits, for example, account for barely eight percent of the total, half the proportion of two-to-four family units—the latter a configuration of miniscule practical importance nationally. It is large-scale structures—those with five or more units—that represent nearly three-quarters of the total. While increasing proportions of these are co-ops or condominiums, this suggests that the national constituency—which in general has supported homeownership typically in one-family configurations, and with it legislative aid—largely bypasses the conventional structures of the city. Indeed, in all of the United States in 1983, there were only 191,000 privately financed, unsubsidized, unfurnished apartments completed in buildings of five units or more. The vast bulk of these were in the South and West, and only 16 percent of the total were at rents of $500 or more—the bare threshold of New York City starts.[6]

The eye of the Manhattan visitor is bemused by the ever higher residential towers—with their matching rents—but a more modest configuration is securing increasing attention. It is striking to note the increasing proportionate role of two- to four-family housing in new construction. While hard hit in the years of the fiscal crunch, since 1981 it represents more than one in five of the city's permitted units (see Exhibit 1). This contrasts with barely one-quarter to one-third of this proportionate representation in the country as a whole. These are the buildings that dot Canarsie and play an increasing role in Staten Island as well. They provide a hybrid mechanism, with many of the tax virtues of homeownership and rental operation—the latter outside the strictures imposed by the city, particularly rent control. This configuration is the major "success story" of the outer boroughs. It provides practically uniquely new rental housing at prices competitive with those of suburbia.

From one point of view, this configuration indicates the latent potency of the market if the city could reduce its self-imposed strictures. A less-positive approach suggests that such units are made possible only by avoiding much-needed adherence to the building code (particularly in the illegal three-family configuration) as well as substantial subsidization through underassessment. Without denigrating the criticisms, there is much to be learned from their comparative success. Is there an expansion opportunity that the city should be reviewing?

The potential of small-scale holding in New York is further indicated by the frantic activity in illegal subdivision of rental units into facilities for the Yuppie generation. Rent-controlled apartments are exploited by the fortunate through subletting and key money. City officials have voiced a demand for maintaining controlled units for true primary residences, but this is honored more in the breach than by observance. The market strength is obvious. It is symbolized by the increased speculative purchase of condo units for rental. But the city lacks the policy mix to channel this vigor into significant housing-start action.

The sum of the present system ensures scarcity, and with it high cost. Speculators and extant holders reap windfalls; this is a penalty not only for residential aspirants, but ultimately the city's economic base.

The Governmental Sector

Housing production in New York City has become the ward of governmental subsidy and regulation. The federal, state, and city governments have all been significant players. The importance of this process in shaping the present matrix deserves study.

No city in the United States has a longer nor a more comprehensive involvement in housing than New York. More than just following the conventional wisdom, New York has been a pioneer—inspiring other central cities and setting the pattern for many federal housing programs. Notable examples include the tenement-house laws of the nineteenth century, public housing involvement in the early twentieth century, and today's multifaceted rehabilitation initiatives.

New York's first housing law dates from 1648, when the city regulated chimney construction and ordered that "hogs and goats be pastured only in fenced areas."[7] In response to the squalor of tenement construction in the mid- to late-nineteenth century, Tenement House Acts were legislated in 1867 and 1901. These inspired further Multiple Dwelling Laws in 1929, 1955, and subsequent years.

But regulation was only part of the input. In 1920, New York State permitted cities to abate real estate taxes on newly constructed housing. New York City applied this incentive to its fullest measure. In a decade period, over 750,000 housing units were built and over $300 million in property taxes abated. The 1920s also witnessed the start of Limited Dividend Companies (LDC) providing low-income housing with the assistance of below-market-rate financing and partial real estate tax exemption. The LDCs constructed over 10,000 housing units, mainly in the late 1920s and early 1930s.

Of much greater import was Public Housing authorized in New York City in 1934—three years before the federal public housing program was enacted. New York City's first public housing venture was a 135-unit project built on the lower East Side in 1936. A half-century later, the New York City Housing Authority encompasses 2,800 buildings containing 174,000 housing units. The Housing Authority provides shelter to over 480,000 people—a population larger than the city of Buffalo.[8] Its electric bill exceeds that of the State of Utah.[9]

The 1950s and 1960s witnessed New York City taking full advantage of newly available state and federal housing programs. Notable examples included Mitchell-Lama (a state- and city-sponsored effort resulting in the production of over 120,000 rental and cooperative housing units), state Redevelopment Corporation housing (12,000 units), and numerous federal programs such as Title I, and Sections 207 (64,000 units), 221(d)(3) (6,600 units) and 608 (28,000 units).[10] These initiatives were followed by later, mainly federal, subsidized efforts in the 1970s such as Section 8, which assisted the construction of over 11,000 new housing units.

This multifaceted litany of housing offerings resulted in considerable throughput. From 1928 to 1982 over 500,000 housing units were built and another 57,000 units rehabilitated with public assistance.[11] Yet much of what has been described in history: The major housing pump-primers of yesteryear, such as Public Housing, Mitchell-Lama, and Section 8, either no longer exist or are merely maintaining what they built in the past. The housing themes today are modest effort and making the most of the limited funds which are available.

This more subdued role, as opposed to the expansive, perhaps hubristic, tenor of yesteryear, is reflected in New York City's current public sector housing involvement. The total authorized budget for FY 1985 of the Department of Housing Preservation and Development (HPD) is some $360 million.[12] This is less than two percent of the total net expenditures for the city as a whole.* While this total does not include taxes foregone through the J-51 and 421 programs, it is a relatively modest level of commitment. It should further be noted that the bulk of the expenditures reflect federal contributions, rather than those generated by the city itself. These latter make up barely one-third of the total.

New York City's current housing effort is characterized by an emphasis on rehabilitation as opposed to new construction and on assuming a caretaker's role for marginal housing (see Exhibit 6).[13] The latter is exemplified by the care and feeding of *in rem* structures, buildings taken by the city on non-payment of taxes. Nearly one-half the CDBG-funded expenditures by HPD in 1985 will be devoted to its *in rem* inventory; such activity represents fully one-third of the total HPD budget.[14] The city's housing caretaker role is manifested in other ways ranging from the appointment of receivers on almost 1,200 units in 1984, to making almost 14,000 emergency repairs, and sealing/demolishing almost 4,000 deteriorated buildings in the same year.

---

* This does not include the New York City Housing Authority nor other departments which may contribute to the city's housing stock, or its governance, such as the Buildings Department, Landmarks Preservation Commission, City Planning Department, etc.

When the flow of activity is examined over the years, there is an evolving substitution of modest rehab for more significant efforts—the latter provided principally under Section 8. In 1981, for example, there were nearly 4,000 substantially rehabbed units under that program alone.

In addition, in the early 1980s, Section 8 new construction averaged in excess of 1,500 units a year—approximately 15 percent of total housing starts for the city as a whole. The imminent demise of much of Section 8 is poorly compensated by an increase in moderate rehab financed by the federal government. Present upscale city housing activity is nearly exclusively the domain of the currently debated §421(a) and J-51 programs. These tax-reduction efforts have been crucial: J-51 itself, in terms of unit activity, far outweighs all of the other housing rehabilitation efforts under the aegis of HPD, while the §421(a) and (b) programs combined were applied on more than one-half of recent housing starts (see Exhibit 6).

The city faces the reality of abrupt declines in the federal funding which has been central to its recent efforts. Yet there is no clear municipal housing policy with which to replace the federal prop. In the words of Carol Lamberg, Executive Director of the Settlement Housing Fund, "This year [1984], New York will receive funds from the Federal Government for the following: about 125 units of public housing; a few hundred units of Section 202 housing for the elderly; 10 or so mixed-income rental housing (HoDAG) developments for perhaps 1,000 units . . . ; 900 units of Section 8 moderate rehabilitation; 3,000 or so units of moderate rehab . . . grants with vouchers to go with some of them; only 589 units of Section 8 for existing housing; Section 235 interest-rate subsidies for about 500 units. . . ." Pointing out that New York State, through its grant program, will provide relatively small subsidies, she concluded, "If all goes well, we will have four thousand units of rehab or new construction, and another six hundred units of assistance for existing housing."[15] In a universe of more than 2.5 million occupied housing units, that does seem a modest figure, indeed. And even this level will be reduced by additional federal cutbacks.

Housing Futures

Most American cities are prisoners of the past, with little in the way of alternative economic activities to replace those which are disappearing. The pattern of shrinkage may be accelerated or slowed by local

EXHIBIT 6

Major New York City Housing Programs — Description and Activity

Program	Description		1978	1979	1980	1981	1982	1983	1984	(Plan) 1985	1985 CDBG Funding (Millions)
I. Loan/Guarantee/Other Subsidy Programs											
Article 8-A	offers rehabilitation loans at 3 percent interest and 20-year terms to owners of multiple dwellings occupied by lower-income tenants ($5,000).	·Units Rehabbed	1,472	2,700	4,869	6,640	7,230	7,398	7,613	7,895	
		·Loans Closed ($ Million)	$ 1.5	$ 4.6	$ 8.9	$ 13.0	$ 15.4	$ 15.3	$ 15.9	$ 16.6	$15.5
Participation Loan	offers a 1 percent interest loan in combination with privately financed market-cost mortgage money to finance repairs/renovations on deteriorating multiple dwellings ($8,000–$10,000).	·Units Rehabbed	392	776	1,904	3,322	3,321	3,571	2,793	2,400	
		·Loans Closed ($ Million)	$ 2.5	$ 11.4	$ 30.3	$ 53.9	$ 54.8	$ 61.1	$ 52.2	$ 48.0	$24.0
Neighborhood Preservation Program	NPP provides a range of rehabilitation services in selected neighborhoods.	·Mortgage Commitments ($ Million)	$ 9.2	$ 14.9	$ 24.3	$ 31.7	$ 38.6	$ 55.1	$ 39.5	$ 36.0	$ 3.2
		·Units Repaired	4,726	4,703	5,668	8,937	10,650	13,043	11,584	10,200	
Section 8	provides significant subsidy for multifamily new construction and rehabilitation (federal subsidy).	·New Construction	1,897	2,799	778	1,537	2,208	1,738	1,362	1,000	NA
		·Substantial Rehab	851	1,920	3,275	3,967	1,281	3,477	967	500	
		·Moderate Rehab	NA	NA	NA	NA	NA	2,317	2,882	161	
Other	Small Home Improvement Program (SHIP) provides loan fund applied by Neighborhood Housing Services (NHS); Home Improvement Program (HIP) provides improvement loans; Real Estate Mortgage Insurance Corporation (REMIC) insures rehabilitation/refinancing mortgage loans.	·HIP Units	NA	NA	NA	NA	418	914	1,461	NA	$11.7
		·REMIC Units	1,252	1,383	1,370	2,608	403	NA	NA	NA	
II. Real Estate Tax Exemption/Abatement											
J-51	provides a 12-year *exemption* from taxation on an increase in assessed valuation resulting from alterations and also permits *abatement* of real estate tax equaling 90 percent of the certified reasonable construction costs.	·Applications Approved ($ Million)	$ 71.4	$ 79.2	$122.3	$154.9	$152.3	$121.7	$ 66.4	NA	NA
		·Units Approved	48,161	41,251	73,808	73,705	73,087	83,296	60,330	NA	

Section 421	provides for an 8- to 10-year phase-in of property taxes resulting from the construction of new residential units. §421(a) applies to multiple dwellings, and §421(b) to one- and two-family homes.	· §421(a) – Units	2,690	2,346	3,679	5,778	1,449	3,852	2,678	NA
		· §421(b) – Units	NA	122	723	1,020	1,236	1,492	1,565	NA

III. *Caretaker Functions*

Article 7-A	provides for court-appointed administrators to manage multiple dwellings where the owners have been unable/unwilling to provide essential services/maintenance.	· Units	NA	NA	NA	NA	1,839	1,200	1,159	1,200	$ 1.4
		· Financial Assistance($000)	NA	NA	NA	NA	$ 832	$ 575	$ 621	$ 800	
Demolition and Sealing	removes the danger and blighting influence of open, vacant buildings through demolition and sealing.	· Buildings Demolished	1,455	1,888	2,235	2,065	1,974	1,532	1,456	1,500	$18.8
		· Buildings Sealed	4,795	5,293	6,484	5,962	4,226	2,656	2,342	3,250	
Emergency Repair Program	makes/provides emergency repairs/services where serious violations exist that the property owner refused to correct.	· Repairs Completed	20,450	21,762	26,329	38,186	37,503	17,321	13,348	15,000	$ 6.2
In-Rem Central Management	The *city* manages, maintains, and eventually disposes of properties acquired for non-payment of real-estate taxes.	· Total Buildings	NA	8,593	9,106	8,417	7,809	9,083	9,983	10,110	$91.2
		· Total Units	NA	100,995	101,352	76,361	76,162	88,466	91,457	95,267	
In-Rem Alternative (Community) Management	There are numerous efforts to foster community/tenant/other private-interest management, and ultimately ownership of the in-rem stock. Examples include the Tenant Interim Lease (TIL) program, Community Management Program (CMP), and Private Ownership and Management Program (POMP).	· Total Buildings	81	708	635	647	523	488	507	527	$33.3
		· Total Units	1,664	7,377	14,969	14,787	12,464	11,457	11,643	11,172	

Total indicated programs (CDBG): $205.3
Total housing programs (CDBG): $240.5

NA = Not applicable, or information not available.

Source: City of New York, *The Mayor's Management Report 1978* (New York, NY: City of New York, Series); City of New York, *City Fiscal Year 1985 Community Development Program* (New York, NY: City of New York, June 6, 1984); City of New York, *Housing Database – Public and Publicly Aided Housing* (New York, NY: City of New York, August 1983).

policy, but the negative direction—at least in the near-term future—is obvious. New York City's case is different. The challenges of optimizing the relationship between its residents and the new economic activities which characterize its future are substantial—but at least the potential vitality and absorptive capacity of the latter are evident. New York has a choice of futures, with housing policy playing a central role in defining the city's capacity to effectively cope with tomorrow. While, as discussed below, we do not see a sharp increase in the total household numbers of the city, the shrinkage which characterizes so many other municipalities does not apply—assuming the city can maintain its economic base. The major dangers lie in the potential for growing conflict between the shelter housing aspirations of the poor and the post-shelter housing agenda of the city's more affluent population.

Future Housing Demand

The issues of forecasting housing demand in New York City partake of all of the uncertainties of this exercise conducted elsewhere—with an extra fillip specific to the New York scene. The very number of its residents, present and prospective, is controversial. Dwarfing this dimension, however, is the issue of household size and numbers—the critical input of demand. In common with defining housing policy nationally, the greatest area of uncertainty is that of headship rates, i.e., for a given population of specific age characteristics, how many households will be formed.

Nationally, headship rates increased dramatically from World War II until 1980. The increases in real housing costs experienced at that time, the decline in real housing buying power as a function of the recession, and perhaps even a crisis of confidence in the future caused an abrupt blip (a long-term deviation?) in this vital phenomenon. Thus, while national Census forecasts for the first four years of the 1980s suggested the formation of 1,700,000 new households on average, the real incidence rate was reduced to 1,300,000. Even the divorce rate declined in the face of economic uncertainty—and with it, a key parameter of household formation and dwelling unit absorption.

In 1980, New York City's average size of household was 2.54 persons—roughly 10 percent under that of the nation. Will this relationship continue, or will the increased cost—and decreasing availability of housing in New York—regroup its inhabitants to yield a smaller demand for housing from a given population? If the necessity for a second and even a third income in order to sustain a household were to continue, there would be, by very definition, fewer households.

The historic trend data are worth reviewing. New York City's population decline of nearly 800,000 people from 1970 to 1980, from a housing point of view, was nearly offset by the decline in household size, with a concomitant relatively small decline of some 50,000 households; i.e., the population loss was more than ten percent, the household equivalent less than two percent.

By 1980 in Manhattan, for example, fully half of the 705,000 households consisted of one person, an additional 193,000 of two people. By way of contrast, only 42,000 households on the Island had five or more members. Nor is this unique: Even in the Bronx half of all households were one or two persons. In 1984 the median number of persons per rental unit in the city was 1.89; for owner households it was 2.41. Virtually half the city's total housing stock was occupied by one- and two-person households. Density levels had fallen to roughly two rooms per person. Indeed, within the controlled stock, sheltering the city's oldest, longest-term residents, there were only .413 persons per room.

The second parameter which must be detailed in viewing the future is the size, by age category, of the total population that is anticipated. Again, for the nation, this is a far simpler process than for a geographic subset. We know the number of present residents who will be reaching the years of household formation, certainly for the next fifteen years to come. Subject to the influence of migration—which, though far from trivial on the national level, is dwarfed by natural increase—this provides a reasonably sound starting point for population extrapolation.

In New York City, on the other hand, the visions of future total population vary most substantially. The New York State Housing Authority, for example, for the purposes of its own demand forecasts, anticipated an increase in New York City's population on the order of 19 percent, with a net addition of 36 percent in household count for the decade of the 1980s.[16] It is sadly unique in this estimate; the New York State Department of Commerce, in its preliminary official population projections for New York State counties as of 1983, generated a tactful 1990 forecast within a few thousand of the 1980 equivalent.[17] Current Census Bureau forecasts, though they show some measure of stabilization from the city's substantial population loss rate of the 1970s, are slightly more modest.

Utilizing the State Department of Commerce forecast of population by age category and assuming a continuation of the headship rates within New York City as of 1980 yields no change in the number of households to 1990. The State Department of Commerce extrapolation of population, when taken to the year 2000, reverses field and brings the household number in New York below its 1980 level.

These estimates are, at best, simply that. Much depends upon the housing buying power changes within the city, as well as its demographics. Certainly, however, they indicate that if there were to be a continuation of the population loss of the 1970s, it would no longer be cloaked by household-size decline. Rather, New York's housing game of musical chairs suddenly would have too few players—and some empty housing units as well. Has the subdivision of the population gone as far as it can go? It is a very long time since the Rand Corporation in its economic analysis of New York City's Mitchell-Lama housing program[18] had as one of its major policy recommendations an increase in the number of two- and three-bedroom units for middle-income families with children.

While the dangers of generalizing from momentary exigencies, of extrapolating trend lines from a moment of time, are made clear by this example, there are a few rules which are evident: the first and foremost is that if the city's economic base should falter, it will be reflected not in a person-per-dwelling-unit fashion, but rather in a decline of housing demand. At a moment in time when New York City rents have no parallel elsewhere in the world, recital of potential vulnerabilities seems absurd. The demographic characteristics and their tight linkage to housing suggest a measure of danger, however.

Secondly, there has been a long, sad, negative relationship of income, and with it, housing buying power and minority status. Unless this relationship is broken, even assuming a near stability in terms of the total number of New York City's inhabitants, the shrinkage potential of white, non-Hispanic numbers in the 18–54 and 55–64 age categories is particularly ominous. At best, it suggests a distinct decline of rent-paying, house-carrying capacity.

The city's shelter crisis could be alleviated by reducing its number of households, but this would be a Pyrrhic victory. The more appropriate response to ensure New York's economic viability–and the concomitant capacity to alleviate the needs of its poor—is expansion of housing opportunity. A decline of demand will not engender housing ease—but rather housing abandonment levels even higher than the 20,000-unit current figure. And decline in demand does not resolve the problem of housing the poor—those on welfare, the homeless, and residents of the *in rem* stock.[19]

Housing the Poor—Public Assistance

In the midst of an economy which by conventional measures is growing substantially, with a civilian labor force that had gone up by only 0.8 percent from the fourth quarter of 1982 to the fourth quarter of 1983, New York's welfare population actually grew.[20] Payroll employment, admittedly including non-residents, increased somewhat more abruptly with a 1.1 percent gain. At the same time, the number of unemployed residents was reduced by fully 12 percent on a year-to-year basis. But the Public Assistance caseload rose 9½ percent from the fourth quarter of 1982 to the fourth quarter of 1983, to a grand total of 904,744 people—a 5.2 percent increase. And this was not a function simply of home relief, i.e., of people receiving supplementary benefits, but rather extended over nearly all categories. This absolute figure was the highest level since the second quarter of 1978 when the city was still emerging from the fiscal crisis and both local and national economies were relatively quiescent. Only 1.9 percent of public assistance households had employment earnings, and even this small percentage seems to be declining.

It is the Aid to Dependent Children program whose participants make up by far the largest proportion of welfare recipients of the city with more than eight in ten of the total. There are 516,000 children on public assistance in New York—roughly a quarter of the total of all minors in the city. The poor have children; non-poor parents reside elsewhere. New York City's aged inexpensive housing stock is a particularly weak vessel with which to contain them, at a time of an increasingly hostile attitude toward the youth of even the affluent.

Only 43,172 welfare families are reported in public housing as of January 1984.[21] Allowing for some illegal doubling up, as well as the city's increasing role as the housing operator of last resort, suggests that the private market provides shelter for the bulk of all welfare households. For those unfamiliar with welfare, it should be noted that so-called SSI (Supplemental Security Income) recipients—the aged, the blind, and the disabled—are separately counted, with a total of some 208,000 within this category over and above the welfare recipients per se. More than a million New Yorkers receive food stamps; nearly a quarter of them do not receive welfare.

In every survey of world cities, New York has had the dubious distinction of being one of the costlier places in which to live. It is a cruel place to be poor. In December of 1983, for example, 68 percent of its public assistance households living in private housing received the maximum state shelter allowance. The overall average was $173; the equivalent allowance paid to four-person households was $202; to one-person households, $143. Yet Section 8 federally established Fair Market Rents (FMR) for equivalent-size households were at least twice as high at that time (e.g., the FMR for existing housing units suitable for a studio apartment was $311, $372 for a one-bedroom, $436 for a two-bedroom, $540 for a three-bedroom, and $599 for a four-bedroom unit).

The affluent of New York find housing costs a devastating reality: The rent levels permitted by government to welfare recipients are below even the *current maintenance* costs of typical city accommodations, with no allowance for any other charges. Allowing for smaller units, in parallel with the shrinkage of household sizes, still leaves the annual increment levels of welfare rents well below the CPI—or any other meaningful measure of inflationary pressure. Where are the necessary resources for upgrading to be found? And what is the administrative linkage which could ensure that additional rents would yield better housing?

Housing the Poor—The Homeless

Relatively small in number, but increasingly striking as a symbol, is the issue of the homeless in New York. While Paris historically has had its deracinated sleeping above subway grates, in the shelter of bridge arches, and wherever the police will permit them, New York City—while far from free of this manifestation of societal frictions— long viewed the homeless as a relatively minor problem. In common with other major municipalities, New York hid its homeless on Skid Row. But the Bowery is rapidly becoming a fashionable area, the no-man's land under the Third Avenue El is no more, and the equivalent of Uncle Sam's Flophouse is vied for by the new Yuppie tenantry flocking to the post-industrial city.

The process of deinstitutionalization of mental patients—the effort to mainstream them, i.e., bring them back into the fullness of society (to say nothing of an effort to save some money)—has resulted in a decline of persons in New York State's institutionalized mental facilities from 60,000 to 15,000 in the space of a decade. Reflecting some of the individuals who no longer can find shelter within mental institutions, and in part undoubtedly resulting from the mismatch between the city's resident population and its job base, there is an increasing number of homeless in the city. A walk through the bus terminals, the public comfort facilities, the railroad stations, and the like, to say nothing of countless hallways, gives some indication of the magnitude of the problem.

There are no definitive data on the number of homeless. Advocates of their cause have suggested that perhaps one percent of the nation's population fits this description, while others have suggested a far lesser magnitude. The Governor and the Mayor indulge in an unproductive sarabande—the latter suggesting that it is the state's responsibility for having "dumped" the homeless through deinstitutionalization, the former implying that the increase in number is rather a result of a supposed failure of the city to reinvent the jobs with which the homeless might once have secured the resources adequate to buy appropriate shelter.

Indeed, it is becoming increasingly evident that one of the prices of political peace in the city is expensive forms of action—some real, some symbolic—to provide municipal facilities for the homeless. The old single-room occupancy hotels, long viewed by housing reformers as disasters to be eliminated as quickly as possible, are now deified by default of any other solution. Their very existence is currently immortalized by rigid protective devices to forestall their reuse for other purposes.

Emergency housing currently is budgeted at well over $200 million, more than twenty times the equivalent of three years ago. The costs per capita are in excess of $10,000 annually. The results at best are a holding operation yielding inferior shelter and current scandal.[22]

The city is the sad heir to a significant share of its nominal housing stock through abandonment. Efforts are being made to recycle it for the benefit of the homeless—but the scale of the problem mocks the results. Who are the homeless? Can the basic provision of shelter suffice? Or are broader social inputs required? No one knows; rival assertions battle in the media. In the meantime the problem is growing.

New York City is not unique in facing this challenge, but it suffers from the law of large numbers. A fractional incidence in smaller settings yields a relatively modest, much more manageable population; in New York, on the other hand, it can easily secure critical mass. The civil liberties of today no longer tolerate the deadline behind which the poor were made invisible a generation ago.

The concept of the city providing emergency aid in the face of disaster—of temporary necessity—has long been established. The fear in this case is that, in the very act of providing the level of housing accommodation for which critics of the present municipal administration are calling, a permanent new group of shelter-dependent individuals may be established. Their ultimate needs may well absorb much more of fiscal capacity than can presently be foreseen. In the meantime, press releases based on top-of-the-head special pleading substitute for hard data. Regardless of the precise figure, it should be noted that a nightly average of more than 5,000 people received lodging in city shelters in the fourth quarter of 1983; this in turn was up 37.6 percent and 72 percent, respectively, from one and two years previously. The equivalent figure in the winter of 1984 is pressing the 20,000 mark.[23]

Housing the Poor: Coping with the In Rem Problem

The very definition of *in rem* housing catches the observer between two worlds. The first is the sphere of functional reality. There is a substantial part of New York City's housing stock which has functionally been abandoned; only a fraction of this abandonment is signaled by tax delinquency. Part of it is by owners whose taxes may be reasonably up-to-date, but whose interest in the building's operations have ended. Their tax payment at most is much more a function of speculative value, even of the stripped lot, than for the extant housing entity.

The legal domain of *in rem* is more limited.[24] In order to be within it, a building must be not only tax delinquent for a significant period of time, but also have been moved into a vesting procedure by the city. The latter process is organized by a so-called "tax sweep," i.e., typically by borough or subset of borough, a thoroughgoing investigation of tax delinquency and subsequent taking. If this is not done currently, there may be buildings which functionally, at least by definition of tax delinquency, should be in *in rem*—but are not. The number, therefore, depends upon whether the city moves to make *functional reality statistical reality—to move buildings which have fallen out of the interests of the private sector into the public domain.*[25]

The precise number of *functionally abandoned* buildings, by this definition, i.e., receiving no landlord care, is far larger than the *legal domain* of those parcels taken by the city. And unless the city has a strong policy of maintaining the taking program, the temptation to avoid "taking" may cause the gap to widen. By default of adequate statistical information on the former, however, we are reduced to presenting materials on the latter. These, as shown in Exhibit 7, are substantial enough in themselves. While some of the city's caretaker functions outside of the domain of the *in rem* process were capsulized in our earlier Exhibit 6, it is the latter which is by far the more important.

Data on the *in rem* housing inventory and its management are provided in Exhibit 7 for 1979 through Budgeted 1985. Basically, the program has averaged an inventory of 8,000 to 10,000 buildings through those years. Slightly less than half of them are occupied; the balance—5,000 to 6,000—are vacant. These buildings have within them a total of roughly 100,000 units; again, half of them are in occupied buildings, the balance in unoccupied ones. The city in recent years has fostered a policy of relocating remnant tenants out of poorer buildings, or those which are nearly vacant, to attempt to compact them—to facilitate management, reduce costs, and hopefully provide a higher level of housing amenity. This is symbolized by the rising ratios of occupied buildings to total from 1979 through 1985.

By 1985, there were some 45,000 occupied units within the city's domain, a far-from-trivial number; its scale represents the equivalent of one-quarter of all the units under *all* public housing programs—federal, state, and municipal. The *in rem* occupied units make up roughly two percent of the city's total of all rental housing. It is the new housing for the very poor. While the average gross income of public housing households as of January 1, 1984 was close to the $10,000 mark, surveys indicate that the *in rem* equivalent hovered at best at about 70 percent of that level.[26]

New York is not alone in discovering that the city itself becomes the houser of last resort. The conventional vision views tax-delinquent parcels as temporary aberrants—the result of financial distress, marital discord, or other personal fiscal tragedy—resulting in a building passing into municipal ownership. Again, the conventional wisdom envisions this as a revolving-door relationship: abandoned bicycles and automobiles are auctioned off by the police; the equivalent holds for

190

EXHIBIT 7
New York City In-Rem Housing Inventory and Management

Profile	1979	1980	1981	1982	1983	1984	1985 (Plan)
				Inventory Profile			
Buildings							
Central[1]	8,593	9,106	8,417	7,809	9,083	9,983	10,110
Alternative[2]	708	635	647	523	488	507	527
Total	9,301	9,741	9,064	8,332	9,571	10,490	10,637
Occupied Buildings							
Central	4,347	3,801	4,928	4,582	3,430	4,190	4,407
Alternative	708	635	647	523	488	507	527
Total	5,055	4,436	5,575	5,105	3,918	4,697	4,934
Total Units							
Central	100,995	101,352	76,361	76,162	88,466	91,457	95,267
Alternative[3]	7,377	14,969	14,787	12,464	11,457	11,643	11,172
Total	108,372	116,321	91,148	88,626	99,923	103,100	106,439
Units In Occupied Buildings							
Central	52,144	39,933	47,386	44,674	31,756	34,471	39,439
Alternative[3]	7,377	14,969	14,787	12,464	11,457	11,643	11,172
Total	59,521	54,902	62,173	57,138	43,213	46,114	50,611
Occupied Units							
Central	31,875	24,269	23,184	25,370	26,739	29,601	34,067
Alternative[3]	7,377	14,969	14,787	12,464	11,457	11,643	11,172
Total	39,252	39,238	37,971	37,834	38,196	41,244	45,239

191

Management Profile

Alternative Managment							
% of Buildings[4]	6.6%	14.3%	15.9%	14.0%	12.5%	10.8%	10.7%
% of Units[5]	15.7%	33.3%	34.4%	30.1%	28.0%	26.1%	22.8%
Percentage Occupancy[6]							
Central	61.0%	61.0%	80.0%	81.0%	84.0%	86.0%	86.0%
Alternative	NA	NA	NA	NA	NA	NA	NA
Percentage Rent Collection[7]							
Central	30.0%	—	—	—	—	85.0%	85.0%
Alternative	—	—	—	—	—	90.0%	90.0%
Sales (Buildings/Units)							
Central	0/0	380/ 878	236/3040	376/2276	720/4124	419/2247	493/2182
Alternative	100/2400	37/ 589	50/1630	112/2263	104/3049	73/1935	106/2779
Total	100/2400	417/1469	286/4670	488/4539	824/7173	492/4182	599/4961
Program Cost (CDBG Funded)							
Central ($ Million)	—	—	—	—	—	$ 76.9	$ 91.2
Alternative ($ Million)	—	—	—	—	—	$ 32.2	$ 33.3
Total ($ Million)	—	—	—	—	—	$108.1	$124.5

[1] Central (city) management
[2] Alternative (community group, tenant, private real estate) management
[3] Assumes all units under alternative management are in occupied buildings which are fully occupied
[4] Percentage of occupied city-owned buildings under alternative management. City-supplied data.
[5] Percentage of occupied city-owned units under alternative management. City-supplied data.
[6] Percentage of units in occupied buildings which are occupied (central management only)
[7] Percentage of owed rents collected (approximate figures).

NA = Information not available or applicable.

Source: City of New York, *The Mayor's Management Report* (New York, NY: City of New York, Series); City of New York, *The In-Rem Housing Program* (New York, NY: City of New York, Annual Series); City of New York, City Fiscal Year/1985 *Community Development Program* (New York, NY: City of New York, Annual Series).

buildings. The only operating issue is the time until an auction can be arranged. The very concept is one which does not conceive of a building without market value—and market aspirants as well. The municipal role at most is a temporary holding operation serving merely to bridge the gap from one private owner to another.

Sadly enough, long-held concepts tend to have a life force of their own, extending into periods into which they are no longer appropriate. The very longevity of the *in rem* phenomenon of New York indicates that this is not a temporary aberrant, but rather a fact of life, one which can best be dealt with by professional organization rather than "pick-up" expedience.[27]

It should be noted that New York City has moved in this direction. The tenant-consolidation process and increased rent collections within *in rem* buildings are solid accomplishments, although far from uncontroversial. Despite efforts at moving the *in rem* inventory into alternative forms of ownership, the pool of structures within its aegis has been virtually unaltered. Central Management as of 1985 was coping with 34,000 occupied units; the alternative approaches, i.e., tenant co-ops, neighborhood management groups, etc., are at one-third that figure (see Exhibit 7). In 1976, the city had some 2,500 buildings which were municipally owned. It has had 9,000–10,000 for the last seven years. Current city costs, borne by CDBG, are over $100 million a year, about $2,000 per occupied apartment.

The private market might well find some of the properties—as, for example, on the lower East Side—increasingly attractive, but typically for the politically suspect gentrification process. The non-profit groups that have been involved in operations have had far from an unsullied record, some of them clearly providing much more image than substance; even within this domain, there has been some feeling of cream-skimming, i.e., that the best of buildings, and those suitable to their operations, have already been taken out of the inventory—as witness the relatively large scale of the buildings which are under alternative management.

As indicated elsewhere, by default of any other inspiration, the abandoned structures are seen as a possible housing opportunity for the homeless. Their vulnerability as typically the oldest, least well-maintained, least mechanically and physically sound part of the city's housing inventory—to say nothing of their modest individual structure scale—raises issues in this regard. On the other hand, current expenditures for the homeless, running well in excess of $10,000 a year per household, suggest the potential of damming up this flow of funds—and with the resulting pool, providing for rehabilitation of the *in rem* housing stock.

But these are not necessarily conflicting resolutions. What is required here as a first step is a much more rigorous classification, mapping, and thoroughgoing inventory evaluation. At present, what we have is rather a holding operation: The political competence of the city is inadequate to cope with the possible, positive potentials. The resolution is, rather, to keep costs acceptable.

The city has explored all of the conventional wisdom of tenant management, non-profit group management, private realty-firm operation, and an infinite level of variation and partnerships among them. Unfortunately, the relative success or failure of these several groups is obscured by their partisans. The track record now is long enough. A period of evaluation followed by stronger policy recommendations is drastically needed. There is a potential of vacant land usable directly by the market, of other areas and buildings that may require additional but reasonable inputs. At present, we have immobility. The battle for turf within the city—of the new post-industrial affluent and the poor—is not confined to viable neighborhoods, but continues even within the mortuary of the *in rem* structures.

The *in rem* experience, as a whole, deserves review. The city's motives in moving to a fast-take procedure, cutting short the nominal four years of tax delinquency before *in rem* proceedings could ensue to a one-year period, were based on the belief that tax-delinquency was merely inexpensive borrowing by owners. Secondly, in the very act of permitting longer periods of tax delinquency, the private holder of property, after a long period of non-payment of taxes, would abandon the structure in the face of the debt which had accumulated on it. Further, there was the hope that if the city took buildings earlier, they would be in much better condition to be maintained, i.e., that the ravages of functional abandonment would simply not be as far along in time. While examples of each and every one of these elements has been cited at one time or another, there has not been a significant study of how well the present process has worked.

The problems of the poor are so compelling, their needs and the limited tools which are brought to bear on them so striking, as to create an emotional backlash. How can the city "give away" tax abatement or other forms of subsidy, much less raise the spectre of secondary displacement through potential neighborhood enhancements which might bring the rich in—and force the poor out? It is no longer enough that there be no fear of direct displacement, i.e., housing for the affluent built over the old railroad yards. The fear now, which inhibits action, is that in the very act of upgrading a blighted neighborhood, sooner or later, peripheral areas will be preempted—and the poor have nowhere to go.

Sometimes these are fears raised by the poor themselves— sometimes by the middle-incomed and more affluent beneficiaries of the current immobilization process. While much question has been raised as to the sheer extent of the gentrification processes which have taken place, there are enough examples to generate major political barriers.[28]

The fiscal crisis is a decade old, the half-life of fear long past. In its place is a hubristic belief that New York's economic growth is beyond question, requiring little in the way of accommodation. The city's increased dependence on self-raised revenues, with the decline in federal transfer payments, is recognized—but seemingly nonintegrated into the politics of its housing efforts. The J-51 and 421 debates exemplify the problems and the policy issues at work.

The Conflict Between the Shelter and Post-Shelter Imperatives— The J-51 Dispute

The city in terms of housing policy is caught between its several roles: as a focal point for the affluent and near-affluent, which for the moment we have entitled the "post-shelter society," and its mission in providing shelter and appropriate environment for the less fortunate— the "shelter economy." The dispute on J-51 and other forms of tax abatement or exemption provides a useful illustration of the issues that emerge from these schizoid goals and their resolution.

Enacted in 1955, the J-51 program provided long-term tax abatements on extant assessments, and exemptions on the value of new improvements, to owners who rehabilitated multifamily housing (and later to convert non-residential buildings to residential use). It was originally conceived as a program which would induce owners of coldwater tenements to upgrade their buildings, and succeeded admirably in that goal. Certainly by 1980, such dwelling units had been reduced to a handful. Increasingly, however, the program became an important tool in upgrading middle-income and luxury units as well. In recent years, the city has probably secured as many units through rehab and conversion as it has through new construction.

But its very success and widespread use led to growing opposition. How could the city forego taxes to the benefit of the affluent while the less fortunate suffered? And true, many of the loft buildings that were being converted for residential purposes were half emptied of their old industrial tenantry. But the very paucity of the jobs they incorporated made the latter more precious to those who held them—or hoped to do so.

In the course of the last several years, the program was initially circumscribed in terms of its areal application, and then a ceiling of $38,000 in total value (post-rehabilitation) for privately financed units was clamped on as well. While there are exceptions to both of these rules of the game, they are at the discretion of the Housing Commissioner rather than being as of right. Given the cost structures of New York, as well as the uncertainties of rehabilitation generally, the stipulation that any project whose cost exceeded $38,000 per unit would lose all its J-51 potential is a particularly punitive measure.

Discretionary programs in New York are subject to too much in the way of political vagaries to yield much in the way of dependable throughput. So, despite some allowance made for moderately rehabbed units in which the bulk of the tenantry remains in occupancy, as well as some publicly financed efforts, the program is now at a virtual standstill. Even the efforts of the Community Preservation Corporation (CPC), one of the nation's most successful non-profit groups in the United States in modest rehabilitation, have been hurt by the uncertainties introduced into the program.[29] And CPC's efforts have nominally been excluded from the new strictures. The conversion of buildings for the more affluent can be done only at breathtaking prices.

Yet substantial studies have indicated that on a purely fiscal analysis, the city literally can "make money" by housing the affluent even at the cost of foregoing real estate taxes.[30] The sheer diversity of the "skin 'em and bone 'em" mechanisms of New York's tax fabric, coupled with the relatively low utilization of municipal services by the tenantry typically housed in more recent years under J-51, yields a net balance.

The loft space of the garment district is underutilized, and much of the downtown cast-iron area is in a similar state. But these prime areas have been largely ruled off-limits for the purposes of loft conversion. Yet it is rehabilitation—and particularly substantial conversion—which, if conducted on large scale, might bridge the cost gap between those fortunate enough to have long-term tenancy in a rent-controlled or rent-stabilized structure and the carrying costs of new facilities. The combination of exclusion of potential sites and/or structures on the one hand, and the virtual demise of the J-51 program on the other, means that the meager few units which are legally available have near-monopoly status—and staggeringly high costs. What this yields, in turn, is a decreasing range of choice for New York's new post-industrial technocracy: It is either fight, and pay extraordinary shelter costs; or switch—to friendlier climes—outside the city.

The other side of the coin, however, is all too vividly pressing. The jobs that are left in the old industrial areas may be shrinking in numbers, but they are still substantial in absolute scale, and there is little on the horizon to serve as surrogates for their present holders. Would the generation of wealth, of ratables, of ancillary service jobs through broader conversion capacity more than offset the displacement phenomenon? And even if it did, is this reason to sacrifice the job of the sewing machine operator or warehouse worker who may not find a casual one-for-one substitution in the new domain? The answers that are being given at present to these somewhat rhetorical questions are to hold on to the old as long as possible, even at the risk of inhibiting the growth of the city of the present, and probable, future. From a housing perspective, however, the fastest way to resolve New York City's housing shortage—and to provide a much greater degree of realism to prices—would be conversion practically at will in Manhattan and its potential colonies in Brooklyn and Queens. But this is a resolution which clearly has been rejected.

In a city in which, at least as of 1984, there were still 174,000 renter-occupied old-law tenement units, i.e., dating back to the turn of the century or before, and more than one-half million additional units built prior to 1929, the need for rehabilitation is evident. Would some of the rehabilitation undertaken under J-51 have taken place regardless of its existence? Yes, and certainly to that degree it has been a windfall to some developers—but there is substantial evidence to indicate that this is only part of the story.

Old units plus new money equal good housing; without that capital input, they must falter and ultimately prove inadequate to meet the test of decent occupancy. Newspaper discussion has followed that of political opponents of the program, both of them focused myopically on giveaways in core areas of Manhattan where demand is postulated as virtually unlimited. There has been a failure, however, to take a broader perspective of the city's needs as a whole. The issues of optimizing the city's fiscal balance and its long-term economic future within the present political climate of the environment are brought home by the conflict over the extension of the 421(a) program.

The principle of "trust not in the faith of princes" is exemplified by housing developers' experience under this program. As administered by the New York City Department of Housing Preservation and Development, it was designed to provide partial tax exemptions for the construction of new residential units back in the dark dismal days of the fiscal crunch. Tax exemption was granted during construction and the first two years of rent-up and then declined on a sliding scale. The process was such that after ten years the project was fully taxable. There were no income limits for tenants; however, a maximum initial rent, reflecting the tax savings, was nominally established and approved by the city. All units were under the aegis of the Rent Stabilization Association, and thus subject to limitations on increases. At the end of the tax-exemption period, however, this latter stipulation was to be abrogated. These were to be free-market units.

The city made a commitment, enormous amounts of money were expended as a result, and the bulk of the multifamily housing that has been constructed in the city within the last ten years has fallen under the program.

One may quarrel with the application of the effort, with the lack of limitations on its use, and with any of a variety of other elements. What is most crucial, however—and harmful to the future—is the fact that the city has now reneged on its contract. Buildings whose abatement will expire through May 15, 1984 have vacancy decontrol, but rent stabilization continues in them and what happens in the long run is left to the political gods.

The substantive rights or wrongs of the issue are again, let us repeat, less consequential than the functional implications. Housing in its very definition is a long-term good. The rules of the game of ownership and management are subject to all the vagaries of the market—and these are substantial enough to make it a high-risk investment. When, however, to these is added a unilateral capacity to renege on contract—as is the case in New York—the issue becomes not why is there so little rental housing constructed in the city, but rather why any of it is constructed.

The very continuance of the program is much debated at this writing with some exemptions for state or federally funded projects. Essentially, the golden area south of 96th Street in Manhattan has been removed from its coverage, or alternately will require off-site guarantees of contributions toward "social housing." The thesis is that whatever would be built in those areas will be built regardless—with the secondary undertone of "Why can't we get some action in the hinterlands?" Nearly 90 percent of the units that came in under the 421(a) program in 1983 were in the restricted zone, with little spill-over elsewhere.

Current estimates of the tax savings under the project, at least in its first year, are approximately $4 per square foot in terms of rents, i.e., a 1,000-square-foot apartment would have savings of approximately $325 a month—but are they savings to tenants or merely windfalls for the developer? If the former, will there be a population of consequence to the city's future which will go elsewhere within its domain—or will they leave? Since housing policy is made on a factual and/or research vacuum in New York, the reality is that no one knows. The city in housing policy responds much more to rhetoric and dances more to the drum of media politics than to any more meaningfully inspired strategy.

The Conflict Between the Shelter and Post-Shelter Imperatives— Condo and Co-op Conversion

The trend toward condo and co-op conversion in New York City dates well into the 1970s. The scale, however—though it attracted much alarm in that decade—was relatively trivial compared with things to come. As summarized in a study conducted by the U.S. Department of Housing and Urban Development, *The Conversion of Rental Housing, Condominiums and Cooperatives*,[31] the proportion of the total rental supply converted through August 31, 1979 was less than one percent of the stock, and even this figure represented only offering plans. Since some of these plans undoubtedly did not succeed, the actual count may be somewhat fewer than the figure shown.

The inflationary pattern of the early 1980s caused an enormous boost. When coupled with the changing economics of developing rental housing within the city—to say nothing of owners' disinclination to operate rental facilities under the threat of rent control and/or stabilization—there were much more monumental results. As shown in Exhibit 8, from 1981 through 1983, more than 1,000 buildings, with some 103,000 housing units, were moved into the co-op pattern. During the same years, condominium conversion, earlier relatively rare, grew rapidly with a total of some nearly 100 buildings—with more than 11,000 units—filing for shifts from rental to ownership. In both cases, there has been a shift from eviction to non-eviction formats, given the relative strictures against the former format.

EXHIBIT 8

New York City Shift from Rental to Ownership

	Co-op (plans/units)		% Eviction to Non-Eviction	Condo			% Condo to Co-op
	Eviction	Non-Eviction		Eviction	Non-Eviction	% Eviction to Non-Eviction	
1981	334/27291	138/10328	242.0/264.2	9/938	6/532	50.0/176.3	3.2/3.9
1982	315/19587	92/13635	233.7/143.7	33/3799	12/1274	275.0/298.2	14.7/15.3
1983	181/16479	149/16512	121.5/99.8	14/1530	21/3166	66.7/48.3	10.6/14.2
Total	730/63357	379/40475	192.6/156.5	56/6267	39/4972	143.6/126.0	8.6/10.8

Source: Jack Richman, N.Y.C. Real Estate Board, Telephone Communication 10/15/84.

It should be noted that the filing of a conversion plan does not indicate the level of marketing. And on this latter, very important point, there are no definitive data. Similarly, we do not know how many of the nominally "owned" units actually, either on a temporary or longer-term base, are utilized as rental. There is evidence from newspaper offerings, however, that the purchase of condominium units both nationally, as well as in New York City, is increasingly the purview of small-scale speculators holding them as rental units typically with returns from tax cover and a hope for level of appreciation in the future, rather than a loss of rental units per se. But in any case, the three years of 1981 through 1983 suggest that somewhere between five and six percent of the total city rental stock had at least been filed for conversion.

Again, the point must be emphasized that the shift from rental to ownership is not unique to New York. Clearly, however, the scale of the phenomenon has few precedents elsewhere. The city either purposefully (or more probably, inadvertently) has fostered this market choice. Alan Oser, in an article in *The New York Times*,[32] has pointed out that, statewide, condominium owners pay an average of one-third less tax than do owners of single-family homes of comparable market value. Similarly, those who rent them out on a free market also have an advantage over owners who operate stabilized or controlled rental buildings. This is accentuated by the possibilities of condominium values rising while rental values under stabilization are held back by rent regulation in more conventional structures.

The assessment stipulation dates back to a state law adopted in 1964 which calls for condominium buildings to be assessed as though they were single units, like a rental apartment house. Though each apartment is a separate tax lot, the sales price of individual units cannot be used as a measure of market value of the building or as a basis of reassessment. In the words of the bill cited by Oser, "The sum of the assessment of the individual condominium units cannot exceed the assessed value that would be placed on the complex if it were not a condominium."[33] While there have been efforts made to rectify the situation, they have been cut short by protest groups. Thus, the city's tax coffers are reduced by state fiat.

Is this a subsidy to the potential condominium or co-op owner—or is it rather a windfall for the owners of structures and/or the converters thereof, which are moved from rental into conversion? Economic theory would suggest that if full assessment were at least imputed as of the time of a filing, this would be capitalized back as a reduction of the value of the structure to be converted. The ultimate sale of an individual unit to a co-op or a condominium occupier thus would be at the same price as is presently the case. But, economic theory has a sad habit of varying substantially from reality.

In the meantime, we can only conclude that the city is foregoing an enormous amount of potential tax revenue. Even a $1,000-per-unit tax increment, assuming that the filings of the first three years of the 1980s were to be successful, suggests a flow of funds in excess of a hundred million dollars a year to the city. Again, we must repeat, the precise division of this additional tax between the owners of structures that move into the conversion process and their ultimate occupants cannot be determined. It should be noted that even if the latter were exclusively penalized under current tax laws, at a marginal tax rate of 40 percent, Uncle Sam would be picking up some $40 million of this figure.

Certainly when one views the arguments on assessment procedures in the city, it is evident that they are conducted at a level of isolation from the real world of arithmetic; rather, they focus on abstractions, i.e., "the brow-beating of already hard-pressed condo/co-op buyers." We would strongly suggest that a very large measure of this is a protective device for structure values inflated by the artificial reduction in appropriate tax levels. It is much more a tribute to political potency of the groups involved than any measure of logic and/or equity. In a city which subsidizes nearly all of its occupants, this is far from the greatest of subsidies. Its recognition, however, is long overdue.

Criticism of condo/co-op assessment procedures should not be taken as a stricture against the growing use of these devices in New York. They represent an essential adaptation of New York's high-density housing accommodations to the ownership imperatives built into high marginal rates of taxation and their inflationary environment. Without them, the upscale owner-aspirant would be driven from the city in order to accomplish his or her tenure objectives. The sheer gap between equivalent housing unit values in rental versus ownership forms indicates the vitality of the latter. A rough measure of the splitting up of nominal ownership in rental structures is provided by the capacity of those fortunate enough to be in residence at a time of conversion to turn over their newly acquired property at substantial increments. Landlord buyouts of tenants are at levels scarcely dreamed of by the advocates of displacement allowances for the victims of governmentally inspired renewal efforts.

Is this a process which should be permitted to continue in its own market-driven fashion with relatively low levels of adoption permitted for non-eviction plans? Or as some would have it, much greater restrictions on the whole conversion process? The rise of a stable, upscale homeowner group within the city is a premier goal of most other American metropolises. In New York, on the other hand, judging from the variety of bills presently on hand which would impede the process, it is a fearsome objective. The response epitomizes the near-paranoia that characterizes the development processes that are at work. How can these best be reconciled?

Closing

The clash between the old and the new—of rich and poor, of those inside the system versus those outside it—is older than New York City in its present configuration. It is one of the few constants of the City's history.[34] Although often inefficient, costly, and leaving physical scar tissues in the City's fabric, its resolution is successful enough to yield the extraordinary artifact which is New York. What is different in our own era, however, is the renewed challenge of alternative physical and functional locations for economic activity. New York City has gone through and largely surmounted the changes from an industrial to a post-industrial city, unlike most of its equivalents elsewhere in the United States.

In order to close the loop, however, a much more aggressive and productive housing posture is called for. The city and its people will have to adjust to substantial reductions in federal aid. New York has always supported a social fabric and housing ventures unique unto itself. The know-how and competence are there; what will be called for is the capacity to raise revenues. New York's economic base and fiscal vitality, therefore, become of increasing importance, not merely to the rich, but even more so to the poor: The former can leave; the latter have no place else to go. Housing is central to the city's vigor; it is housing not only for the poor, but for the more affluent as well.

There has been substantial experience gained even in the ten years of near housing blight that followed the fiscal crunch. The shelter mechanisms do not have to be invented: The market is presently waiting for product, but it will not wait forever. The missing ingredient is political will. The pulling together of a strong constituency may require much more in the way of inventive merchandising, of linking the cash flows derived from upscale housing, with specific targeting to social efforts; of making clear that New York's social inputs require a mix and match of shelter and job opportunities.[35] The penalties of housing failure will be felt by the city's economy as a whole—and its poor most stringently. The price is evident; the prize, a most substantial and important one.

Success, however, depends upon a much broader comprehension of the dynamics of the city as an economic entity than has presently been promulgated. The forces that presently call for statsis—for reducing adaptive change—are evident; the pressures and fears which make them powerful are all too real. The city's future depends upon their reassurance and a vision of the future—a vision of the future which is brought into physical being.

Notes

1. U.S. Department of Commerce, Bureau of the Census, *1984 New York City Housing and Vacancy Survey*. Special Census tabulation.
2. City of New York, Human Resources Administration, *Project Bulletin*, November 1984, p. 2.
3. Researchers in New York City's housing must move from data source to data source. (For historical perspective on this issue, see Housing Study Guild, "Pertinent Data for New York—Recent Housing and Property Studies," May 1934.) The summary produced by New York's Department of City Planning shown below (*New Housing in New York City in 1981-82*, December 1983), provides further insight into the decline in the city's capacity to generate housing. After a wartime lag that limited the net increase in the city's housing stock from 1941 through 1950 to under 150,000, there was an enormous burst of activity, which yielded in the following twenty years a net increase of more than one-half million. This is in very sad contrast to the decade of the 1970s, with an increment level on the order of 83,000 units, while the net change in 1981 and 1982 combined barely reached 10,000. All this was represented by Manhattan, with the increase in Queens and Staten Island offset by the losses of the Bronx.

   It should further be noted that the minor increment of 1981–1982 was nearly exclusively a tribute to the positive impacts of conversions, with the net dwelling units added by this means (units added through conversions less units lost by conversion) representing some 70 percent of the net increment. Indeed, while the conversion process has long been criticized, this imbalance, with conversion additions far in excess of removals, has dominated the past 40 years of the city's housing picture.

Official Recorded Annual Net Change of Dwelling Units
New York City and Boroughs

| | Number of Dwelling Units | | | | | | |
| | Dwelling Units Added | | | Dwelling Units Deducted | | | |
Year	New Units Completed	Conversions	Total	Units Demolished	Conversions	Total	Net Change
New York City							
1941–50	165,590	56,918	222,508	52,369	23,441	75,810	+146,698
1951–60	323,330	56,567	379,897	121,865	15,587	137,452	+242,445
1961–70	348,045	37,911	385,956	100,269	13,878	114,147	+271,809
1971–80	165,615	28,506	194,121	101,744	9,142	110,886	+ 83,235
1981–82	15,994	9,722	25,716	13,628	2,080	15,708	+ 10,008

Source: City of New York, Department of City Planning, *New Housing in New York City 1981–82* (New York, NY: City of New York, December 1983), p. 25.

4. Unpublished data from The Port Authority of New York and New Jersey.
5. City of New York, Department of City Planning, *Housing Database—Public and Publicly Aided Housing* (New York, NY: Department of City Planning, August 1983), p. 43.
6. Bureau of the Census, *Current Housing Reports, Characteristics of Apartments Completed in 1983* (Washington, D.C.: U.S. Government Printing Office, 1984).
7. The historical material in this section is derived from the Citizen's Housing and Planning Council, "Housing in New York City—A Chronology" (New York, NY: CHPC, 1965). See also, City Club of New York, "New York's Housing Crisis: Challenge to the Next Mayor" (New York, NY: no date). See also City Club of New York, "A Housing Program for the City" (New York, NY: March 1954).
8. *The New York Times*, June 25, 1984.
9. *Ibid.*
10. See City of New York, *Housing Database—Public and Publicly Aided Housing*, pp. 4–5.
11. *Ibid.*, pp. 42–43.
12. City of New York, *Adopted Budget Fiscal 1985—Expense Revenue, Capital* (New York, NY: City of New York, 1984).

13. City of New York, *HPD Handbook of Programs* (New York, NY: Department of Housing, Preservation, and Development, 1984).
14. City of New York, *City Fiscal Year 1985 Community Development Program* (New York, NY: Department of City Planning, June 1984).
15. Carol Lamberg, "Public Tools to Enhance Affordability," in New York City Housing Partnership, Inc., *New Homes for New York Neighborhoods* (New York, NY: Housing Partnership, October 15, 1984), p. 150.
16. See New York State, Division of Housing and Community Renewal, *An Analysis of the Housing Needs of New York State* (New York, NY: Division of Housing and Community Renewal, April 1984), pp. 4–20.
17. State of New York, Department of Commerce, *Preliminary Official Population Projections* (March 4, 1983—processed).
18. J.S. DeSalvo, *The Mitchell-Lama Program* (New York, NY: Rand, June 1971).
19. There are many other dimensions of housing the poor in New York City; for example, how to deal with Single Room Occupancy (SRO) hotels. For historical discussion of the SRO issue, see Judah Gribetz, "The SRO Building—A Case Study of Housing Myopia" (Address—April 3, 1965). For further discussion of SROs, see the Center for New York City Affairs, "A Program for Tenants in Single Room Occupancy and for Their New York City Neighbors" (New York, NY: New School for Social Research, June 1969). See also, *The New York Times*, January 1, 1973; September 22, 1974; May 6, 1983; and August 3, 1984. See also note 22 in this paper.
20. The data on welfare recipients which follows is from the City of New York's Human Resources Administration, *New York City's Social Report*, First Quarter, 1983 (New York, NY: Human Resources Administration, April 1984).
21. New York City Housing Authority, *Tenant Data, as of January 1, 1984* (New York, NY: Housing Authority, 1984).
22. An excellent summary is by Jeffrey E. Glen and Alan Kleinman of the New York City Law Department and the Mayor's Office of Single-Room Occupancy Housing in an unpublished paper, *Single Room Occupancy*, December 1984, processed.
23. *The New York Times*, November 15, 1984, Section 6, page 12.
24. See *New York Law Journal*, December 28, 1977.
25. For further discussion of *in rem*, see Citizens' Housing and Planning Council of New York City, Inc., *In Rem: Recommendations for Reform* (New York, NY: Citizens' Housing and Planning Council, September 1981), and City of New York, *The In Rem Housing Program* (New York, NY: HPD, Annual Report).
26. Michael A. Stegman, *The Dynamics of Rental Housing in New York City* (New Brunswick, NJ: Center for Urban Policy Research, 1982).

27. Robert W. Lake, *Real Estate Tax Delinquency: Private Disinvestment and Public Response* (New Brunswick, NJ: Center for Urban Policy Research, 1979).
28. The relatively small levels of gentrification are shown in Daniel E. Chall, "Neighborhood Changes in New York City During the 1970s," *Federal Reserve Bank of New York* (Winter 1983–84).
29. The New York City Community Preservation Corporation, *1983 Annual Report* (New York, NY: Community Preservation Corporation, November 1983).
30. See George Sternlieb et al., *Tax Subsidies and Housing Investment* (New Brunswick, NJ: Center for Urban Policy Research, 1976); Kristina Ford, *Housing Policy and the Urban Middle Class* (New Brunswick, NJ: Center for Urban Policy Research and Citizens' Housing and Planning Council, 1978).
31. U.S. Department of Housing and Urban Development, *The Conversion of Rental Housing Condominiums and Cooperatives* (Washington, D.C.: Government Printing Office, 1980).
32. *The New York Times*, November 4, 1984, Section 8, p. 1.
33. *Ibid.*
34. See, for example, James Ford, *Slums and Housing* (Cambridge, MA: Harvard University Press, 1936).
35. See, for example, the recommendations of the Development Commitments Study Commission, *The New York Times*, August 19, 1984.

PART III

The Changing Shape
of the Economy

It is hard to believe that in many of the post-World War II years the economy and macroeconomic activities as a whole were largely left— at least in their technical aspects—to economists. By the mid-1960s, the National Bureau of Economic Research, originally put in place for the study of the business cycle, was searching for a new set of problems. Just twenty years ago, the hubris (Greek for inflated vanity!) of the economists and politicians was such as to believe that not only did we understand all the inputs into economic vagaries, but we had a tool kit completely adequate to their mastery. All that was required for economic stability in the future was "fine tuning." One looks back at this era of faith with the same fond amusement that a contemporary historian views the treaty for the division of the New World between Spain and Portugal some 400 years earlier. They both reflect a complacent sense of being in control of the world—perhaps even a denial of the existence of forces outside the immediate purview of the ruling power.

The Spanish/Portuguese fix probably lasted longer than did the era of America's economic complacency. Its inception was marked by the Prudential Insurance Co. giving 100-year, fixed-rate loans (yes, they really did!) in the early 1950s and its termination, barely twenty years later, by a Republican president invoking price controls in the face of what then seemed to be runaway inflation. And that before the first oil crunch!

In any case, all the papers in this collection are permeated, at the very least implicitly, by the issue of economic uncertainty. In one generation we have enjoyed 3½-percent mortgages and deplored those that reached close to the 20-percent mark. We have seen the United States economy dominate the world—and feared the inversion of this relationship. These are changes which truly are complacency shakers!

And this was at the national level; the internal turbulence was even more substantial. As earlier noted in this volume, for example, the decline of New York and its reinvention—as well as the regional shifts moving at a seemingly inexorable direction from north to south, from east to west—were even more accentuated.

There is a flywheel in our thinking, however, which tends to make concept run after reality. The nominal forecaster is much more frequently someone who merely gives labels (to say nothing of writing learned essays) on what has already taken place. Intellectual response lags not only new initiatives, but sometimes their slowing down or reversal. Thus, the perceived market wisdom of investment in the Southwest was appropriate to the age of energy shortage, an era of the flight from the dollar. Houston became the new symbol of America; Detroit was left far behind. Washington was now the capital of a system of state capitalism; finance capitalism and its geographic node—New York—seemed to have no future.

But just as the learned were extrapolating short-term blips, generalizing from what we now know were far from uninterruptible processes, the pendulum swung the other way.

The first of the three articles in this section, "Frost Over the Sunbelt," written by James Hughes and myself, and published in 1983 in *American Demographics*, looks at the vulnerability of some of the industries that relocated in the Southeast, particularly in manufacturing. It raises the issue of whether they will provide a long-range growth basis, or whether the process is merely transient. The textile industry certainly found the Southeast more hospitable than its original home in New England, and non-union steelmaking shifted ferrous metal production from the soon-to-be labelled Rust Bowl. But was this really the end of the road, or were the new areas doomed to the same process as yet other shifts took place?

In our estimation, the answer to that question was—and would continue to be—the latter. Selling cheap labor in the United States is a loser's game in a world filled with poor countries. Secondly, the energy/extractive industries have had a boom–bust cycle evident throughout history—and we were somewhat cynical as to whether this had been repealed. So with some trepidation we advanced a cautionary thesis and suggested a new look at the Northeast.

How long this reversal of the tide will hold is open to question. Not least of the uncertainties is the issue of new technology. For that reason I was particularly delighted by an invitation to do an essay on information technology and demographics for a conference held jointly by Columbia University and the Wharton School of the University of Pennsylvania on that topic. The staff at the Center was finishing work on a major study of factory-closing legislation and the issue of deindustrialization. The invitation provided an incentive for a longer-term forecast which Jim Hughes and I responded to in the paper, "A Note on Information Technology, Demographics, and the Retail Response," which is included.

As a founder and former partner in one of the early software firms on Boston's Route 128, I had learned, much to my financial regret, how easy technological strides come to lip, yet how very difficult they are to market; how resistant systems and folkways can be to the potential of the machine, to say nothing of how cantankerous the latter is. The article permitted a range of thinking and association, which is a rare luxury involved as we are more typically in contract research. The addition of retailing to the original mandate was an effort to bring the analysis from ethereal generalization—always a temptation—to the practical. The effort developed a life force of its own and may raise more issues than it resolves, particularly on the role of credit, the use of specialized mailing lists, and the conflict between electronics and conventional print media in the realities of shopping at home.

The last essay, "American Industry: The Continuous Revolution," is taken from a major study completed at the Center on changes in the economy and factory-closing law. Supported by a foundation grant, my colleagues, led by Robert Burchell and myself, were given the opportunity of studying a new, dominant concern in the United States: the future of how we organize ourselves in order to make our livings. I wrote the chapter presented here in order to provide a review and setting for the study as a whole. Hopefully, it possesses enough unity to stand by itself—and stimulate/provoke the reader to respond to the issues which it raises. The critics of the economy—Lester Thurow, Robert Reich, and Robert Lekachman, to name a few—have challenged the long-run capacities of our system to deliver the better life. How realistic are their appraisals?

I will look forward to comments and criticisms on this—as well as the other pieces.

10

Frost Over the Sunbelt

George Sternlieb and James W. Hughes

Where's the Action?: Reality Comes to the Sunbelt

The life of the marketer and locational specialist of the 1970s was simple: "When in doubt, go to the Sunbelt." The North Central states—America's aging industrial heartland—were faltering; the Northeast, in the conventional view, had long since been relegated to the broom closet of corporate locational optimization. At the end of the decade, Sunbelt targeting by business and marketing efforts was the unquestioned route to securing guaranteed yields, rivaled only by "upscale" segmentation and "baby boom life-cycle riding" strategies.

The nation's total population increase of 11.4 percent between 1970 and 1980 was far outpaced by the South (20.0 percent) and West (23.9 percent); the populations of the North Central (4.0 percent) and Northeast (0.2 percent) Regions were near stagnant. For every additional person gained by the Northeast (76,000) over the decade, the South and West combined (20.9 million) secured 275 additional residents. The latter also prevailed over the North Central states' gains (2.3 million) by a more than nine-to-one ratio.

Thus the 1980 Census results codified the common wisdom, and projected it to the present decade. The critical mass of America's consumers would continue to reposition itself to the Sunbelt. And this

Reprinted with permission from *American Demographics*, © June, 1983. Ithaca, New York.

was given emphasis by the patterns of job growth activity. In the six years from 1975 to 1981, as the United States crawled out of what was then considered the sharpest recession since the Great Depression, the Northeast added less than one new job for every ten that existed in the depressed base year (1975) while the North Central states added less than one in eight. In contrast, the economy of the South flourished, with an increase of one new job for every four, and that of the West boomed, gaining one in three.

Life was simple for the market researcher. One merely had to add Horace Greeley's injunction—"Go West, Young Man"—to the reality that the South had "risen again." And any forecast based on the evidence would carry the day in the future.

But projections are a sometimes thing. The major issue, as American industry finds itself looking for handholds with which to crawl out of the crevice (or Grand Canyon!) of the latest recession, is whether the affirmed experience of the 1970s can provide an adequate guide to the 1980s.

The Foundations of Prosperity

The ethos of the shift of northern industry to the South seemed overwhelming. The principles of growth receptivity, with little in the way of government-imposed inhibitions; of cheap and abundant quantities of land, labor and housing; and of Congressmen with seniority who knew that their constituents valued the importing of jobs (and who had long established themselves at the principal faucets of the Defense Department) were seen as permanently anchoring the foundations of the new prosperity. They were joined in the 1970s and broadened in their areal implications to the West and Rocky Mountain states by the two energy crises—the oil embargo and the fall of the Shah. Energy-related employment, for example, grew nationally from 1976 to 1981 by over 43 percent, outspeeding even high technology, the heralded work-force expansion of which was a more modest, but not trifling, 32.6 percent (Exhibit 1).

Thus, as the decade of the 1970s came to a close, the political and natural resource endowments of the Sunbelt census regions were uniquely matched to America's high-growth employment sectors. The Northeast and North Central states, in contrast, were saddled with the nation's sunset industries.

EXHIBIT 1

Partitioned Employment Sectors: 1976–1981
U.S. Total
(Numbers in Thousands)

Sector	1976	1981	Number	Percent
Old Line Industry	18,547.8	20,306.4	1,758.6	9.5%
High Technology	3,074.3	4,075.4	1,001.1	32.6
Energy	757.7	1,084.9	327.2	43.2
Services	26,354.2	33,288.3	6,934.1	26.3
Government	15,322.0	16,408.0	1,086.0	7.1

Note: For sector definitions see source below. Tabulations exclude wholesale and retail trade.

Source: George Sternlieb, James W. Hughes and Connie O. Hughes, *Demographic Trends and Economic Reality: Planning and Markets in the '80s* (New Brunswick, NJ: Rutgers University, Center for Urban Policy Research, 1982). Appendix A.

Cracks in the Foundation?

But growth obscures a multitude of sins and weaknesses. (In addition, hindsight is also the scholar's best friend!) In retrospect, the sheer explosion in the energy-related extractive industries tended to submerge the difficulties that other natural-resource-centered activities were beginning to experience.

For most of the 1970s, the value of money went down as the value of selected commodities zoomed. Many of the latter were to be found in the mineral-rich states, while the former was still concentrated in the historic financial bastions of the older regions. But price increments in grain, for example, which even through the mid-1970s had nearly kept pace with the initial energy-cost spiral, began to falter—and with them, some of the prosperity of the North Central states. The latter was obscured by the flywheel of expectation, reflected in agricultural land speculation, which far outran what society was willing to pay for its product.

The surging prices of gold and silver, as the flight from paper money took wing, obscured the less fashionable stumbling of much more significant basic areas, such as the molybdenum of Colorado, the copper of Arizona, and the taconite of the North Central states.

But the oil boom covered all the states fortunate enough to enjoy its presence with the glow of wealth. The major imperative of every market-driven investment sector was to insure its representation in the new, guaranteed capital-gains situations of Denver and Houston. And location in the capitals of oil land often involved paying "hysteria premiums" both in costs and in foregoing the conventional wisdom of tenants in hand before construction. The central business district of Houston in 1950 contained more than 95 percent of the region's total of eight million gross square feet of office space; it can now view—both with pride and (perusing some of the vacancies) with consternation—an inventory of 34 million square feet. The growth of the major downtown office node has been accompanied by a large number of overbuilt suburban ventures, even more tenantless. The SMSA total is now in excess of 130 million square feet; the vacancy rates at this writing are zooming.

Denver, a relatively sleepy Rocky Mountain metropolis distinguished a generation ago only by smogless skies and railroad and service employment, was hit by the Midas touch of oil. Suddenly it became the beneficiary of pension fund investments both from here and abroad. The latter joined with other real estate speculators in a near hallucinogenic frenzy, producing nearly 14 million square feet of office space either completed or well through the pipeline, all within the space of a handful of years. Much of it is without tenants—and in some cases equally bereft of long-term financing.

The Manufacturing Dilemma

The flight of manufacturing activity—both old-line and high-tech sectors—from the North to the South, and increasingly to the West, epitomized the triumph of the Sunbelt. In 1960, the Northeast (33.6 percent) and North Central (33.4 percent) regions evenly shared two-thirds of the total manufacturing employment in the country (Exhibit 2). By 1981 this combined share diminished to little more than half. In turn, by the latter date, the South listed three out of ten of the nation's total manufacturing employees and had become the dominant manufacturing locus of the country. Concurrently, the West emerged as a burgeoning industrial powerhouse, evidenced by an increase in manufacturing employment of 62.3 percent versus an absolute decline in the northern regions as a whole.

But the complement of this success was vulnerability to the new-world realities of manufacturing, and the declining potency of this sector within the United States. Between 1981 and 1982, for example, the nation lost 5 percent—over one million jobs—of its manufacturing base.

EXHIBIT 2

Manufacturing Employment Change: 1960-1981[1]
by Region and Division
(Numbers in Thousands)

	1960		1981		Change: 1960-1981	
	Number	Percent	Number	Percent	Number	Percent
U.S. Total	16,725.6	100.0	20,133.4	100.0	3,497.8	20.4
Northeast Region	5,620.6	33.6	5,016.2	24.9	−604.4	−10.8
Middle Atlantic Division	4,172.8	24.9	3,503.9	17.4	−668.9	−16.0
New England Division	1,447.8	8.7	1,512.3	7.5	64.5	4.5
North Central Region	5,579.9	33.4	5,991.8	29.8	411.9	7.4
East North Central Division	4,586.4	27.4	4,644.6	23.1	58.2	1.3
West North Central Division	993.5	5.9	1,347.2	6.7	353.7	35.6
South Region	3,650.5	21.8	6,082.4	30.2	2,431.9	66.6
South Atlantic Division	2,013.1	12.0	3,040.4	15.1	1,027.3	51.0
East South Central Division	823.2	4.9	1,350.9	6.7	527.7	64.1
West South Central Division	814.2	4.9	1,591.1	8.4	876.9	107.7
West Region	1,874.6	11.2	3,043.0	15.1	1,168.4	62.3
Mountain Division	248.9	1.5	564.9	2.8	316.0	127.0
Pacific Division[2]	1,625.7	9.7	2,478.1	12.3	852.4	52.4

Notes: [1] Employees on nonagriculture payrolls as of March of the respective years.

[2] Excludes Hawaii and Alaska.

Source: U.S. Department of Labor, Bureau of Labor Statistics, *Employment and Earnings*, Monthly.

Thus, in the midst of world recession, the seemingly inexorable growth patterns of the South and West are suddenly open to question, spearheaded by a weakened manufacturing activity, and joined in by the abrupt disruption of energy development. These regions have suddenly surfaced as equally—or even more—vulnerable to the new economic calculus which dominates the United States.

New Parameters

The extractive oil boom which followed the development of the Overthrust Belt through the Rockies, and even the energy hegemony of mighty Texas and Houston alike, has now been questioned. The vacant office towers of Denver are a tribute to forecasts of $40 plus per barrel of oil; they seem to have much less reason at $34. Indeed, their very existence may well be questioned as the foundations of

OPEC begin to rock. The Houston banks—long the frontrunners in rates of return for the industry nationally—now painfully reflect on the difference in business as the number of drilling rigs is halved and the synthetic fuels industry lies stillborn.

Success begets success. The web of secondary and tertiary development that evolves when new sources of primary wealth are generated needs little amplification. What is sometimes forgotten, however, is that if the dependent sectors do not develop a life force of their own, they will in turn falter when the initial locomotive slows down. Thus, in hitherto ever-booming Houston, one discovers major shopping centers whose mortgage holders now are extremely nervous—and with cause. Similarly, the real estate boom of the Mountain states is leaving a wake of bankruptcies behind it.

The commodity-rich areas of the United States, whether in grain, oil, copper, or non-differentiated labor, are suffering from the slowing of the world economy—and the increasing homogenization of its skills. The very virtues of the South and West, from a planning and marketing perspective, thus are increasingly threatened. As the allure of the sure-thing areas of a very few years ago begins to be challenged, there is an intriguing reassessment taking place of some older sites, which may have much more in the way of stability, and perhaps even the potential of economic leapfrogging into the future.

The comparison of decennial snapshots, particularly those of 1970 and 1980, fails to distinguish shifts in internal dynamics over the intervening period. The forces of growth at the end of the decade were far different from those operating barely five years previous.

Unemployment

The rules of the regional game have been challenged. The cheap labor and non-unionized work force of the South may have been enormously alluring compared to the more structured situation of the North, but these advantages are minimized as we move from a national to a world economy. In this latter context, even the poorest-paid worker of the South may prove to be non-competitive.

Within the distortions and noise of a sputtering economy, are new patterns of areal vigor—and trauma—beginning to emerge? From September 1981 to September 1982—the last period for which data is available at this writing, total unemployment in the United States rose from 7.6 percent to 10.1 percent. And certainly no region—nor state—was exempt from this devastating sweep. It is striking, how-

ever, to note that the Northeast Region—even incorporating, as it
does, the still heavily industrialized states of New Jersey and
Pennsylvania—seems to have weathered the economic storm best.

By September 1981 the New England Division (perhaps
hereinafter to be referred to as the Gilded Snow Belt?) had the lowest
unemployment rate, 7.1 percent, of any division in the country (Exhibit 3). The contrast with the South, whose unemployment equivalent
was 9.1 percent, is particularly striking. But even this rising threshold
was exceeded by the West's 9.5 percent rate.

The North Central Region, devastated by the dominance of non-
competitive heavy industry, clearly still leads the unemployment
parade. Much of the Sunbelt's increase in unemployment is a function
of migrants seeking the new promised land rather than an absolute
reduction in employment. A case can be made, however, that the
victories of the Sunbelt in securing a substantial migration of manufacturing from the North may have been only transient. The new recep-
tors are the manufacturing meccas of the development world. Even
golden California has an unemployment level which has ballooned to
9.7 percent, more than 25 percent higher than that of the New England
Division.

Unheralded Successes

The unemployment dilemmas of the Sunbelt and the apparent
"sturdiness" of the Northeast and New England are tributes to a shifting economic order. The new defense industries, for example, have
much less to do with the hardware of yesterday than an equivalent
buildup a few years ago would have inferred. While naval shipbuilding
is safely ensconced in the home states of the former potentates of the
Armed Services Committee, there is $300 million worth of electronics
to every Agena class ship; and the new technology is not produced in
Louisiana or Mississippi.

The New Hampshire syndrome of low taxation combined with a
very strong thrust toward minimizing economic frictions may be controversial, but it has been seized upon by other areas of New England.
Even once super-heavily taxed Massachusetts has joined the circle of
jobs first, equity later—regardless of the party of the incumbent governor. The unique educational infrastructure of the area has become the
focal point of an America increasingly dubious of the future of its old
industries.

EXHIBIT 3

Unemployment Rates:
Regions, Divisions and States

	September 1981	September 1982
NORTHEAST REGION	*6.9*	*8.7*
New England Division	*6.1*	*7.1*
Maine	6.3	7.5
New Hampshire	4.5	6.3
Vermont	4.7	5.7
Massachusetts	6.6	7.4
Rhode Island	6.8	8.6
Connecticut	5.6	6.5
Middle Atlantic Division	*7.2*	*9.3*
New York	7.0	8.4
New Jersey	6.3	8.6
Pennsylvania	8.2	10.9
SOUTH REGION	*6.8*	*9.1*
South Atlantic Division	*7.0*	*8.5*
Delaware	6.9	8.0
Maryland	7.0	8.1
District of Columbia	9.7	10.7
Virginia	5.6	7.4
West Virginia	8.4	14.0
North Carolina	6.0	8.7
South Carolina	8.2	10.7
Georgia	6.2	7.5
Florida	8.1	8.2
East South Central Division	*8.3*	*12.1*
Kentucky	6.9	10.6
Tennessee	8.3	11.4
Alabama	10.2	14.3
Mississippi	7.8	12.2
West South Central	*5.8*	*8.3*
Arkansas	7.9	9.4
Louisiana	7.9	10.6
Oklahoma	3.4	5.8
Texas	5.4	8.0

EXHIBIT 3 (continued)

	September 1981	*September 1982*
NORTH CENTRAL REGION	7.9	10.9
East North Central Division	9.0	12.3
Ohio	10.0	12.3
Indiana	9.1	11.4
Illinois	8.0	12.1
Michigan	10.7	14.5
Wisconsin	6.3	10.2
West North Central Division	5.2	7.4
Minnesota	4.4	7.2
Iowa	5.9	7.7
Missouri	7.0	8.8
North Dakota	3.8	4.8
South Dakota	4.2	4.6
Nebraska	3.6	5.6
Kansas	3.9	7.1
WEST REGION	6.9	9.5
Mountain Division	5.7	8.7
Montana	5.8	7.4
Idaho	6.3	7.7
Wyoming	3.3	5.5
Colorado	4.9	7.6
New Mexico	6.8	9.9
Arizona	6.0	10.7
Utah	6.1	7.7
Nevada	6.2	10.4
Pacific Division	7.4	9.8
Washington	8.8	10.9
Oregon	8.9	10.0
California	7.0	9.7
Hawaii	5.7	7.9
Alaska	7.9	7.7
U.S. TOTAL	7.6	10.1

Source: U.S. Department of Labor, Bureau of Labor Statistics, *Employment and Earnings*, Vol. 29, No. 11, November 1982.

Nor is this a New England exclusive. While Silicon Valley is viewed as the focal point of the new twenty-first century imperative, it should be noted that the concentration of IBM, Bell Labs, and General Electric in New Jersey, New York and Massachusetts is at least of equivalent scale and certainly dwarfs the efforts at creating a "Silicon Prairie" in the Dallas or Fort Worth areas. The health sciences are particularly concentrated in New Jersey and continue to expand.

Increasingly, the assembly work and manufacture of the hardware of high tech no longer are headed South, but rather to the Far East. In essence, therefore, the *downside* risk, an often overlooked measurement, may well be minimal in the once passed-over area of the Northeast.

Equally compelling is the renewed vitality of New York City. While the outer boroughs are shrinking, the island of Manhattan is increasingly becoming the dominant world-city. Its 284 million square feet commercial space inventory, eight times that of downtown Houston, has a vacancy rate (5 percent) far below the national average (over 8 percent). The flows of capital internationally are now focused much more in the shadow of the World Trade Center than in London or Zurich. While hindered somewhat by the strength of the dollar, the rise of New York (despite all of the well-known inhibitors) to a world-class tourist shopping mecca is particularly noteworthy. Even Long Island, seemingly passed over and aging ungracefully, has suddenly revived through a combination of defense contracting and the gestation of new, small, high-technology concerns.

The Market Research "Snake Dance"

This is not to infer that the Northeast is necessarily the new "Promised Land"—but let us suggest that it is a much less unpromising land than has been accepted in the recent past.

The market research "snake dance"—in which all seers look at the same entrails and follow the same leads—may well have led to an overdevelopment, an overexpansion, an overconcentration of resource in the more obvious national targets. Certainly, the excesses in office supply bear witness to this phenomenon. The midwest concentration of commodity products and heavy industry must wait upon massive revitalization of the GNP. But New England and the New York–New Jersey metropolitan region already have suffered through the peak of "old" industry withdrawals. Within this new reality, the Northeast may rise again.

11

A Note on Information Technology, Demographics, and the Retail Response

George Sternlieb and James W. Hughes

Introduction

This paper is organized into three broad sections. The first details the demographic matrix of 1985: America will be a much more mature nation, a middle-aged society predominantly "paired and nested." The era of explosive labor-force growth will have passed, a period of labor-force shortage arrived. Decentralization and deconcentration trends will continue at regional and metropolitan levels, but older regions—presently typified by New England—may secure increasing vigor. And the demographic and economic parameters of the 1990s indicate a far more receptive environment for technological innovation.

The second section highlights a much more difficult task— forecasting technological impact. The demographic matrix of the balance of the century is relatively "certain" within general boundaries. But there are relatively few technological imperatives with such vigor as to support instant judgment. An overview of the evolution of retailing in America provides an insightful example of the complexities at work.

Reprinted with permission from Faulhaber, Noam, and Tasley's *The Impact of Information Technologies on the Service Sector*, Copyright 1986, Ballinger Publishing Company.

The concepts of stasis and inertia versus the forces of change unleashed by technological innovation are the subject of the final section. Journey-to-work—the linkage between residence and work-places—is evaluated, along with the notion of the "electronic cottage." The impact of the information era may portend households free of spatial ties as they work at their dispersed electronic residences—with information commuting, not people. But just as shopping malls flourish in the face of electronic retailing, so too will the office remain viable. People will not want to be isolated from other people. Thus, the impact of technology must be viewed through a matrix of societal elements which shapes its eventual spatial distributions—and settlement patterns as well.

Demographic Parameters

The confusion between sequence and causation is a hazard of the social sciences. We are dependent upon past relationships for forecasting the future. When these relationships alter—or if they are coincidental in time rather than descriptive of immutable linkages—the predictive failure can be very costly indeed. We are much more competent as historians than as futurists.

This stipulation is essential as we project demographic realities to come. It is made even more significant when we attempt to interpret the applications of communications and information technology both present and anticipated.

In the first domain, for example, it is chastening to observe the demographic forecasts of yesteryear. In the depths of the Depression, the consensus of learned forecasters, typified by the 1933 Hoover Commission Report, envisioned a population peak of 145 million people in the United States in the 1980s.[1]

The post-World War II baby boom (1946 to 1964) was completely unanticipated both in its scale and its longevity. The rapid increase in reproduction was matched only by its precipitous decline. The subsequent baby bust of the post-1964 years was equally unforeseen. We have moved from national population projections for the Year 2000 of more than 300 million to a consensus of 265 to 270 million. The former was a function of the fertility rates of the 1950s, the latter of their abrupt reduction in the 1960s and early 1970s. In retrospect, the tendency for straightline extrapolation based on "clear trends" among the nominally learned is all too evident.

There are, however, three basic demographic phenomena which can be forecast with a reasonable degree of certainty. They revolve around 1. the powerful dominance of the baby boom cohort moving through its life cycle with enormously consequential societal repercussions; 2. the maturing baby bust generation, introducing the concept of shrinkage at each stage of its life cycle; and 3. the rise of the elderly—as yet much more a function of longevity than of a unique size of cohort. These three phenomena will dominate our population change through the balance of the century. Anticipations of their future ramifications feed back even now to our vision of social issues to come.

From an *areal* perspective, there are also three seemingly immutable processes of our time: decentralization, particularly evident in the dominant settlement artifacts—the major industrial cities—of a century we now realize ended with World War II; suburbanization and exurbanization, which has resulted in a continuous broadening of the concept of metropolitan areas; and regional shifts, i.e., the transfer of population and economic activity typically from the Northeast and Midwest to the South and West. So consequential has this last element been as to raise a number of statistical anomalies, i.e., the rise of cities and metropolitan areas as the new growth areas thicken up, and of vast conurbations, perhaps mislabeled metropolitan areas, growing in size while their older forebears decline.

Bounding these elements—and at one and the same time both dependent on them and serving as accelerants—are transformations of the American labor force, and technological/economic functions as well. The demographic dynamics, summarized subsequently, set the basic stage for the future.

The Population Context

The United States is passing through the pressures exerted by the enormous increments of population growth which have characterized the post-World War II era. From 1950 through the mid-1980s, our population increased by nearly 60 percent. But this is a process which is now slowing. The baby-boom upsurge of the 1950s, marked by an 18.5 percent population increase nationally between 1950 and 1960, gave way to the baby-bust era of the 1960s and 1970s, with decade population increases on the order of 13.4 and 11.4 percent, respectively. The dynamics set in motion over these last three decades will dominate the demographics of tomorrow. *Much of the adaptation and receptivity to new technology and information systems will be shaped by them.*

The stress points of the 1970s are illustrated in the age structure data of Exhibit 1, which highlights the reduction in the absolute number of children under the age of 14 years in the 1970s (the baby-bust generation), with a decline of more than 6 million; and the enormous growth of young adults in the 25 to 34 years of age range (the maturing baby boom), who increased by half. Indeed, nearly all of the population increment of the 1970s was in the 25 to 44 years-of-age sector (20.6 million out of 22.7 million). The growth in older Americans barely compensated for the loss of the young.

The three basic propulsive forces were thus made evident in the 1970s: the sheer size—and now the aging—of the baby boom generation; the continued growth in the elderly; and a relative dearth of new, young adults on the horizon. While the baby-boom echo, as a function of the sheer size of the cohort at risk, is illustrated by the resumed growth in the under five-years-of-age population between 1980 and 1983, it is but a shadow of the earlier vitality that produced its parents.

EXHIBIT 1

Total Population Age Structure, U.S. Total Population
(Including Armed Forces Abroad): 1970 to 1983
(Numbers in Thousands)

	1970	1980	Change: 1970 to 1980 Number	Change: 1970 to 1980 Percent	1983	Change: 1980 to 1983 Number	Change: 1980 to 1983 Percent
Total	205,052	227,704	22,652	11.0%	234,496	6,792	3.0%
Under 5 Years	17,166	16,457	−709	−4.1	17,826	1,369	8.3
5 to 13 Years	36,672	31,080	−5,592	−15.2	30,116	−964	−3.1
14 to 17 Years	15,924	16,139	215	1.4	14,633	−1,506	−9.3
18 to 24 Years	24,711	30,347	5,636	22.8	30,148	−199	−0.7
25 to 34 Years	25,324	37,593	12,269	48.4	40,334	2,741	7.3
35 to 44 Years	23,150	25,882	2,732	11.8	29,492	3,610	13.9
45 to 54 Years	23,316	22,737	−579	−2.5	22,342	−395	−1.7
55 to 64 Years	18,682	21,756	3,074	16.5	22,219	463	2.1
65 Years and Over	20,107	25,714	5,607	27.9	27,384	1,670	6.5

Sources: U.S. Bureau of the Census, *Statistical Abstract of the United States: 1984* (104th Edition), Washington, D.C., 1983. U.S. Bureau of the Census, Current Population Reports, Series P-25, No. 949, *Estimates of the Population of the United States, by Age, Sex and Race: 1980 to 1983*, U.S. Government Printing Office, Washington, D.C., 1984.

Presented in Exhibit 2 are the age structure shifts projected from 1983 to 1990 and then through 1995. By that terminal date, the demographic profile of America is dominated by the aging of the baby-boom generation. Over 73 million Americans will be between 35 and 54 years old—a dramatic expansion without parallel in our past. Its companion—a shrinking number of young adults—is indicated by the relatively small increments in their historic absolute number. The much-feared accession rate to the elderly will be substantial, but it will really become dominant only in the next century.

America of 1995 will be a much older nation, with its population concentrated in middle-aged to near-middle-aged groups. It will be much less dominated, at least from a numerical point of view, by the youth orientation of past decades. It should be noted in this context that, subject to changes in immigration flow, population projections to 1995—at least for people over the age of ten—are relatively secure in scale. The demographic matrix of the next decade has already been set in place.

EXHIBIT 2

Population Projections by Age, U.S. Total Population (Including Armed Forces Abroad): 1990 and 1995 (Numbers in Thousands)

	1983	1990	Change: 1983 to 1990		1995	Change: 1990 to 1995	
			Number	Percent		Number	Percent
Total	234,496	249,731	15,235	6.5%	259,631	9,900	4.0%
Under 5 Years	17,826	19,200	1,374	7.7	18,616	−584	3.0
5 to 13 Years	30,116	32,183	2,067	6.9	34,443	2,260	7.0
14 to 17 Years	14,633	12,940	−1,693	−11.6	14,071	1,131	8.7
18 to 24 Years	30,148	25,777	−4,371	−14.5	23,684	−2,093	−12.0
25 to 34 Years	40,334	43,506	3,172	7.9	40,489	−3,017	−6.9
35 to 44 Years	29,492	37,845	8,353	28.3	41,994	4,149	11.0
45 to 54 Years	22,342	25,391	3,049	13.6	31,378	5,987	23.6
55 to 64 Years	22,219	21,090	−1,129	−5.1	20,951	−139	−0.7
65 Years and Over	27,384	31,799	4,415	16.1	34,006	2,207	6.9

Note: Census Bureau Middle Series Projection.

Sources: U.S. Bureau of the Census, Current Population Reports, Series P-25, No. 922, *Projections of the Population of the United States: 1982 to 2050* (Advance Report), U.S. Government Printing Office, Washington, D.C., 1982. U.S. Bureau of the Census, Current Population Reports, Series P-25, No. 949, *Estimates of the Population of the United States, by Age, Sex and Race: 1980 to 1983*, U.S. Government Printing Office, Washington, D.C., 1984.

Regional Population Shifts

Of considerably less certainty are future regional settlement patterns. In the 1970s, accelerated population growth in the South and West on a national scale brought with it a new vocabulary—of "Sunbelt" and "Frostbelt"—to the general media. But more significantly, it represented the visible product of the long-term pyramiding of successive technological innovations.

Before the turn of the century, F.J. Kingsbury isolated three factors portending significant changes in the population distribution between the city and its surrounding countryside—the trolley, the bicycle, and the telephone.[2] Each of these entrants into American life was seen as expanding the periphery of urban settlement. Kingsbury perceptively suggested that alterations in society's course are often underlaid by the pyramiding of seemingly unimportant and inconspicuous developments into forces of major consequence.

Current modifications of America's demographic evolution have been facilitated by the same general categories of technological innovation recognized by Kingsbury—public and private transportation and communications. Advances in air transport and dry-bulk cargo shipping, the Interstate Highway System, and the increasing sophistication of place-independent computer linkages, have served to substantially homogenize time and space, and radically alter patterns of connectivity.

Predecessors of these innovations gave impetus to the suburbanization process in earlier decades. In the 1970s they advanced to the national scale and facilitated increasing disparities in interregional population growth. And the processes at work have propelled themselves into the 1980s. In Exhibit 3, we have shown the changes in the regional distribution of America's population from 1980 through 1984. The conventional wisdom of population shifts to the South and West at the cost of the Northeast and Midwest is still valid. Roughly 90 percent of all of America's population growth in the first four years of the 1980s was in the former areas; the latter, at least from an aggregate demographic perspective, remained virtually static.

The pattern of change from mid-1983 to mid-1984 indicates a potential break from the past. The slowing down of the natural resource economy—of the mineral base of Texas and the Rocky Mountain areas—introduces new uncertainty. Wyoming, for example, actually lost population, but this may be only a recession-born blip. The new information economy, however, may be much less resource-dependent than its predecessor. The world economy which it makes possible further deepens the problems of those domestic areas whose raison d'être rests on suddenly challenged bases. The copper states are depressed both by fiber-optic cables and alternative mineral exploitation throughout the world.

The future will hold equally significant, and equally unanticipated, developments. In the early 1970s, New England was still considered an economic laggard, depleted by the loss of its historical industrial mainstays over the preceding half-century. Spearheaded by new innovations, the information and technological era has reversed New England's economic fortune. Although its 1980 to 1984 population growth still lags the nation, a base for future growth has been established.

Will a similar path be open to other aging industrial regions? The Sunbelt–Frostbelt disparities of the 1970s were linked to shifting energy costs and the obsolescence of the industrial infrastructure of the past. But the age of energy "shortfalls"—and with it the rush to Texas and the Mountain states—may be over, raising questions as to the long-term pulling power of these areas. The new information era has not only resurrected New York City as the national—and now worldwide—financial capital, but has also given it much greater potency, challenging the role of the "regional cities." The inertia of past spatial demographics will be continually challenged as the future economy unfolds.

Long-term shifts of population—and with them, jobs, residence place, entertainment facilities, and all the infrastructure of modern-day life—render obsolete old facilities in left-behind areas, and demand an accelerated level of new capital provisions in the high-growth areas. With them comes the capacity—at least the potential—for crest-of-the-wave innovation, for the employment of new means of communication and transportation which do not face the competition of the already-in-place infrastructure of the older sections of the nation. One out of four houses built in the South dates from 1970 or later; the equivalent for the Northeast is one in ten.

Central City Population

The subject of population change and the concomitant alteration of economic functions in central cities is an enormously complex one. In our own estimation, we do not see the pattern of population decline, shown in Exhibit 4 for selected cities from 1950 to 1980,

EXHIBIT 3

Estimates of the Resident Population of States, July 1, 1983 and 1984
(Numbers in Thousands. Includes Armed Forces Residing in Each State.)

Region, Division, and State	Estimate		April 1, 1980 (Census)	Change, Number	1980–84 Percent
	July 1, 1984 (provisional)	July 1, 1983			
United States	236,158	234,023	226,546	9,612	4.2
Northeast	49,728	49,502	49,135	592	1.2
New England	12,577	12,486	12,348	228	1.8
Middle Atlantic	37,151	37,016	36,787	364	1.0
Midwest	59,117	58,890	58,866	251	0.4
East North Central	41,601	41,478	41,682	−81	−0.2
West North Central	17,515	17,412	17,183	332	1.9
South	80,576	79,637	75,372	5,204	6.9
South Atlantic	39,450	38,852	36,959	2,491	6.7
East South Central	15,028	14,931	14,666	362	2.5
West South Central	26,098	25,854	23,747	2,351	9.9
West	46,738	45,994	43,172	3,565	8.3
Mountain	12,553	12,348	11,373	1,180	10.4
Pacific	34,184	33,646	31,800	2,385	7.5
New England					
Maine	1,156	1,145	1,125	32	2.8
New Hampshire	977	958	921	56	6.1
Vermont	530	525	511	18	3.6
Massachusetts	5,798	5,763	5,737	61	1.1
Rhode Island	962	956	947	15	1.6
Connecticut	3,154	3,139	3,108	47	1.5
Middle Atlantic					
New York	17,735	17,663	17,558	177	1.0
New Jersey	7,515	7,464	7,365	150	2.0
Pennsylvania	11,901	11,889	11,864	37	0.3
East North Central					
Ohio	10,752	10,736	10,798	−46	−0.4
Indiana	5,498	5,472	5,490	8	0.1
Illinois	11,511	11,474	11,427	84	0.7
Michigan	9,075	9,050	9,262	−187	−2.0
Wisconsin	4,766	4,746	4,706	60	1.3
West North Central					
Minnesota	4,162	4,144	4,076	86	2.1
Iowa	2,910	2,904	2,914	−4	−0.1
Missouri	5,008	4,963	4,917	91	1.9
North Dakota	686	681	653	34	5.2
South Dakota	706	699	691	15	2.2
Nebraska	1,606	1,596	1,570	36	2.3
Kansas	2,438	2,426	2,364	74	3.1

EXHIBIT 3 (continued)

Region, Division, and State	Estimate		April 1, 1980 (Census)	Change, Number	1980-84 Percent
	July 1, 1984 (provisional)	July 1, 1983			
South Atlantic					
Delaware	613	606	594	18	3.1
Maryland	4,349	4,299	4,217	132	3.1
District of Columbia	623	623	638	−16	−2.4
Virginia	5,636	5,556	5,347	289	5.4
West Virginia	1,952	1,962	1,950	3	0.1
North Carolina	6,165	6,076	5,882	283	4.8
South Carolina	3,300	3,256	3,122	178	5.7
Georgia	5,837	5,732	5,463	373	6.8
Florida	10,976	10,742	9,746	1,229	12.6
East South Central					
Kentucky	3,723	3,713	3,661	62	1.7
Tennessee	4,717	4,676	4,591	126	2.7
Alabama	3,990	3,961	3,894	96	2.5
Mississippi	2,598	2,581	2,521	77	3.1
West South Central					
Arkansas	2,349	2,325	2,286	63	2.7
Louisiana	4,462	4,440	4,206	257	6.1
Oklahoma	3,298	3,310	3,025	273	9.0
Texas	15,989	15,779	14,229	1,759	12.4
Mountain					
Montana	824	815	787	37	4.7
Idaho	1,001	987	944	57	6.0
Wyoming	511	516	470	42	8.9
Colorado	3,178	3,416	2,890	288	10.0
New Mexico	1,424	1,399	1,303	121	9.3
Arizona	3,053	2,970	2,718	335	12.3
Utah	1,652	1,618	1,461	191	13.0
Nevada	911	897	800	110	13.8
Pacific					
Washington	4,349	4,302	4,132	217	5.2
Oregon	2,674	2,658	2,633	41	1.6
California	25,622	25,186	23,668	1,955	8.3
Alaska	500	481	402	98	24.4
Hawaii	1,039	1,018	965	74	7.7

Source: U.S. Bureau of the Census, *Commerce News*, CB 84-233, Public Information Office, Washington, D.C., December 28, 1984.

EXHIBIT 4

Population Change, Selected Cities – 1950 to 1980

City	1950[1]	1970[2]	1980[3]	Change: 1950-1980		Change: 1970-1980	
				Number	Percent	Number	Percent
Boston	801,444	641,071	562,994	–238,450	–29.8	–78,077	–12.2
Buffalo	580,132	462,768	357,870	–222,262	–38.3	–104,898	–22.7
Chicago	3,620,962	3,369,357	3,005,072	–615,890	–17.0	–364,285	–10.8
Cincinnati	503,998	453,514	385,457	–118,541	–23.5	–68,057	–15.0
Cleveland	914,808	750,879	573,822	–340,986	–37.3	–177,057	–23.6
Detroit	1,849,568	1,514,063	1,203,339	–646,229	–34.9	–310,724	–20.5
Minneapolis	521,718	434,400	370,951	–150,767	–28.9	–63,449	–14.6
New York City	7,891,957	7,895,563	7,071,030	–820,927	–10.4	–824,553	–10.4
Newark	438,776	381,930	329,248	–109,528	–25.0	–52,682	–13.8
Philadelphia	2,071,605	1,949,996	1,688,210	–383,395	–18.5	–261,786	–13.4
Pittsburgh	676,806	520,089	423,938	–252,868	–37.4	–96,151	–18.5
St. Louis	856,796	622,236	453,085	–403,711	–47.1	–169,151	–27.2

Notes: [1] April 1, 1950 Census.

[2] April 1, 1970 Census.

[3] April 1, 1980 Census.

Sources: U.S. Bureau of the Census. County and City Data Book, 1956 (A Statistical Abstract Supplement), U.S. Government Printing Office, Washington, D.C., 1957; and U.S. Bureau of the Census, Commerce News, "Three Cities of 100,000 or More At Least Doubled Population Between 1970 and 1980, Census Bureau Reports," CB81-92, Public Information Office, Washington, D.C., June 3, 1981.

reversing markedly in the future. The long-term nature of the forces underlying this decline makes this evident.

The development of the horse-drawn streetcar in the late nineteenth century was the initial instrument which stretched the city beyond its circumscribed pedestrian limits. The ability to transmit electricity from a central power station to a moving vehicle, and the development of an efficient electrical streetcar motor, further accelerated movement to the countryside. The diffusion of the telephone and advances in the economical transmission of electricity (including the switch from direct to alternating current) also facilitated population decentralization. But at the same time, they also permitted *employment* centralization, increasing the number of people who could be gathered at a central locus within a fixed period of time.

The advent of widescale automobile ownership after World War II merely accentuated the suburbanization process. It permitted the working-out of long-standing social desires that had been evidenced in the late 1920s. The data of Exhibit 4 were virtually preordained by the technological introductions of a half-century before.

At present, despite much publicity, the often-heralded return of older suburbanites and/or Yuppies to the central city simply has not occurred; future demographics, particularly the slowing growth of household formation, are distinct negatives. *The homogenization of space—and increasingly of time—available through information technology has made much of the historical functions of the older core areas obsolete, or at best, opened them to very substantial and increasingly successful competition.* The major dynamics of dispersion and decentralization made possible by the technology of yesterday can only be accentuated by future innovation; within this latter context, there is little, at least on the horizon, which is unique and specific to central cities, and which might provide them with a new surge of competence and pulling power.

Household Change

The impact of technology is a function of the societal matrix which serves as a shaping device. Within this context, the shifts in America's household configurations are particularly important. The 1970s were the years of nominally unorthodox households—singles and "mingles"—and a relatively slow growth in traditional married couples. Overall, however, there was an enormous expansion in the number of American households. Housing buying power, at least in the beginning of the 1970s, was relatively high; a variety of household types, therefore, had the capacity to seek out independence. In our own estimation, however, the future will be quite different.

In Exhibit 5, we have projected household growth increments by age, type, and tenure, from 1983 through 1995. (The 1983 and 1995 totals are presented in Exhibits 6 and 7.) The pattern is one which reflects the maturing of America. First and foremost is a decline in the scale of household formation: Absolute household growth will average only 1.2 million per year in the early 1990s, as compared to 1.7 million in the 1970s.

Secondly, and equally evident, is the continued dominance of ownership. Again, this has significant ramifications for the adoption of new technology. On the one hand, owners may be more desirous—or perhaps even more capable—of long-term capital investment in their domiciles. A second, and perhaps less salubrious (from the viewpoint of technological innovation, at least) element, is the decline in renter

EXHIBIT 5

Projected Household Growth Increments by Age, Type, and Tenure: 1983 to 1995
(Numbers in Thousands)

| | Total | Family Households | | | Nonfamily Households | |
| | | Married Couple | Other Family | | Male Householder | Female Householder |
			Male Householder	Female Householder		
			Owner Households			
All Households	11,038	8,005	251	1,031	624	1,124
Under 25 years	−184	−117	−13	−12	−30	−15
25 to 34	44	34	−1	11	15	−16
35 to 44	4,742	3,809	114	448	250	120
45 to 54	3,839	3,011	105	389	164	171
55 to 64	−609	−439	−21	−44	−21	−84
65 yrs. and over	3,206	1,709	67	238	244	948
			Renter Households			
All Households	3,417	1,247	96	734	563	778
Under 25 years	−811	−318	−17	−118	−192	−166
25 to 34	39	57	−12	2	2	−10
35 to 44	2,089	854	74	539	414	209
45 to 54	1,155	460	46	228	231	191
55 to 64	−146	−55	−11	−11	−38	−31
65 yrs. and over	1,092	249	17	94	146	585

Source: CUPR Household Projection Model.

households. While not precisely coterminous with multifamily housing, at best this is indicative of relatively modest increments in large-scale, physically integrated housing configurations. This may have some limiting impact in adoption of equivalent-scale, centrally located innovation.

Unlike the 1970s, household growth will be dominated by married couples, typically two-worker households, concentrated in the 35- to 54-year-old householder age segment. At least in historic terms, these are people moving into the peak income-earning years, with a greater capacity for capital investment. Time will tell whether they have as much desire for crest-of-the-wave "electronics" as they exhibited in the 1970s. At least the more youthful among them are chil-

EXHIBIT 6

Owner and Renter Households by Age and Type
U.S. Total: 1983
(Numbers in Thousands)

	Total	Married Couple	Male House-holder	Female House-holder	Male House-holder	Female House-holder
		Family Households	*Other Family*		*Nonfamily Households*	
			Male House-holder	*Female House-holder*	*Male House-holder*	*Female House-holder*
Owner Households						
All Households	54,494	38,853	1,195	4,427	3,513	6,507
Under 25 years	1,097	759	47	80	163	49
25 to 34	8,985	7,060	162	553	872	338
35 to 44	11,149	8,895	263	1,103	589	299
45 to 54	9,525	7,499	240	929	401	456
55 to 64	10,519	7,709	210	777	440	1,383
65 yrs. and over	13,219	6,929	273	986	1,048	3,982
Renter Households						
All Households	29,423	11,055	821	5,043	6,001	6,504
Under 25 years	4,597	1,670	152	727	1,071	977
25 to 34	10,119	4,377	254	1,812	2,175	1,501
35 to 44	4,871	1,997	178	1,222	970	504
45 to 54	2,829	1,109	111	588	553	468
55 to 64	2,555	893	74	346	562	680
65 yrs. and over	4,451	1,009	51	348	670	2,374

Source: U.S. Bureau of the Census, Current Population Reports, Series P-20, No. 388, *Household and Family Characteristics: March 1983*, U.S. Government Printing Office, Washington, D.C., 1984.

dren of the electronics age, already shaped by casual ease of access to the computer. This, combined with personal means, may yield a much greater level of adaptation to the era of high technology than we have yet seen.

Labor Force Constraints

It is changes in the labor force that may well be the most important manifestation of the demographic matrix, both in terms of the economy of tomorrow and of technological adoption as well. The United States from 1970 through 1982 was unique among its principal

EXHIBIT 7

**Household Projections by Age, Type and Tenure
of Households, U.S. Total: 1995
(Numbers in Thousands)**

		Family Households			Nonfamily Households	
			Other Family			
	Total	*Married Couple*	*Male House-holder*	*Female House-holder*	*Male House-holder*	*Female House-holder*
		Owner Households				
Under 25 years	913	642	34	68	135	34
25 to 34	9,029	7,094	161	564	887	322
35 to 44	15,891	12,704	377	1,551	839	419
45 to 54	13,364	10,510	345	1,318	565	627
55 to 64	9,910	7,270	189	733	419	1,299
65 yrs. and over	16,425	8,638	340	1,224	1,292	4,930
Total	65,532	46,858	1,446	5,458	4,137	7,631
		Renter Households				
Under 25 years	3,786	1,352	135	609	879	811
25 to 34	10,158	4,434	242	1,814	2,177	1,491
35 to 44	6,960	2,851	252	1,761	1,384	713
45 to 54	3,984	1,569	157	816	784	659
55 to 64	2,409	838	63	335	524	649
65 yrs. and over	5,543	1,258	68	442	816	2,959
Total	32,840	12,302	917	5,777	6,564	7,282

Source: CUPR Household Projection Model.

overseas trading partners in terms of total civilian employment growth (Exhibit 8). While it expanded in the brief twelve years by more than 25 percent (almost 21 million jobs), it was actually declining in Germany and Great Britain. Even Japan's performance—an 11.6 percent growth rate (6 million jobs)—was dwarfed in comparison.

The level of capital investment in production facilities in the United States was severely impacted by this phenomenon. The cost of money in the 1970s increased very substantially; at the same time, labor was relatively freely available and—particularly at unskilled levels—relatively cheap. The temptation to maximize the use of the latter—and minimize the former—was pervasive.

EXHIBIT 8

Total Civilian Employment in the U.S.,
Four Largest European Nations,
and Japan: 1970 to 1982[1]
(Numbers in Thousands)

	1970	1982	Change: 1970 to 1982	
			Number	Percent
United States	76,678	99,526	20,848	26.5
Four Largest European				
Countries, Total	89,290	88,920[2]	−370	−0.4
France	20,320	20,980[2]	660	3.2
Germany	26,100	25,090[2]	−1,010	−3.9
Great Britain	23,780	22,460[2]	−1,320	−5.6
Italy	19,090	20,390	1,300	6.8
Japan	50,940	56,857[3]	5,917	11.6

[1] Includes self-employed, other non-payroll, and agricultural employment.

[2] Preliminary.

[3] Third Quarter.

Source: Janet L. Norwood, "Labor Market Contrasts: United States and Europe," *Monthly Labor Review*, Volume 106, Number 8, August 1983, pp. 3–7 (for U.S. and Europe); OECD, *Labor Force Statistics: 1969 to 1980*, Paris, 1982, and Quarterly Supplements (for Japan).

The situation is very different, however, as we turn to the future. The Bureau of Labor Statistics projects a total labor force growth from 1982 to 1995 of only 21 million (Exhibit 9). Thus, we will move from a pattern of labor force expansion which in the 1970s averaged 2.4 million participants a year, to 1.8 million in the 1980s, and to 1.3 million in the first five years of the 1990s—barely one-half that of the 1970s. The technological imperative—assuming that we have passed through the era of economic "shocks"—is evident. *The 1970s, from a demographic point of view, were far from a salubrious era for technological implementation; the 1980s are much more positive; and the 1990s, drastically so.*

America—subject to changes in immigration—is going to be short of labor. This will be manifested in a broad variety of areas. One has only to glance at the increment in individuals over the age of 65, from 20 million in 1970 to 34 million in 1995, to see one reflection of the increased demand for personal services—and this in the face of a drastic shrinkage in the labor force. Technological innovation will be the key to closing the gap.

EXHIBIT 9

Civilian Labor Force, by Sex and Age, 1970–1982, and Middle Growth Projection to 1995

	Labor Force (in thousands)					Participation Rate				
	1970	1980	1982	1990	1995	1970	1980	1982	1990	1995
Total, age 16 and over	82,771	106,940	110,204	124,951	131,387	60.4	63.8	64.0	66.9	67.8
Men	51,228	61,453	62,450	67,701	69,970	79.7	77.4	76.6	76.5	76.1
16 to 24	9,725	13,606	13,074	11,274	10,573	69.4	74.4	72.6	74.7	74.5
16 to 19	4,008	4,999	4,470	4,123	4,043	56.1	60.5	56.7	62.3	62.9
20 to 24	5,717	8,607	8,604	7,151	6,530	83.3	85.9	84.9	84.4	84.1
25 to 54	32,213	38,712	40,357	48,180	51,358	95.8	94.2	94.0	93.8	93.4
25 to 34	11,327	16,971	17,793	19,569	18,105	96.4	95.2	94.7	93.7	93.1
35 to 44	10,469	11,836	12,781	17,469	19,446	96.9	95.5	95.3	95.6	95.3
45 to 54	10,417	9,905	9,784	11,142	13,807	94.3	91.2	91.2	91.3	91.1
55 and over	9,291	9,135	9,019	8,247	8,039	55.7	45.6	43.8	37.4	35.3
55 to 64	7,126	7,242	7,174	6,419	6,311	83.0	72.1	70.2	65.5	64.5
65 and over	2,165	1,893	1,845	1,828	1,728	26.8	19.0	17.8	14.9	13.3
Women	31,543	45,487	47,755	57,250	61,417	43.3	51.5	52.6	58.3	60.3
16 to 24	8,121	11,696	11,533	10,813	10,577	51.3	61.9	62.0	69.1	71.6
16 to 19	3,241	4,381	4,056	3,778	3,761	44.0	52.9	51.4	56.8	58.2
20 to 24	4,880	7,315	7,477	7,035	6,796	57.7	68.9	69.8	78.1	82.0
25 to 54	18,208	27,888	30,149	40,496	44,852	50.1	64.0	66.3	75.6	78.7
25 to 34	5,708	12,257	13,393	16,804	16,300	45.0	65.5	68.0	78.1	81.7
35 to 44	5,968	8,627	9,651	14,974	17,427	51.1	65.5	68.0	78.6	82.8
45 to 54	6,532	7,004	7,105	8,718	11,125	54.4	59.9	61.6	67.1	69.5
55 and over	5,213	5,904	6,073	5,941	6,008	25.3	22.8	22.7	20.5	19.9
55 to 64	4,157	4,742	4,888	4,612	4,671	43.0	41.3	41.8	41.5	42.5
65 and over	1,056	1,161	1,185	1,329	1,337	9.7	8.1	7.9	7.4	7.0

Source: Howard N. Fullerton, Jr., and John Tscheller, "The 1995 Labor Force: A Second Look," *Monthly Labor Review*, Volume 106, Number 11, November 1983, p. 5.

It will be services, judging from past trends both here and abroad, which will dominate employment growth. As shown in Exhibit 10, even the success stories of the 1970s—Germany and Japan— showed little increment in goods-producing employment; indeed, Germany actually had a small decline. It is the service sector throughout the advanced industrial economies which represents the future.

In this context, while the exhortations for productivity increases to survive within an increasingly competitive world economy have been directed toward manufacturing, services have been the real pro-

EXHIBIT 10

Total Civilian Employment in the U.S., Selected European Nations, and Japan by Economic Sector: 1970 to 1982[a] (Numbers in Thousands)

	United States	France	Germany	Great Britain[b]	Italy	Japan
Agriculture[c]						
1970	3,567	2,821	2,262	782	3,839	8,860
1981	3,519	1,800	1,402	647	2,731	5,570
1982	3,571	(d)	1,371	(d)	2,525	(d)
Goods Producing[e]						
1970	26,080	7,917	12,465	10,531	7,586	18,190
1981	28,995	7,208	10,885	8,028[f]	7,722	19,700[g]
1982	27,070	(d)	10,480[f]	(d)	7,594	(d)
Service Producing						
1970	49,031	9,605	11,442	13,071	7,656	23,890
1981	67,883	11,968	13,261	14,373[f]	10,003	30,540
1982	68,888	(d)	13,251[f]	(d)	10,277	(d)

[a]Small adjustments made to the overall employment data in Exhibit 8 could not be made to certain sectoral data. Includes self-employed, other non-payroll, and agricultural employment.

[b]Includes Northern Ireland.

[c]Not available.

[d]Not available.

[e]Manufacturing, mining, and construction.

[f]Preliminary.

[g]Includes utilities.

Sources: Janet L. Norwood, "Labor Market Contrasts: United States and Europe," *Monthly Labor Review*, Volume 106, Number 8, August 1983, pp. 3–7 (for U.S. and Europe); OECD, Labor Force Statistics: 1969 to 1980, Paris, 1982, and *Quarterly Supplements* (for Japan).

ductivity laggards. As labor shortfalls loom—and as a by-product, labor costs increase—the imperatives of mechanization in the service sector are evident. Demographic and economic parameters strongly suggest a far greater degree of receptivity to new technology, born of necessity. But predicting its impact is far more problematic.

Predicting Technological Impact

While we have suggested the level of uncertainty in forecasting demographics, much less is our capacity to envision the technological future—and perhaps even more strikingly the levels and pace of adaptation to the alternatives that it makes possible. It is not yet a generation since the concept of the computer utility dominated the technical literature. This was a vision of super high-speed central computers whose capacities were so unique as to require relatively few of them, with users tied in via dedicated wire networks. Project MULTICS, the principal effort in this regard, cost the General Electric Company its taste for competing in the computer field—and this despite enormous levels of financing and a massive input at MIT. At least as of this writing, the freestanding, small-scale computer linked as a peer to a broad network—with no central point necessary—is now being viewed as the pattern for the future.

The uproar on video games as a defiler of youth—with commercial versions absorbing somewhere on the order of 25 billion quarters in 1982 and even greater market penetration predicted with new technological lures—has moved to the land of the Hula-Hoop. The best selling toys of 1984 were not computers (they were not even electronic), but rather the Cabbage Patch doll and its incidental number of accessories and knockoffs. Modernity fell out, dolls fell in.

But technological innovation can have far-ranging ramifications, changing our folkways. Dedication to location was evidenced in the past by the vast network of baseball leagues. Does anybody still go to the Class A League Albany Senators? The memory of the Newark Bears and the Jersey City Giants has passed into legend. But they have been replaced by new TV loyalties, seemingly independent of place. The Dallas Cowboys are now advanced as "America's Team" in football.

In a recent suburban garden apartment study conducted by the Center for Urban Policy Research, respondents tended to describe their locations in terms of highways and shopping centers, not municipalities. Areal orientation remains; its axes and artifacts, however, are altered. The immediacy of the local movie theater and its accompanying handful of stores in small-town America has largely disappeared, but the regional shopping centers have become "teenage villages." Adaptation has many forms; there are relatively few technological imperatives with such vigor as to support instant forecasts. Retailing provides an insightful example of the complexities at work.

The Retailing Evolution

The ambivalent nature of technology in altering areal patterns and organizational formats is exemplified by retailing. The pattern of communications of 100 years ago revolved around major city wholesalers who concentrated the products of small-scale manufacturers, and/or imports, and in turn maintained traveling sales forces which serviced the decentralized pattern of small merchants located at every crossroads location, USA. As so ably pointed out by Chandler in *The Visible Hand. . .* , prior to the Civil War, with the exception of the industries that rose to service the railroads, manufacturing was conducted in very small individually owned facilities.[3] The railroads provided the transit facilities for the drummers, and for delivery of goods. The communications line typically was the mail service—again, typically carried by the railroads—as well as the telegraph, which commonly used the same rights-of-way.

Given the seasonal character of a largely agricultural society, credit provision was central, both from retailers to consumers, and from wholesalers to retailers as well. Despite the early rise of advertising, its media and potency were relatively limited. Quality was essentially locally certified, and this was increasingly the case as individual retailers grew in scale. As late as 1910 a minority of Americans lived in urban areas, with localism a dominant. The rise of cities was accompanied—and perhaps aided, as well—by a synergistic relationship between the expansion of local newspapers and local retailing. The growth that ensued permitted the development of the classic department store, an optimization of the economics of central place that was to continue practically to our own time. The high-speed press fostered this expansion. The newspaper was king, and retailing its most prominent patron.

Certification of quality was a function of having bought at Bambergers', or Lazarus', or Altman's, or any of the other major downtown facilities. But this dominance of what was in effect local branding, paralleling the equivalent hegemony of local advertising media and communications, was challenged in the years immediately prior to World War II—and has nearly disappeared in recent decades.

While the first rise of national magazines of significant circulation occurred around the turn of the century, the rise of true national brands was a function of the development of radio. There had been pioneers before in exotic consumer goods, such as brands of cigarettes; soon they were joined in by a broad variety of other nondurable consumer goods. This was the era of Jello and Chase and Sanborn coffee.

For the upscale market, the national magazines had increasing style/brand potency, and with it centralization of manufacture. Just prior to World War I, for example, there were more than a thousand individual manufacturers of pianos in America. Steinway and Baldwin, in tune with *Vanity Fair* and the early version of *The Saturday Evening Post*, soon signaled a very substantial curtailment, with an equivalent process taking place in automobiles. To make a genius of the obvious, this was just the beginning as we moved into the television era, which provided a much broader spectrum of information, of dynamic visuals, of national—and increasingly international—brands. The role of local retailers as certifiers of quality gave way before the rise of these national entities whose very scale permitted the development of technology. The relationship was an enormously dynamic one. Color television without the potential availability of advertising dollars would, at the very least, have waited for another generation—and perhaps forever.

What was the impact on retailing? In the very act of providing brand certification, the goods in question became commodities. The package of services, of aura, and most of all, credibility given by the local retailer was subsumed by the manufacturer, and certified by national media. The *Good Housekeeping* Seal was alive implicitly before it was formalized. Grocery stores might decry the very low markups available and lack of price protection on national merchandise, but they had to carry the goods: They were literally pulled through the channels of distribution. The rise of the discount house and other forms of reasonably efficient distribution left the old mechanisms—and their historic areal distributions—in disarray. *Where you bought something became much less important than what you paid for it. The definition of staples/commodities was enormously broadened by the new communications channels.* And Main Street America became obsolete.

Paralleling this development, and to a certain degree contravening it, was the rise of the chain store operations. These called for a rigorous standardization of operation, an assumption of replicability of market and location, and the capacity to merchandise and administer from a central node. Starting up roughly around the turn of the century, their dominance of the urban scene was epitomized by Sinclair Lewis's *Main Street,* with the presence on every Main Street in America of Thom McAn, A & P, J.C. Penney, and the like. And the scale of these operations—without the abilities of our new high technology—was considerable indeed. J.C. Penny, for example, prior to its current consolidation, had more than 1,600 units; A & P at its peak, more than 30,000.

The technologies involved were all in place three generations ago: rail and then truck shipping, telegraph and telephone for communications, and dependable mail service both for parcels and unit-control purposes (i.e., detailed information on a daily base of items sold, stock needs and the like, forwarded to a central location for information processing and response). While chain store dominance of small-town America has been decried, it permitted a substantial broadening of market centers, which flourished as a function of, and undoubtedly facilitated, the thickening of urban America which so vigorously characterized the 1920s.

None of these institutional developments can be characterized simply as either centralizing or decentralizing in their nature. There is strikingly little in current technology which so far has altered that generalization. Machine-readable unit-control tickets were envisioned in the 1920s—and came into being in the beginning of the 1950s. So far they have merely replicated the information available utilizing flocks of clericals. At least in the United States, video-text shopping has been notable by its failures. A more vigorous effort in this regard under government auspices is being promulgated in Western Europe, particularly in France. Again, however, the vision of shopping at home, while continuously reinforced by the vigor of mail order, has not significantly altered the broad spectrum of retail merchandising. The modern suburban shopping center, in its replacement of Main Street, is much more a tribute to the national highway program (and, if anything, a belated tribute) than it is to communications or information technology per se.

The influence of technologies and informational processing *past* is evident in the retailing configurations *present.* These in turn certainly have impacted on the areal distribution of economic activity and population concentrations as well. As of the moment, while there is much in the way of new information/communications technology which could produce significant shifts in the near-term future, there is little in the way of market success. Even the computer has facilitated but not basically altered extant functions.

Mail order, which a generation ago was viewed as a leftover remnant of an understored, rural America, has expanded. In substantial part this is a tribute to the speed, cost efficiency, and excellence of reproduction made possible by modern color-printing mechanisms, particularly when linked with the consumer targeting and partitioning made possible by the computer.

Video text, which would be the next logical development in non-store retailing, is certainly technologically feasible. As of the moment it requires the equivalent of a Sarnoff, with the level of commitment and fiscal competence that was mobilized to deliver color television. The threshold conditions are so substantial as to have defeated the several entrepreneurial groups that have assaulted it in this country. Even at its most grandiose, it is difficult to believe that it would serve as a passive surrogate for present-day shopping, so much of which, particularly in the suburban shopping center, serves as a recreational/social outing as much as for retail purposes.[4] The two-worker household may lean more heavily on nonstore marketing—but the heft of sales is traditional.

The pre-punched computer control tag has replaced some of the clericals, hard-wired sales registers linked to computers have abated some of the problems of sales audits, and new self-service fixturing combined with brand identification has limited the expansion of sales help. These and similar elements clearly will be pursued in the future. Similarly, warehouses have given way to the distribution center with concomitant declines in the carrying costs of inventory. This is linked with a far greater capacity to limit costs and target merchandise in short order with real-time information processing. And it has altered labor force requirements and the loci of employment.

Credit

The subject of the provision and sources of credit over time deserves much more attention (and competence of treatment!) than we are able to give it. The old pattern of credit provision by wholesalers to retailers and, in turn, by them to individual customers of a century ago, gave way in time to a bifurcation: Small retailers continued this pattern; the larger ones went into the credit business on their own. By working directly with manufacturers and depending only upon normal trade terms—indeed, sometimes paying cash—they were able to bring down price. In turn they extended credit to their consumers based on their own fiscal competence, and became increasingly dependent on the profitability of consumer credit per se. The range of price, merchandise offerings, and credit certified the unique position of the central city retail giants. They, in turn, assured the pulling power and dominance of the cities they occupied.

Each institution individually provided credit to the same customers; the amount of credit checking and general paper work was enormously redundant. The rise of central credit facilities (i.e., American Express, Visa and their equivalents) represents a very substantial compaction of this process. Enormously more credit transactions can be undertaken with a reduction of staff per transaction as a function of centralization and the automation of procedures which it permits. While precise data on this point are lacking, it is clear that the competence of the new information technologies has permitted an enormous expansion of credit. While person power per transaction has been reduced, the sheer growth of the operation has provided even more in the way of jobs than would otherwise be the case.

Not the least important reflection of the centralization of credit (even some of the major department stores are foregoing the exclusive use of their own credit cards) has been a lifeline extended to relatively small-scale operations. Local vendors now can be represented in shopping centers and other high transient areas where they do not know their customers, but still extend credit based on central information processing. *Personal knowledge gives way to formalized centralized information processing. The former is coterminous with sales place, the latter relatively independent. The rejuvenation of decentralized retailing is in part a reflection, therefore, of the centralization of consumer credit.* The back room of the local retailer, once devoted to unit control, to credit files, and perhaps as well even to payroll and sales audit, now can be transported through hardwire to an infinite range of locations—and with them the jobs which are involved.

The Retail Dynamic and the Limitations of Technology

Perhaps the most consequential innovation of the last 50 years in retail distribution has not been a function of technology, but rather, conscious or unconscious systems analysis. This has revolved around the substitution of the customer as order picker for paid labor. Beginning in the depths of the Depression, this was pioneered by the early supermarkets. Clerks behind counters who served as order pickers gave way to bulk stocking (initially in packing cases with, at most, primitive fixturing). The customer served as order picker. The results in terms of efficiency of distribution, largely as a function of the reduction of labor costs, were truly revolutionary.

Efforts at high-tech approaches to the same functional juncture— i.e., how do you go from wholesale lots (cases) to individual orders— have failed because of the low costs made possible by this process. Thus, as early as the 1920s, there were efforts to mechanize order picking with primitive electromechanical devices. And similarly in the 1940s and 1950s Grand Union failed with the same approach. Home delivery of foods, attempted in Sweden through centralized warehousing and customer-telephoned orders—accompanied by some measure of electronic gadgetry—foundered on the same rock. Within this context, the development of the shopping cart was much more consequential than the new code marking and the laser registers which have come in its wake. At this writing, the latter innovations have made possible the use of lower-class labor (or is it the same class of labor with poorer educations and less arithmetic capacity?) but are dwarfed in consequence by the much more basic systems change. So efficient has been customer order picking as to be adopted now in a variety of nonfood areas, as witness the fixturing of the modern-day liquor store, hardware store, home improvement center—and increasingly soft goods merchandise emporiums as well.

Information technology has been more significant in providing, as we have earlier indicated, access to broader-based areally dispersed selective networks of specialized consumers. This has been fostered by specialized publications—the *Radio Controlled Modeler*, *The American Orchid Review*, and literally thousands of other media. It is complemented on a broader base by the increasingly sophisticated utilization of census data for specialized mailing, i.e., the *Sharper Image* catalog and the ready-to-wear offerings of rugged clothing for the "*L.L. Bean*ized" urbanite. The total scale of these latter efforts has been enormously facilitated by the rise of credit mechanisms independent of specific retailers.

Stasis and Inertia

The basic locomotion devices employed in the journey to work have been relatively little changed in a half-century. As far back as 1929, the United States turned out as many cars per capita as it did last year; and while the trolley has given way wholly to the bus, the commuter railroads have altered little or at all. (If we might interject a parochial note, in our own state of New Jersey we are presently replacing railroad commuter cars from the class of 1928.)

The revolution of suburbanization, we would suggest, has been as much a function of affluence as of technological revolution. Within the latter domain, it is much more a tribute to the national highway program than to communication devices, at least in its first generation (roughly through 1970). It was the Depression of the 1930s, plus five years of wartime constraint, that inhibited the complementary dispersion of population and economic function which was the appropriate complement of the information and transportation innovations of the 1920s, principal among them the telephone. The omnipresence of this incredibly inexpensive device as a facilitator of both centralization and decentralization has often been cited; its prominence is worthy of reiteration.

But even given the constraints of the 1930s and World War II, there was a very long gap between technological competence and societal reaction. The first major enclosed suburban mall dates from the early 1950s, but the large-scale suburban shopping center really did not come into full blossom until the succeeding decade. It was not until the 1970s that the major part of office construction moved out of the central city.

There is a powerful flywheel of custom which leads to inertia. This is particularly the case when it is linked with the enormous sunk costs and slow replacement cycles that characterize American society. We have both the conservative virtues and demerits of long-term affluence and development. A good housing year is one in which starts are roughly equal to two percent of the extant stock, portions of which go merely to replace facilities that are scrapped. In New York City, for example, over the last ten years new housing starts have averaged on the order of 10,000 units a year. Given a base of nearly 2.8 million, this would suggest a building replacement cycle on the order of 300 years. While equivalent data on industrial facilities suffers from changes in their nature over time, the average age of the gross stock of fixed non-residential business capital hovers around the 10-year mark.[5] *Thus, there can be a much more abrupt response to changes in information technology on the part of production facilities than holds true in terms of settlement patterns.* The latter are complicated by the enormously potent role that housing plays in the United States as a source of per-

sonal savings. More than 60 percent of the equity of Americans is
frozen in personal housing ownership.[6] The conflict between these
two elements—the first with a 50-year "replication cycle," the latter
with one only a fifth as lengthy—is particularly striking as we move
toward the end of the twentieth century. It has served as a stabilizer
of older settlement patterns. Much of what we see as suburbanization
or regional shift is a belated response of the latter to new economic
spatial imperatives.

Journey to Work and the Electronic Cottage

The Journey-to-Work data available from the 1980 Census illus-
trates in considerable detail the growing congruence between work
and residence place. Journey-to-work times have not expanded;
indeed, there is some indication of their contracting. The central city
as the major focal point clearly has given way to peripheral, point-to-
point, commutation, and with this, a growing dominance of private
means of transport as against public conveyors.

The incongruity between the vast amounts of funding that the
latter are absorbing, versus their declining utilization, raises some very
real issues as to their continuance. The degenerative spiral of declining usage leading to increased fares and/or declining maintenance/
service leading to further patronage declines, seems to characterize
our older facilities. These tend to set up frictions in commuting to
places which are dependent upon public transit—particularly rail transit.

The prototype is New York City. As the commuter linkages
begin to generate much more in the way of friction (cost, time, and
comfort), there is a split in response. On the one hand, we have
those who can afford to live proximate to the workplace—typically
Manhattan—doing so. The long-term decline of Manhattan's
population—a process that has nearly 70 years of antecedence—now
seemingly has, at the very least, plateaued. But a growing proportion
of its job base is maintained by commuters—and there is some indication that their faithfulness to this process has been and will be
reduced in time. Thus the rise in peripheral locations (northern New
Jersey being a premier example) of competing office facilities yields a
shift to closer proximity of workplaces and residence place. Just as the
cutting and styling and selling operations of New York's garment
center lofts could remain there while the sewing shops moved to

cheaper locations with linkages of interstate trucking, so we see back-room office facilities moving peripheral to the city—and sometimes at far greater distance. This latter process in information handling has its equivalent technological enabling mechanisms: the era of the computer and high speed communications linkages. And clearly, the end of this dynamic is not at hand.

In 1983, with roughly similar-sized populations, New Jersey secured four times as many new housing units—and northern New Jersey alone, twice as much office space—as New York City. While final data for 1984 are lacking at this writing, current estimates suggest an equivalent disproportionate development. And jobs are increasingly footloose. They can follow as well as lead people.

The close linkage of workplace and residence place is exemplified by journey-to-work patterns. In 1980, there were approximately 75 million workers 16 years of age and over resident in metropolitan America. Of the 29 million of them who lived in central cities, fully 25 million worked inside the SMSA of their residence. The combined total of those working inside another SMSA—or working outside SMSA's—barely exceeded the three-million mark.

This is confirmed when the data on workers living outside the central city are viewed. Fully 38 million of the grand total of 45 million for whom data are available worked inside the SMSA of their residence—but only a third within the central city.[7] The basic technology of communications and information processing now being implemented has been available for at least 20 years. The lag, again caused by the flywheel of custom, leaves a gap between technological competence and market fulfillment. But this is rapidly receding into the past.

There are countervening forces at work as well. Estimates by Regina Armstrong at the Regional Plan Association, for example, suggest that roughly one-half million jobs in the New York region are dependent upon foreign investment. And more than 100,000 of these jobs stem from foreign firm operations in Manhattan.[8] A tribute to this hegemony is the new wave of national centralization of banking, brokerage, and insurance facilities within the city. The World Trade Center may have been a premature title; it is now representative of a potent reality.

It is evident that information technology has subverted localism in terms of banking. Despite the scar tissue of legislation left over from the Depression, the de facto nationalization of banking is at hand. It is evidenced by the Bank of America consolidating 2,000 employees in New York City; its international equivalent is revealed by the enormous flow of foreign establishments into the city.

Question must be raised in this context, however, as to what happens to the old regional centers with the rise of a national and world economy. Philadelphia, at least in banking, is becoming a branch city. Even Chicago is threatened by the same fate.

Some measure of the rise of the new dominance of New York in this context is shown in Exhibit 11, which indicates the flow of international phone calls from various major cities in the United States. New York City alone accounted for more than 20 percent of them. More than twice as many overseas message units were generated by New York City as by Los Angeles. When New York City, northern New Jersey, Long Island, and the four New York State counties north of New York City are added together, the New York Metropolitan region accounts for almost 30 percent of the total.[9] While some of this flow undoubtedly represents non-business calls (proportionate to New York's enormous ethnic population), there is no question of its uniqueness.

The ambiguous role of new information technology as a centralizing and or decentralizing example is exemplified in the growing challenges to the monolithic role of utility companies. The latter had cen-

EXHIBIT 11

Overseas Message Units

Area Code	
New York City 212	22,718,027
Los Angeles 213	9,310,028
San Francisco 115	4,535,474
Chicago 312	4,028,709
Northern New Jersey 201	4,639,122
Connecticut 203	2,129,146
Westchester, Putnam, Orange, and Rockland Counties (NY) 914	1,897,576
Nassau-Suffolk, Long Island (NY) 516	1,705,740
Total (USA)	115,001,763

Source: AT&T Communications. Secured from: Mitchell L. Moss, "New York Isn't Just New York Anymore," *Journal of the International Institute of Communications*, July/September 1984. Vol. 12, No. 4/5.

tral places as their focal point. The new technology is much more spatially ambiguous. For example, NYNEX derives a disproportionate share of revenues from its largest business customers, with three percent of them providing a third of its business revenues; one percent of New York Telephone's business customers generate 25 percent of its revenues. Fully 85 out of 100 top revenue-producing customers of New York Telephone Company are located in Manhattan; the borough in and of itself contains 46 percent of New York Telephone's business access lines, and contributes 35 percent of its total revenues.[10]

The very scale of the major customers, however, permits them to develop bypass operations for their own proprietary use and/or participate in alternative, inexpensive approaches geared to large-scale users. An example is the New York Teleport being built by Merrill-Lynch, Western Union, and the Port Authority of New York and New Jersey. This is a communications complex nearing completion on Staten Island designed to connect customers in the New York metropolitan area with all outside calling points. The customers, in turn, are linked directly to the Teleport by fiber cable rather than through New York telephone facilities. Heavy line users were once substantially tied to central city, but how close to the central "exchange" does one have to be in order to take advantage of these efficiencies of scale?

Present technology involving laying of fiber cables, interestingly enough, is following the rights-of-way of the railroads. Does this suggest office development will be areally defined by the railway line disposition put in place nearly a century ago? Or is there a greater measure of freedom even within today's parameters, much less those of tomorrow? Cable television, for example, provides a second bypass threat to the New York Telephone Company. Commercial data transmission services will soon be available connecting directly to New York and the American Stock Exchange, with links to the Teleport, thus enabling subscribers to completely bypass the local loop.

On the one hand, we can envision this type of development as permitting large-scale firms to stay in what is a high-cost location—and making permanent its job base and related settlement pattern as well. But even if technology is so limited as to require this close proximity, the potential feedback on the cost structures of those firms which are not able to take advantage of the new elements must be viewed with some trepidation. Telephone service (and indeed many other elements of New York) is a very high, fixed-cost operation. A reduction in the user base could require catastrophic increases in the prorated charges to the balance of the utility's customers. This in turn could speed decentralization.

These possibilities are far from unique to New York. We would suggest, however, that they are most potent in our older metropolises with fixed capital costs which are particularly sensitive to reduction in usage. This has already been evidenced in the case of the subways and public transit in general—and these may only herald things to come.

As pointed out by Mitchell L. Moss, however, there are requirements imposed by a world economy which may have very serious feedback, given the limitations of New York City as a whole—and Manhattan particularly.[11] The 24-hour business day is premier among them. The very costs of infrastructure, and the requirements for providing services and information on a worldwide base, impose equivalent staffing requirements. And New York City is not an easy place within which to provide required security. The trans-Hudson City of Manhattan—northern New Jersey—may play a much more imposing role in the future in this regard. This may impose limitations on the growth of Manhattan and the other boroughs as well.

The perfection of communications opens up a variety of alternative locations. The very cost strictures of the city and its limited capacity to provide housing for middle management constricts crucial labor force flows. The elite can buy space proximate to work while youthful aspirants are willing to accept very poor housing conditions in order to be close to the dynamo. But other less-affluent and/or less-flexible home seekers are driven away.

Amidst an enormous flow of plenty seen by visitors to New York is the harsh reality of median 1983 renter household incomes under $13,000—and of median homeowner (including co-ops and condominiums) incomes of $25,000. A thin veneer of the rich glamorizes the eye and distracts it from a rather broad spectrum of the poor. However, the sheer animal vitality of the city and its increasing focus (as pointed out very presciently a dozen years ago by Eli Ginzberg) on production services, provides a rare base of opportunity.[12] Even here, however, there is some indication that an increasing proportion of this growth is going to commuters. In 1979 roughly six percent of Manhattan's jobs were held by New Jerseyans. Estimates by the Port Authority indicate that approximately 23 percent of the growth in jobs in that borough over the last 5 years have flowed to New Jerseyans. Ultimately the jobs will follow the people.

New forms of coaxial cable, optical fiber, and micro-wave

transmission facilities—as well as yet-unknown and unseen mech-anisms—will be put in place. What they suggest is an increase in bifurcation: of centralization of functions on the one hand, and a capacity to spread them out on the other. *In this context we would suggest that technology is an enabling element rather than a determinative one. The impact of technology must be viewed through a matrix of societal elements which shape its ultimate areal resolution—and settlement patterns as well.*

Nowhere is this requirement more evident than in predictions of a society of "electronic cottages." The pinnacle of industrial urbanization was the central city that emerged in the nineteenth century, built on massed population, productive power and industrial technology. In contrast is the view that the end point of the communications revolution is the electronic cottage. The information era will bring decentralization, just as the industrial era wrought centralization. Households will be free of spatial ties as they work at their dispersed residences: Information will commute, not people. A vision of post-industrial cottage industries is raised; knitting is replaced by information work.

The reality to come will not be nearly so extreme. Just as the regional shopping center flourishes despite the potential of electronic retailing, so too will the office remain a viable workplace. People will still want to be with people. As Naisbett has suggested, the more technology we pump into society, the more people will seek the "high touch" of the office and shopping mall. "The gee-whiz futurists are always wrong because they believe technological innovation travels in a straight line. It doesn't. It weaves and bobs and lurches and sputters."[13]

Notes

1. President's Research Committee on Social Trends, *Recent Social Trends in the United States* (New York: McGraw-Hill, 1933).
2. F.J. Kingsbury, "The Tendency of Man to Live in Cities," *Journal of Social Science*, Vol. 33, November 1895.
3. Alfred D. Chandler, *The Visible Hand: The Managerial Revolution in American Business* (Cambridge, MA: Harvard University Press, 1977).
4. For a more positive view, see William A. Gordon, "Electronic Retailing: Trends and Implications," *Urban Land*, October 1984.
5. U.S. Bureau of the Census, *Statistical Abstract of the United States: 1984* (104th edition), Washington, D.C., 1983, p. 542.

6. "Survey of Consumer Finances, 1983," *Federal Reserve Bulletin*, September 1984, pp. 679–692.

7. U.S. Bureau of the Census. *Census of Population: 1980. Journey to Work: Metropolitan Commuting Flows*, Washington, D.C., 1984.

8. Regina Armstrong, "The Future of New York in the World Economy," Regional Plan Association, unpublished paper.

9. Mitchell L. Moss, "New York Isn't Just New York Anymore," *Journal of the International Institute of Communications*, July/September 1984, Vol. 12, No. 4/5, pp. 10–14.

10. Goldman-Sachs, Nynex Corporation Report, December 19, 1984.

11. Mitchell L. Moss, "New York Isn't Just New York Anymore," *Journal of the International Institute of Communications*, July/September 1984, Vol. 12, No. 4/5, pp. 10–14.

12. Eli Ginzberg, *New York is Very Much Alive: A Manpower View* (New York, NY: McGraw-Hill, 1973).

13. John Naisbett, *Megatrends* (New York, NY: Warner Books, 1982), p. 41.

12

American Industry: The Continuous Revolution

George Sternlieb

Structural Change, Innovation, and Worker Displacement

Was the comparative stagnation of the American economy in the 1970s and early 1980s merely a reflection of noise, of transient phenomenon? Or was it rather a new message of stress requiring major adjustment? Is the post-1982 upturn a result of a last flare of Keynesian deficit spending, doomed to pass of its own weight? Is there a unique set of technological circumstances, prevalent in our own era and dominating the future, so different from those of the past as to require basic shifts in the governance of our economy? Has the competitive nature of the world's economy so changed, given the near worldwide homogenization of space, expertise, and flows of funds, as to imperil the comparatively unstructured reliance on the market which has dominated the American scene? Or is there rather a conjunction of a number of periodic cycles, none of which is aberrant to history, whose coming together at one moment in time has imposed relatively unique stresses—but which will recede? A premier example is the secular downturn in both the United States and the world economy in the 1970s, perhaps as a culmination of the oil crunch, whose full implication in terms of economic strictures has not been fully appreciated, combined with the enormous accession rate to the labor force which has dominated—perhaps uniquely—the recent American scene.

253

The basic parameters are evident. There are two interwoven but relatively distinct phenomena which are taking place within our society at the same time. The first of these is the pruning of obsolete facilities and the replacement of their functions in more efficient settings. This is far from a novelty. It is characteristic of industries and firms which are intent and competent to stay in business. Success in these endeavors may well be dependent upon a vigorous implementation of the process.

The second strand is part of the monumental structural shift of our economy. The gauge of this process is the rise of new sectoral activities and the decline of others. The process is seemingly irreversible, certainly within the near-to-intermediate future. The goal of this process must be to redirect capital and labor as rapidly, as efficiently, and as painlessly as possible. Long-term investment, perhaps even continuing in "sunset" businesses, by very definition represents less than optimal use of resources in both the private and public sphere. Frictions which significantly inhibit the dynamics sketched above are enormously costly. It should be stressed that this holds true both for accounting within a particular firm and, equally consequentially, in terms of the total national weal.

None of these questions is unique in time. They are as old as industry itself. But is our current situation of such drastic proportion as to require new major government-mandated change in the responsibilities of management to buffer labor from the impact of change? What has brought the issue to the fore in public attention is an increasing awareness of a seeming decline in America's competitive cutting edge. In the face of an ever-homogenizing world labor market and, increasingly, expertise and capital flows as well, the conceptual tools of the past are increasingly criticized. The threat of the unknown sometimes produces near hysteric reactions. Thus, on the best-seller lists of our time, cheek by jowl are items on the reduction of unwanted fat and descriptions (many of them spurious) of the Japanese as super-managers. And, obviously by default in this latter case, the decline and fall of the Caucasian in the face of alien elements, a leitmotiv with age-long antecedence, is evident.

All of these elements in turn are seen through a filter, half alluring, half threatening, of the technological revolution which is at hand.

The structuring of the roles of capital, labor, and government in the United States has typically reflected past experience rather than the necessities of the future. While the discontinuities between American practices and those of our principal industrial competitors have been substantially exaggerated, in general labor in the United States has been rewarded with higher levels of current income, if perhaps less in the way of mandated safety net legislation. This approach, which has been enormously successful, is now under challenge. The epitome of this challenge is the changes that are proposed under the general title of "plant closing law"—broad, mandated changes in the freedom of management to close or move plants and equipment.

It is fifty years since the last major realignment of management and labor under the New Deal. This strengthened the institutionalization of labor's rights and powers by increasing the capacity to unionize, and thus extended the use of collective bargaining. Is this process adequate for our time? Or is a more sweeping, structured set of changes called for in order to preserve the peace and to facilitate the sweep of America's progress into the new economic world which is in the making? The powers of the collective-bargaining process have been severely curbed by the regional shifts within the United States to non-union settings; are they adequate to provide a safety valve in a competitive, fast-changing world economy?

Within this context, a strong case can be made that the economy is much too important to be left in the hands of economists; certainly an even more vigorous thrust, strongly fortified by recent past events, would suggest the same strictures in terms of leaving it to the mercies of the political sector. It is and must be, in all practicality, a political economy in the classic sense of that terminology, aware of the necessities of constituency building, but placing them within a cost/benefit context that does not sacrifice the future in terms of the immediacies.

The Precedent of Automation

One of the curious phenomena of our age is that of self-flagellation: "The sky is falling" has always had its supporters, perhaps because it provides an opportunity for evading responsibility for making things work, perhaps as a rationalization of personal frustration. In this context, it is worthwhile to step back in time to a period in which America's economic competitive hegemony was still unquestioned, but the fear of new technology symbolized by the then-new term automation (invented by students at the Harvard Business School at the beginning of the 1950s) was rampant.

So substantial was the fear of displacement "by the machine" in the early 1960s, that a presidential commission on the impacts of automation was implemented (National Commission on Technology,

1966), plus a substantial output of analytical work by other authors as well. As Jack Barbash, Professor of Labor Education and Economics at the University of Wisconsin, stated in a 1963 publication, "In the 1930s the dominant note in the tone of industrial relations was union recognition; in the wartime period, wages; in the immediate post-war period, fringe benefits with special emphasis on health insurance and pensions. The leitmotiv of the contemporary industrial relations scene is expressed by one variation or another of technological change and its popular equivalent, automation" (Barbash, 1963, 44).

Barbash notes that "When union responses to technological change are taken together with responses to problems of health care, we can begin to see how collective bargaining is constructed, piece by piece . . . health, welfare and pensions constituted the first major extension of the new collective bargaining. Now the welfare orientation is being further extended to cover a wide range of employment consequences of technological change" (Barbash, 1963, 56).

The original dismay with automation receded. The question at hand, however, is whether this provides a parallel to our present situation. Are we encountering a needless faltering of faith in the competitive capacity of the economy in its ability to generate new employment opportunities to replace the old, and indeed an overstatement of the actual amount of displacement that has taken place? Or is the 1960s' reaction to automation rather a premature anticipation which now has caught up with the reality?

The reaction to innovation is merely one aspect of the motivating forces that have focused on changing the balance of power between labor and management. A variant of it, as we will note later in more detail, is the issue of the requirement of a massive change in goods delivery only being securable politically within the context of worker protection. The assertion is made that given the realpolitik of our time, this realignment is the price of technological progress, of shifting the economy onto the new fast tracks of the twenty-first century.

Much more bleak has been the erosion in one of the dominant themes of western society, at its strongest in the United States, and that is the very theory of progress: the belief that today is better than yesterday, and tomorrow will be better yet. While there has always been an undercurrent of refrain toward "getting back to the good old days," the much more common focus of American culture has been the general acceptance that new is better. Without argument as to its merits, "think small" through most of U.S. history would have been antithetical to the governing drives of our system. Indeed, part of the shock value of such books as *The Limits of Growth* (Meadows, 1974) is their attack on what heretofore had been a basic (if not *the basic*) given of Americans' personal belief: a faith in an ever more bountiful tomorrow.

The issues of what it is that Americans do so uniquely well as to justify their standard of living—of fear of external competition—of calls for forms of organization which, if not emulated, will reduce us to the "second team" of world economic hegemony—become particularly forceful. While their growth seemingly has been slowed, given the relative economic prosperity which dominates at this writing (the beginning of 1985), they too have long historical antecedents. Thus, Thorstein Veblen, predicting the Allied victory over Germany in World War I as a function of America's entry into it, pointed to industrial know-how moving initially from England to Germany. The latter learned from the pioneer's earlier mistakes, perfecting the processes and outlook required by industry, only in turn to be supplanted by the United States.

While Veblen, in his essay on the importance of being last, clearly endorsed the new economic hegemony, he raised the issue of whether in the future there would be successors to the United States. These, in his view, would once again learn from us, would be able to perfect the processes, but would leave the elements of archaic practices behind, and in turn seize the torch (Veblen, 1939).

Have we reached one of these turning points? Is ours an era of Toynbeean crisis, of challenge to our system which must be met with major adaptation, with the success or failure of the process determining our futures? Or is it a moment of transient confusion which can, and will be (or perhaps already is being), met without significant alteration of our social fabric?

The Range of Perspectives

There are figures at both ends of the political spectrum who have projected, with considerable public acclaim, the decline and potential fall of the American economy. While both their descriptions and their diagnosis of the underlying disease may vary, the vision is remarkably constant. In turn, this *Götterdämmerung* serves as a springboard for a variety of nostrums. Thus, to the right, the United States is slowly being dragged down by self-inflicted wounds—of slackers, welfare, by a failure of the work effort and by its concomitant, the hedonistic immoral society. Government itself is seen as a reflection and, indeed, an amplifier of these trends. The focus on transfer payments rather than production, the burdening of the economic machine by overwhelming social costs, and the encrustation of the ways and means by which America generates its abundance, are viewed as the cardinal sins. Proposals reflecting this point of view involve a return to the historic virtues of yesteryear, the "unleashing" of the forces of free enterprise, and the severe limitations—if not the very dissolution—of the government role.

To the new left, the projected twilight comes as a pleasing confirmation of the long sought-for decline of capitalism. Capitalism lacks the legitimacy to withstand the changes which are taking place in technology and the sacrifices and adjustments which will be necessitated by its needs. Indeed, the required shifts are so formidable as to require a commensurate revolution in social and business organization. The woes of our society—whether among welfare recipients, the unemployed former industrial elite of the steel mills and automobile plants, indeed, the very decline of our cities—are viewed as cracks in the structure foretelling its near-term collapse. Not uncommonly, the left tends to dismiss international competitive issues as semi-fantasies invoked by union busters, as part of the right wing counter-assault against the remnants of the New Deal and the social revolution which inevitably must come. On the non-Marxist left, a new romantic yearning is evident: Think small, work in personalized units, worker control even of shrinking markets and obsolete processes, scramble in a little isolationism, and you can hold the world—and time—at bay.

Caught in the middle of this battlefield of woeful visions are the meliorists, desperately shouting slogans such as "reindustrialization before it is too late," "ten, five, three," "high tech," or "National Development Bank," and a variety of other magic bullets peddled by one or another advocate.

The factory closing law issue provides in microcosm, the arena in which all of these elements are involved. Should there be significant changes in the relative freedom of management to close, relocate or transfer activities and jobs with minimum advance notification? With penalties in the form of payments limited to those in specific labor agreements? Or is there such a tidal wave of change in prospect as to require new mandated rules of the game set by government?

More insight into the rival views of America's economic society is called for to provide a setting in which to view these issues. Certainly many of the arguments and criticisms of our system, even those from groups which seldom see eye to eye, may have some validity. It is essential, however, that before deciding among them, we secure some grasp of current realities as best we may. The precise dynamics of the American economy's checkered record of the last ten years are being debated. In the section which follows, we attempt a brief retrospective view of some of the principal arguments.

The Current Scene

Real median incomes of American families increased by 38.2 percent from 1950 to 1960, and by fully one-third from 1960 to 1970. The first years of the 1970s continued this trend, the very longevity of which had made it a seeming constant "right" for Americans. But this was a process which aborted. Real median family income peaked in 1973 at $26,175, and declined by fully 10.5 percent to $23,433 by 1982.

Even in 1984, after a nearly unprecedented economic recovery, family incomes had barely resumed their upward march. And critics have raised the issue as to whether the latter is being bought by enormous deficits whose very curbing may bring back the era of "stagflation."

While there are many variables which must be considered before taking these data at face value—changing demography, limitations in measuring sticks, and the like—they do provide one measure of the crisis of economic confidence which dominated the beginning of the 1980s. Their full political potency is still being manifested in national debates on economic and industrial policies.

The battering of the vision of national impregnability was symbolized by the forced withdrawal from the gold standard and the virtual floating of the dollar. Viet Nam claimed many victims, not least among them the relatively stable balance between governmental spending on the one hand, and incomes on the other, which had persisted since the Korean eruption. The guns-versus-butter argument required hard answers. In the face of an unpopular war, it was resolved by taking the seemingly easier way out and avoiding reality. The assurance that both were affordable was a high-water mark in economic hubris. The price was inflation, and under the devastating impact of the latter, the fall of the dollar.

This merely set the stage for the impact of the energy crunch of 1973–74. In combination with its successor of 1979–80, it resulted in the equivalent of a tax paid overseas of roughly 50 billion dollars a year.

In a previous publication, we have pointed to the complementary relationship between American expenditures for automobile purchase and their equivalent for energy for personal driving (Sternlieb, Hughes and Hughes, 1982). These were roughly at parity in 1973. But by the beginning of the 1980s, the absolute dollar level of expenditure on new automobiles for personal use remained at its 1973 level; that for imported petroleum products, however, rose by two-and-one-half times that amount, i.e., from a baseline of under 40 billion dollars to nearly 90 billion dollars.

The United States was forced into a position of coping with this impact not only in terms of our domestic economy, but also in support of much of the balance of the oil-importing world. In very broad terms, the oil surplus nations lent money short-term to American financial institutions and the latter, in turn, served as recyclers on longer-term notes to the balance of the world. American institutional credit certification made it possible for the developing nations to survive. While an international depression comparable to that of the great crash was averted, it was at the price of enormous levels of debt. And this debt still serves as a menacing overhang to the long-term recovery which we are presently anticipating.

Complicating the orderly response to the oil challenge was a crisis of confidence not only in America's government, but seemingly in a variety of allied institutions which had provided stability to our governance and authority to centralized expertise. The shock of Watergate, complicated by the rise of a new youth generation and changing mores, at least in its initial stages came close to shattering the sociopolitical fabric of the United States. The involvement of large-scale industry in the laundering of funds, the spreading wave of involvement exemplified by the large political slush funds and payoff puddles of companies such as Gulf Oil and some of the defense contractors, ITT's involvement in overseas affairs as well as their domestic implications—all left a power vacuum. The primitive legislative responses that ensued rarely were thought out, at best, and all too frequently were much more vengeful than constructive (Lipset and Schneider, 1983).

The unparalleled inflation which arose in the late 1970s was enormously harmful to the American web of industry. The flight from the dollar that ensued, the rise of collectibles from beer cans to stamp collecting and perhaps most of all, housing, has been envisioned as draining money for reinvestment away from productive uses. Inflation made a mockery of corporate income reports. In very large measure, particularly for heavy industry, they reflected inadequate depreciation replacement provision, rather than the growth of potential resources. It was relatively cheap money which permitted the continuous upgrading of America's plant. But now the costs and uncertainties of financing soared.

The shift toward monetarism and the appointment of Paul Volcker as head of the Federal Reserve symbolized the acceptance of the necessity for strong medicine. The clamping down of the federal printing presses caused a skyrocketing of interest rates to levels that have not been seen since the panic situations of the Civil War. The cure, though strong and certainly painful, has seemingly been effective.

The end of the age of collectibles is symbolized by the staggering drop in the price of gold, shifting from more than $800 to less than half that figure. Yet personal savings rates have yet to show renewed vigor: the United States has the dubious distinction of having the lowest personal savings rates of any major industrial country. And while inflation by 1983 had been reduced to levels low enough to surprise just about all of the financial forecasters, the basic rates which are anticipated for the mid-eighties, it should be kept in mind, are those which in a more innocent era at the beginning of the 1970s, occasioned a conservative president, Richard Nixon, to move toward price controls.

Key to this abatement has been the decline in energy costs. It has taken ten years, but the seemingly inexorable relationship between energy consumption and growth in GNP has been at the very least, alleviated: The dominance of OPEC has moved from the front pages to the realm of history (Salant, 1982).

From the viewpoint of the more sanguine prognosticators of the right, the faltering of the economic machine was a relatively small price to pay for a new political realism. The latter is evidenced by massive shifts in the incidence of taxation, a substantial lowering of marginal income tax rates, much more generous corporate depreciation allowance, and a scene set for the basic vigor of America's free market economy to fully rebound. Even the seemingly worn-out smokestack areas of the country, still suffering from winter, now begin to anticipate a new spring.

But is this a true reburgeoning? Is the stagflation of the last ten years nothing but a painful plateau upon which a new base of Ameri-

can prosperity will arise? Or are there, rather, longer-term phenomena
at work? The low levels of inflation of 1984 and 1985 have been purchased through cheap imports. Long-run stability is still endangered
by the scars and "cures" which were the price of a decade of no-
growth. The issues of displacement have receded—but may well be
renewed.

Worker Displacement and Economic Adjustment

The difficulties of pinpointing the reasons for the comparative
decline of American industry are accepted even by the more outspo-
ken critics of the current administration. Robert Lekachman, in the
course of an overall indictment of Reaganomics, admits the decline in
investment is enormously disquieting . . . but then provides as its
explanation that "The sociology of innovative investment is mysteri-
ous." At best, he suggests that the United States is replaying the Brit-
ish parallel when "In the 1880's for no adequate reason, these aggressive, thrusting souls lost their élan, became complacent, and gradually
lost ground to American and German rivals" (Lekachman, 1982, 68).

But certainly one of the principal arguments for a massive
overhaul of capital-labor relationships (and plant closing law is the cutting edge of them) relates to the future of labor in the face of technology. This argument, however, is as old as the formal study of
economics. For example, Ricardo put the invention of machines on a
par with the expansion of international trade and the division of labor,
claiming that all three increase the amounts of goods and "contribute
very much to the ease and happiness of mankind." Thus the new
technology of early nineteenth-century England would have "a decided
tendency to raise the real wages of labor."

Malthus, writing at roughly the same time, was far less sanguine,
feeling technology would ultimately decrease both the value and living
standards of the working class. Indeed, while Ricardo saw demand
increasing in parallel with inventions to save labor, Malthus had considerably less faith in the phenomenon. Ricardo, with great foresight,
pointed out that if the government curbs mechanization, capital would
migrate elsewhere. "This must be a much more serious discourage-
ment to demand for labor than the most expensive employment of
machinery" (Heertje, 1973, 18). But even Say, who was perhaps even
more sanguine about the ability of the introduction of machinery to
improve man's life, was far from sure that immediately displaced

workers would be absorbed by the new wealth and the new incentives to capital investment (Heertje, 1973).

This argument from the early days of the industrial revolution continued through the next century. Babbage, the great pioneer of computer conceptualization, analyzed statistics of 65 textile mills covering the period from 1822 to 1832, to show that as mechanical looms ousted hand looms, the number of hand weavers dropped to one-third the original number, but the number of those operating mechanical looms grew by a factor of five. An almost fourfold increase in production, thus, was accompanied by a 20-percent increase in total number of jobs. He added, however, that "In considering this increase in employment, it must be admitted that the 2,000 persons thrown out of work are not exactly of the same class as those called in employment by the power looms" (Heertje, 1973, 28). And certainly, the greatest critic of the rivalry between labor and technology was less sanguine regarding its results. While Marx followed Ricardo's statement that "machinery and labor are in constant competition," he was far more certain that ultimately the workers would lose out (Heertje, 1973).

The arguments in this sector have two basic parameters which have continued to our own time. The first is similar to that of Babbage's: New jobs are not filled by the workers displaced as a result of technology. Thus Bluestone and Harrison, in their current call for massive change in management powers after examining the revitalization of New England, feel that the trade-off of old jobs for the new sectors has been inadequate. "Jobs in the new high-tech industries and the retail trade and personal service sectors do not come close to making up for the jobs lost through a deindustrialization of the mill-based economy." They point to wage levels falling relative to other regions, an increasingly uneven distribution of income, more part-time and part-year jobs, as well as high employee turnover and limited upward mobility for many of the region's workers (Bluestone and Harrison, 1982, 94–95). Implicit in their comments is the assumption that somehow New England not only could have, but should have, held on to its old jobs in the face of the new competition. They suggest that the flight from unionization has become international and purposeful on the part of management—not a response to competition so much as an episode in the battle for managerial control. In this view, left behind is the wreckage of the New Deal's social compact.

Even the dismal comforts of replacement jobs in the fast-food industries decried by Bluestone and Harrison are more than can be anticipated according to some observers. The vision of massive reductions in employment as a result of the technological revolution has become more prominent. Nobel Prize winner Wassily W. Leontief stated that in the past "machinery replaced the physical labor of human beings, that made the mental efforts of people more important to make the move to jobs that machines cannot perform." Now, he contends: "Smart machines are replacing the mental efforts of a great many people who have no place else to go. Robots and computers are much more efficient. Thus reducing the costs of human labor will not work." Comparing the results to what happened after the industrial revolution of the nineteenth century, he states that, "even if the horses had been willing to eat less oats, the tractors would have replaced them anyway."

What is the answer? "Let us spread the work. We do not have to maintain the horses, but we have to maintain the people." And thus he calls for income and work-sharing procedures (*The New York Times*, 1983).

The fears of labor displacement through automation and technology are not the exclusive possession of Professor Leontief. In the viewpoint of a member of the editorial board of *democracy*, the journal self-described as representing the democratic radical left, the problem is the infatuation, of both the Marxist and capitalist, with technology and the concept of technological progress. Thus, ". . . the political radicals view the problem in terms of the distribution of property and political power. They viewed machines simply as tools to be used for good or evil, depending upon who had the power to use them. They decried opposition to machinery as wrong-headed and worked to divert workers' attention and antagonism away from the machine toward the political system. . . . The Marxist ridicule of all who oppose capitalist-sponsored technological development thus simply seconded the hegemonic social tabu, and further marginalized those who tried to insist upon viewing such development in the present tense. Those who refused to accept technological necessity . . . were dismissed as romantic reactionaries or utopian dreamers."

The article from which these statements are excerpted, far from unrepresentative of pieces in the journal, is essentially a call for an optimization of present-day comfort rather than "selling out" for dubious future progress. There is within it a very specific defense of the Luddites, long figures of ridicule for fighting "the inevitability" of progress (Nobel, 1983, 19–21). This is not to suggest that the radical left excuses "the system." In the words of the editor of *democracy*, Princeton's Sheldon Wolin, "there can be no solutions to the problems of the economic system. . . . Unemployment is a recurrent condition produced by the need of capitalists to adjust the labor force to market conditions and changing technology." Thus, the displacement issue is inherent to the present configuration of governments (*democracy*, Spring 1983, 3).

It is intriguing to note that immediately thereafter, in the same issue, is a summary of the International Machinists' proposed Bill of Rights which calls for major changes in industrial governance. The President of the International Association, Mr. William R. Winpisinger, testifying before the Subcommittee on Economic Stabilization of the House Committee on Banking, Finance, and Urban Affairs, July 1981, further pointed to the deleterious effects of new technology on skilled labor, and suggested that machinists have been replaced by low-skilled machine operators backed up by a relatively small number of service people.

In his view, the government has aided and abetted this process in two related ways: It has supported vocational and technical school training, which most often takes the form of specialized training rather than more general training obtained from collective bargaining-based apprenticeship programs, and secondly, through efforts like the Department of Defense's "Partners-in-Preparedness," has promoted reindustrialization programs without the benefits of labor representation.

He clearly calls for major shifts in management-labor relations to deal with what are described as basic weaknesses of the system; much of their focus relates to the factory closing issue as the distillate of the new stresses.

Within the exigencies and uncertainties of today, it is sometimes easy to forget the prior revolutions in the workplace that have taken place in the United States. The era of the Great Depression coupled the fear of new technology with a no-growth economy. It provides a useful perspective to the present challenge.

The literature of the early 1930s is rife with comments which are remarkably comparable both to the historic and current debates. Thus, in the *Report of the President's Research Committee on Social Trends*, published in 1933, several authors repeatedly raise the issue of technological unemployment. "One is also impressed by the frequency with which new machines displaced laborers, making their services and former tasks no longer necessary . . . there seems to be no way of measuring the future of this displacement, but there are so many new inventions indicating displacement of labor that technological unemployment may be an even more serious problem in the near future than it is now. In the past, expanding industries and population shifts have in time accomplished the readjustments. It is difficult to say whether the numerous new labor-saving inventions may not augment the problem of technological unemployment in the future, but such is the strong possibility, despite a diminishing rate of increase in population."

The writer continues on to question the value of innovation. "It might be well to ask first whether society wishes to encourage mechanical invention in natural science at all. The question appears absurd or academic, yet the changes which many conservatives object to are the result of invention. And even radicals have suggested declaring a moratorium on inventions until society catches up" (Ogburn, 1933, 165).

In that depression-racked era, whether it was manufacturing employment in the broad, which for the first time was declining, or the displacement of more than a half-million workers in the railroad industries in the course of the 1920s, the fear of a radically altered future in which new development would not replace the old is evident. Mixed within the comments are doubts: even accepting the existence of a salutary balance in terms of *numbers* of jobs arising in new occupations to replace those that had become obsolete, what of the specific individuals who lost out in the process?

The agricultural migration off the land in the 1920s involved a total migration estimated at nearly six million. Even this was just the crest of a longer wave whose implications were clearly seen by 1930: "The cotton picker may compel the migration of an unparalleled magnitude in our history from the hill lands as well as the level lands of the Cotton Belt to the cities" (Baker, 1933, 110). While the fear of a depopulation of the countryside, and its consequent impoverishment to the benefit of the cities, may bring a wry smile to the current observer, the scale of the shift which took place is far greater than any recent change in real employment in the various sectors of the United States, and it has no current comparability in forced migration. The process in the long run was successful; the pain involved, however, was enormous. The stresses produced major changes in the government role vis-à-vis capital and labor. Does our present situation present an equivalent challenge?

The Domination of Manufacturing

Total employment in the United States has expanded at a rate which would have completely shattered the critics who scoffed at Henry Wallace's 1948 campaign call for a nation with 60 million jobs. The seemingly swollen ranks of the 40 million non-agriculturally employed at the end of World War II represented an increase of 25 percent from the pre-War baseline. The woesayers, who envisioned a return to Depression levels once the wartime boom was over, were clearly laid to rest with an increment of ten million jobs in the decade from 1945 to 1955. And this was merely a preliminary plateau of things to come. By 1965, the base figure was over 60 million. In the ten years following, there was an even more heroic leap upward, with an additional 16 million individuals joining the ranks of the paid nonagriculturally employed. Indeed, even in the recession-impacted year of 1982, total employment on the same basis in the United States barely slipped from the peak of 1981's 91 million to 1982's 89.6 million. By late 1985 it had risen close to the 100-million mark.

Within this overall ebullience, it is evident that manufacturing employment has played a declining role. From the 1945 peak of 38.4 percent, manufacturing fell steadily to roughly a third of all jobs by 1955, and barely one-in-five by 1982. It is particularly striking to note that 1975, a deep recession year which particularly impacted manufacturing profits, still reflected 23.8 percent of America's paid workers involved in manufacturing, while 1980's equivalent was 22.4 percent, with subsequent slippage to the 1982 low point.

The true growth sectors of American employment have bypassed manufacturing, with at best a virtual stability in absolute job levels in the score of years since 1965. The absolute number of persons employed in manufacturing during those twenty years has been 19.5 million, plus or minus one million (Sternlieb and Hughes, 1984).

In a study of employment trends earlier published by the Rutgers University Center for Urban Policy Research, the elements presented here are elaborated on more fully. It should be noted, however, that while the 1982 median weekly wage level in the goods-production sectors of industry was $331, the equivalent in service production was $223. Thus, in part, the problem is not merely one of job growth per se—an area in which the United States has performed heroically—but rather the stagnancy of the traditionally high-paid manufacturing sector (Sternlieb and Hughes, 1984). And to this must be added a fear of the future. The level of new manufacturing building in the United

States has been extremely lethargic. Even 1984—two years into the recovery—was below the worst year of the mid-1970s' business cycle (Dodge/Sweets, 1984).

As announcement after announcement of overseas fabrication even of high-tech equipment hits the daily press, the future of the smokestack industries takes on an additional somber cast. A survey of 600 high-level business executives, many of them chief executive officers, by *Business Week* indicated a surprisingly negative split on how far to go in salvaging non-competitive industries. Pollster Lou Harris summarized the results bluntly: "The prevailing wisdom is to let these industries go down the drain. A significant minority feels that they are encumbrances on the economy" (*Business Week*, 1983).

At best, high tech, even if employment within its avant garde portals were limited to the United States, is viewed as a very limited replacement activity in terms of total jobs. And it is perhaps of even more limited potential in smoothing the transition out of the older heavy-industry base and to serve significantly to ameliorate the regional stress of the closing of old facilities (Browne, 1983; Thompson and Thompson, 1983). Thus the spectre voiced by Leontief has many antecedents in the past, as well as adherents—and some evidence, presently and prospectively—as well.

The Current Demographic/Labor Force Bulge

The powerful impact of the changing demographic profile of the United States also must be factored in as we approach the issues of adjustment in employment. From 1969 to 1979, for example, the population of the United States aged 15 to 64 years increased by nearly one-in-four, with the bulk of the increase concentrated in the baby boom generation. There is no parallel among the principal industrial countries of Europe or Japan. The amazing labor force absorption performance of the United States in the face of this tidal wave has been largely overlooked. The net addition of new jobs since 1970 in the United States is equal to the total labor force of France or Italy, just slightly lower than the total of West Germany, and triple the rate of Japan (Sternlieb and Hughes, 1984).

The difficulties of adjustment to automation and the increasing application of technology in Europe were buffered by the relatively low population increases of the northern European industrial powers. Given reasonable levels of economic growth, this permitted vast shifts off the land, both within the several countries, and even more strikingly, among their southern neighbors. The flow of the so-called "guest workers" typically from Italy, Spain, and Greece, as well as from eastern Europe as a whole, to the industrial areas of western and central Europe, was enormous, with more than 10 percent of the total labor force in some of the host countries representing "outlanders."

A similar process has been taking place within the United States. Our equivalent of both the European and non-European guest workers has been the flows across our southern border and from the Caribbean. But we have not had as rigorous immigration quotas as held true in Europe, and illegal immigration makes a mockery of our nominal restrictions. There is little in the United States of the necessity for non-citizens to hold a current work permit; in France, failure to produce a permit can result in forced out-migration.

The guest workers, therefore, have at least in substantial part, though far from wholly, provided a "soft landing" in western Europe, their numbers expanding in times of demand and being reduced in periods of recession. The United States, in contrast, has essentially internalized the enormous immigrant flow. The latter, based on legal immigration, represents approximately one-third of the total national increase in population in the last decade, and current estimates indicate that this figure is dwarfed by the flow of illegals.

It is noteworthy in this regard to view the trepidation with which hitherto-successful industrial countries such as West Germany face their own futures, which unlike the United States indicate a rapid burgeoning of the labor force. Thus, Werner Heinz, in an essay on industrial policy in the Federal Republic of Germany, highlights a total West German economy whose basic job parameters are highly reminiscent of those in the United States, i.e., an expanding service sector but a decline in industrial jobs, and warns of an increase in the German work force as a result of large numbers of young people entering the labor force who will be confronted with a decreasing number of jobs (Heinz, 1981, 126).

The situation in the United States has been complicated by the higher levels of labor force participation rates, by some measures nearly uniquely high: "For instance, the United States and Japan have had similar rates of population growth over the past two decades, yet the U.S. labor force has grown much faster than Japan's, because participation rates of women and youth have risen in the United States while they are falling in Japan. . . . In contrast, sharp declines in labor force activity have occurred in Germany and Italy . . . and a more modest decline was posted in France. In 1960, Japan had the highest participation rate—68 percent—of the countries enumerated. By 1981, it was down to 62.2 percent. The United States, conversely, in 1960 was at the 59.4 percent mark; by 1981 it was at 63.9 percent. The bulk of this difference focused around the increased role of women." While the labor force participation rate of women increased substantially in the United States, in Germany and Japan it declined—in both cases quite sharply (Sorrentino, 1983, 23).

The enormous expansion in female employment as a proportion of total work force in the United States thus has few parallels elsewhere in the industrialized world. By 1981, nearly 43 percent of the 100 million persons employed here were women. Their presence was most striking in the growth segments of our economy—particularly wholesale and retail trades, and the services in general. Even in manufacturing, whose total labor force has remained relatively stagnant since 1970, the share of jobs held by women shifted up abruptly.

This has been further accentuated by a little-noticed increase in the labor force participation rate of youth in America. The change in the United States was almost 12 percentage points for persons under 25, from 1960's 56.4 percent to 1980's 68.1 percent. While part of this represents a readjustment in the relative scales of the age groups within the 16–25 range, it further indicates the pressures that have been exerted. "In the United States, more than half the teenagers in the labor force are also in school. The rise of student participation in the labor force has been attributed to several factors, including need for—or preference for—earnings to supplement family income, greater participation in work-study programs, and increases in the proportion of college students in two-year colleges, who have higher activity rates than those in four-year colleges. By comparison, few European and Japanese students work while in school, for a variety of academic and other reasons" (Sorrentino, 1983, 30).

With the advent of the baby bust generation, and the declining rate of labor force participation increase by women, the stresses on the economy to provide jobs to newcomers should abate. We will move from a labor force expansion which in the 1970s averaged 2.4 million a year, to 1.8 million in the 1980s, and to 1.3 million in the first five years of the 1990s (Sternlieb and Hughes, 1985).

Domestic Productivity and International Competition

One of the principal indictments of the United States's management–labor–government relationship has revolved around the issue of declines in productivity: the level of goods and services produced per work hour. There is substantial controversy over the adequacy of our measuring tools in this sphere, with some observers raising the issue of whether conventional instruments are adequate at appraising a service economy (Henrici, 1981). Other critics, typified by Robert D. Reich and Lester Thurow, the principal economic theorists of the Democratic Party, have used data in this sector as a sad barometer of failures of the system to yield the productivity increases which are essential to ensure increases in the standards of living, and ultimately in international competitiveness. To Reich, for example, "decline of relative productivity is the major *reversible* cause of our present economic woes" (Magaziner and Reich, 1982, 2).

In the eyes of some commentators, the rise of Japanese manufacturing competition and the comparative vigor of the French and German economies, have raised significant issues on the adequacy of our present organizational capacities as the United States becomes more deeply involved in the world economy. Key to the cure, as they envision it, is some measure of government input, loosely termed "industrial policy."

Critics of Adam Smith have suggested that while the concept of competition within national boundaries makes for efficiency, when international trade is factored in, it may well make for a more efficient world but at the price of disaster for the specific country that it has impacted (Schelling, 1971). In order to implement the necessary closings of old facilities, greater assurances to labor, it is asserted, are required to permit flexibility in its utilization and reallocation.

In their frequently cited book, Reich and his co-author, Ira Magaziner, point out that while the United States has a relatively small proportion (21 percent as of 1978) of its total wage and salary earners unionized (as compared to West Germany's 42 percent and Japan's 33 percent), the typical working days lost per 1,000 employees (averaging 1970 through 1977) was far heavier in the United States—529 on average, versus Japan's 148 and West Germany's 38 (Magaziner and Reich, 1982). The authors conclude: "The poor pattern of U.S. labor–management relations contributes not only to the nation's decline in competitive productivity, but also the insecurity and lower standard of living for its working population. U.S. managers have lagged behind their Japanese and continental European counterparts in eliciting cooperation from the work force, in encouraging greater commitment to productivity, and using human resources to the fullest." While they admit that some of Japan's and Germany's relative industrial peace has "a number of social and industrial practices that can be traced ultimately to cultural roots," they suggest that the impact of these elements is much exaggerated. Modernization requires buffering the impacts of change on labor (Magaziner and Reich, 1982, 154).

Magaziner and Reich claim that the United States government has "failed to ease the transition of the labor force out of businesses whose long-term competitive position has declined . . . as a result in order to obtain protection, workers were threatened by plant closings and layoffs that are attributable to imports [and] joined the political alliances with businesses that are also threatened by foreign competition. The so-called 'trade adjustment assistance' for workers directly impacted by imports, rather than easing their adjustment out of declining industries, has served primarily to keep workers where they are. The program has offered generous unemployment benefits but only relatively meager job search relocation assistance" (Magaziner and Reich, 1982, 210).

In general, according to the authors, the job retraining programs are poorly attended and are generally directed to providing basic job skills at the bottom levels, rather than helping older, more highly paid, skilled or semi-skilled employees retrain in new jobs. In sum, "the problem of declining businesses will not disappear. Indeed it will accelerate in the coming years as the pace of international competition picks up. . . . The United States needs an affirmative policy for industries in distress, a policy that helps them regain competitiveness when possible, and simultaneously aids workers and regions to adjust to change. Anything less is not a strategy for economic development, but a recipe for slow but sure economic decay" (Magaziner and Reich, 1982, 215).

In essence, the arguments advance the thesis that either we have a strategy structured by government to cope with factory closings, or we will have not only substantial social costs, as well as protectionism, but also an inability to upgrade both the range of our manufactures and the implementation of procedures and technologies with which to make them competitive. Changes in factory closing procedures are viewed as crucial to generating cooperation between labor and management as a foundation for productivity increase and quality control. Japan is frequently cited as the model for future American policy.

Critics of this approach have questioned whether Japan's industrial success has been the result of specific government guidance and have noted the limitations on government-implemented adjustment procedures and meliorative measures when shops outside the elite firms are forced to close down (Trecsize, 1982).

In addition, the fiscal problems of some of the leading western European industrial countries faced with competition have been accentuated by the broad nexus of social interventionary strategies to buffer the impact on workers. Labor peace can be costly. Firms may refuse to locate in areas in which the contingent liability of massive severance requirements overhangs the site. Government aid to displaced workers may buffer dislocation, though perhaps at the price of immobility. The recovery of the United States economy since 1982 has stilled some of the comparative criticisms—but is this merely the lull before a renewed storm? In order to project the future in this vital sphere, a better grasp of the economic dynamics of the recent past is essential.

Managerial Tactics and Capacity

The very definition of the world economy—its ultimate shape, and the counter-revolt which has stirred in the forms of protectionism—is far from clear. At the very least, however, it is causing a substantial review of all of the facets of how we make a living. Not the least among these is the criticism that has arisen in terms of managerial tactics.

There are those who thus would blame much of America's malaise on a supposed Harvard Business School approach: the deification of current value with its emphasis on immediate return as the optimal goal, at the cost of larger strategic formats. This is frequently contrasted with the supposed Japanese investment approach, shaped by government, which provides a longer-term developmental strategy. The very vigor of American stock markets, the much more important position that equity plays versus debt in our corporate balance sheets as compared with other countries, have been criticized. On the one hand, it is this very format which, in combination with reduced capital-gains taxation, has provided a unique flow of funds to new enterprise. But on the other hand, it has supposedly driven management to milk "no-growth" sectors without regard to the impacts on labor and community.

Within this context, there have been a number of striking instances in which the sale of nominally profitable but stock market-unfavored facilities (which are viewed as worthy only of low multiples, i.e., of a meager relationship of earnings to stock values because of their lack of fashionability) has clearly enhanced, at least in the short run, the stock market values given particular companies. Cases in point would be the Motorola sale of its television-production facilities, TWA's unbundling of its airline, or General Electric spinning off its stake in energy—Utah International—six years after its purchase. It is noteworthy, particularly in the last case, that the ratio of sale price to nominal profitability, based on 1982 results, was relatively low—far lower than the multiple awarded General Electric's overall earnings. The prospect that the sale price in turn would be invested in "high tech," moreover, spurred on a substantial increase in the common stock of the parent company.

A number of points proceed from the cases cited above and their equivalent. First, these measures do not necessarily lead to plant closings. They do indicate, however, the comparatively high level of return that is required of investment in basic, non-glamour industries. Glamour industries may have a common stock-to-earnings ratio of twenty or more. Investment in this sphere, yielding as little as a five percent return, thus may be adequate in terms of non-dilution of the stock-to-earnings ratio. More-basic industries, however, are well down in the pecking order, typically with less than half the multiple given their more favored equivalents. This severely rations the flow of new capital accorded the latter and requires much faster levels of payback, much more in the way of instant return to warrant expenditures. Over a long period of time, therefore, the less-favored industries by definition will tend to have a far higher level of old equipment and facility, and with them lower productivity.

By very definition, therefore, the market is serving to move "sunset" industries to the back burner while providing a much more salubrious climate for the financing of new ones. This may well be appropriate in terms of the prospects of investment in the future rather than the past. But by its nature it tends to reify corporate decisionmaking. The very act of setting varying multiples to various industries provides relatively painless flows of capital to the favored, at the cost of those that are viewed in a less positive light.

This has been a long-term reality assuring resources for the future. When opportunities for investments are viewed in a worldwide context, however, they may pose increasing stress on the adaptation of the domestic economy. The relatively low evaluation given less-favored industries in older plants may well mean that they are worth more dead than alive, i.e., the post-tax consequences of writing them off may be much more salubrious than keeping them operating or even selling them as operating entities.

While effective corporate tax rates have declined precipitously, this may not hold true for marginal rates in selected industries. There is a reinforcement element at work. If the corporate treasurer does not have major resources for new investment, the firm probably will not have the advantages of investment tax credits and accelerated depreciation coverage. Thus, the effective tax rate in old industries may be higher than in growth ones. In turn, the temptation to close down and secure maximization of tax cover—or at the very least, minimize real loss—may be considerable. While some effort has been made to blunt the processes outlined above through the controversial capacity to sell unused tax credits, the basic dynamic is evident.

It is striking to note that this process should tend to search out the same targets that the "Atari Democrats," and other believers in the new technology at the expense of old, are calling for, i.e., a much more rapid deployment of assets into the cutting edge. If successful, the trade is between current jobs in old industries versus high growth and the expectation of future employment growth. Again, the latter is essential within a competitive world environment. The question is whether the pace is fast enough to keep America competitive—and Americans working. Secondly, given their developmental lags, these newer facilities make sense only within the context of a stock market which is going to ascribe flows of yield from them at a future date as being worthy of high multiples, thus justifying low rates of immediate return. Does this require capital allocation through government?

The issues that are raised are severalfold. Prime among them is the question of credit crunch, particularly given the high level of federal spending. It has been emphasized by critics of the major diversion of resource into financial manipulation, i.e., epitomized by the merger boom. And, from the viewpoint of the study at hand, the acceleration of the necessary reinvestment process may come to a halt as the resistance of labor, relatively fully exposed to its impacts, begins to stiffen. Thus, while some critics of the American system call for a stabilization of jobs, other advocates of new factory closing law initiatives view the latter as key to the refocusing of America's industrial thrust.

Industrial Adaptation to Change: Is It Adequate?

The point has been made by Bluestone and Harrison (1982) that the preferred industries in the United States, i.e., the new high-growth, high-tech ones, tend to be non-unionized, and tend to have a higher proportion of low-paid, unskilled labor often represented by increased employment of females at the cost of the old backbone, male, blue-collar elite of steel and autos. From the viewpoint of the interventionists, such as the authors represented in *democracy*, the changing pattern of employment opportunity is not merely the following of an inexorable law, but rather a result of political decisionmaking masquerading as divine economic determinism. "The problem, of course . . . is that private decisionmakers in the market, when freed of civic values, might not act in the best interest of the collectivity." Even Adam Smith early recognized that the new urban capitalist might be an untrustworthy sort, with little civic commitment. "A very trifling disgust," Smith observed in *The Wealth of the Nations*, "will make him remove his capital." The critics' view is easily summarized. "Everything is reduced to the crudest form of economic determinism . . . the depoliticization of economic life leaves us with a remarkable image of history and society, one characterized by actions without actors" (Bender, 1983, 12).

To many who want change in our economic ways, what is required is significant state intervention, at the very least to ameliorate the impacts of the changing nature and quality of jobs, and at a more robust level, for a change in the system. Thus, from the viewpoint of Bluestone and Harrison, "deindustrialization" is taking place broadly in the United States. (They mean by this term a widespread systematic disinvestment in the nation's basic productive capacity.) Controversial as it may be, the essential problem with the U.S. economy can be traced to the way capital—in the forms of financial resources and of real plant and equipment—has been diverted from productive investments in our basic national industries into unproductive speculation, mergers, and acquisitions in foreign investments. Left behind, in their view, are "shattered factories, displaced workers, and a newly emerging group of ghost towns" (Bluestone and Harrison, 1982, 6).

In their much-discussed book, *The Deindustrialization of America*, which originated in a research project commissioned in 1979 by a coalition of trade unions and community organizations "concerned with the causes and consequences of plant closings all across the United States," the authors point to increased concentration of American economic power in fewer and fewer hands. The latter are accused of having moved capital, labor, and even equipment abroad. This in turn, in their view, has engendered world competition in which the profitability of American corporations has gone down. Corporations have been driven to conglomeration and short-term expediencies.

"Buying and selling entire businesses and transferring capital from one sector to another at the first sight of trouble constituted a most important corporate strategy for raising short-term profitability during the 1960s and protecting those profits in the face of the economic crises of the 1970s. In the process a great many profitable, formerly independent companies were shut down and a special productivity embodied in skills and viable plant and equipment destroyed" (Bluestone and Harrison, 1982, 164).

The authors suggest that this has been, in large part, a flight from unionization as part and parcel of a market economy, with private individuals and private management more interested in income differentials than the increase in the size of the economic pie, or ultimately the economic viability of the country as a whole (Bluestone and Harrison, 1982, 204). They argue that none of the meliorative strategies, whether those of liberals such as Felix Rohatyn and his call for an industrial development bank, or Lester Thurow with his advocacy of a broad series of measures to ensure movement of capital to new industry (both criticized as ultimately having as their bottom line increased productivity); or even the advocates of encouragement of small companies as major employment growth centers (they suggest that, after all, most of the jobs created by the latter are in the secondary labor market—and provide inadequate opportunity), are adequate to the future (Bluestone and Harrison, 1982). In their place they come out for a vigorous factory closing law initiative, and "a radical reindustrialization" (Bluestone and Harrison, 1982, 235).

To a more structured Marxist such as David Harvey, the crises of capitalism are not accidental. They are rather to be viewed as major periods of rationalization, "shakeouts and shakedowns" which restore balance to the form. But their rationalizing function is no comfort to those caught in their midst (Harvey, 1978, 228).

Regardless of their political hue, whether they hope that "the system" can be saved or indeed anticipate with some degree of pleasure its demise, there is expressed a general feeling that the economic compact of the New Deal has been rendered obsolete. Thus, an editor of the *Harvard Business Review*, in summarizing an article by Robert B. Reich, states that "perhaps it is fair to say that the nation has lost its economic innocence—the genial assurance that American industry would, without government intervention, provide an unfailing engine for bettering the American standard of living." He sums up Reich's critique by stating "We must face the fact that wrenching structural changes will have to be made in the economy if America's industrial base is to regain its full international competitiveness. And these changes, in turn, will require carefully drawn industrial policy both to encourage the flow of capital where it is needed [and] to ease the inevitable dislocation of the labor force" (Reich, 1982, 74).

The debate on the need for formal constant and direct industrial policy continues, barely abated by the 1983 recovery. While the issues of the very existence of the American disease, and therefore the need for structured direction, is under challenge, its proponents view it as a necessity (McKensie, 1983). A crucial part of its implementation is a call for a soft landing for employees of the so-called sunset industries in order to ensure the political acceptability of resource allocation to high-growth areas. According to Reich, for example, there are three strategic choices for nations with regard to declining businesses (Magaziner and Reich, 1982, 198):

> A nation can ease the adjustment of capital out of these businesses by assisting workers with retraining and relocating, by subsidizing the development of new businesses within the same regional community, and by helping firms to salvage those portions of the declining businesses that are capable of becoming competitive on their own.

> A second choice is to protect them through quotas or voluntary export agreements or other means of subsidization.

> A third alternative: Do nothing, allowing the market to do on its own . . . is generally politically unacceptable.

But even among the moderate proponents of industrial policy, the question of whether the United States is politically capable of the choices that are necessary is increasingly evident. Reich, in a recent article in *Public Interest*, is far from sanguine on the results. "How can we insulate [industrial policy] from the predations of narrow interest groups and the vagaries of partisan politics while ensuring that it is democratically accountable? Republican or Democrat, liberal or conservative, that question will continue to be with us" (Reich, 1983).

In general, particularly in the steel industry, efforts at softening the crunch of competition through aid to new technology and facilitating efficient plant development have often gone astray, and have led to the continuation of the status quo through a barrier wall of protectionism. A classic article on the topic which reviews nearly twenty years of governmental intervention highlights this conclusion (Borrus, 1983).

The Mitigation Measures of Organized Labor

The flight to protectionism and a fortress America-type mentality in order to protect extant industries—and more strikingly, extant jobs in their present locations—is becoming increasingly overt on the part of American labor, even parts of it that were long supporters of free trade. The attitude of America's labor organizations has moved far from the era of a half-century ago when even unemployment insurance was viewed as an inhibitor to a much more desirable goal—more pay; when the ideal of union policy was seen as "The most effective safeguard against distress is a rate of wages high enough to allow decent standards of life in the present and adequate savings for the contingencies in the future." As a commentator writing in 1931 stated, "Committed to this policy, the majority of American unions, particularly the AFL, have always resisted compulsory unemployment insurance." It was only the Great Depression which altered these attitudes and began to move the unions in the direction of job stability as a primary goal (Wolman and Peck, 1982).

The issue is not a mere continuance of the developments within labor-management negotiations. Sometimes overlooked by the new critics are the substantial changes and facilitating mechanisms that have been put in place by this means. There is a long post-Depression history of labor management negotiations on the issue of plant closing. The automobile industry pioneered supplementary unemployment benefits (SUB) in 1955. Additional assistance for the permanently displaced, put in place in 1958, called for severance pay. Early retirement benefits were also made available for the older displaced employee. The automobile industry contract negotiations in 1961 provided, for the first time, shorter work-week benefits as well as moving allowances as certain employees were transferred from one plant to another. Similarly, the same pattern of development, with great emphasis on job security measures, was adopted in the steel industry. Within the same context, the revolutionary agreements worked out on the West Coast with the International Longshoremen-Warehousemen Union permitted technological innovations in return for guaranteed annual wages and invested early retirement rights. In the words of one observer, "Labor-management adjustment to technological change is not a destination, but an unending journey" with no one universal solution (Killingsworth, 1982).

It is noteworthy, however, that each of these positive solutions, particularly the longshoremen's, occurred in situations in which there were very considerable savings available to management through work-rule changes. These, in turn, could serve to defray the benefits given the workers. Most particularly they were achieved in the face of relatively little in the way of outside-U.S.A. competition.

Does the homogenization of manufacturing competence worldwide create a very different setting for reconciliation? Has the pace of technological shift accelerated to a point where the pattern of individual industry and specific labor-management negotiations yields inadequate results? It is more than twenty years since the editors of one of the major works on the problems of automation wrote "(The) . . . differentiation between beneficiaries and sufferers from technological change presents us with a moral as well as an economic problem. Society as a whole, by and large, is a beneficiary. Is it morally acceptable for most of us to enjoy the benefits of new technology without utilizing every possible means of minimizing the losses and assisting the adjustment of those who are not beneficiaries, but sufferers?" (Somers, 1982, 207).

Certainly, there has been a broadening of the safety net since this plea. But it has been within the broad parameters of past adaptation. The success of the American economy in recent years has dimmed the attention given its critics. But it has been bought with deficits which cannot be continued. There is little left in the economic larder if the nation should falter.

The end of the story is the beginning: of search amidst uncertainty. Past triumphs do not assure future success. They do, however, bear witness to a capacity which should not be underestimated.

References

Baker, O.E. "Agricultural and Forest Land." In President's Research Committee on Social Trends, *Recent Social Trends in the United States*. One-volume edition. New York, NY: McGraw–Hill, 1933, pp. 90–121.

Barbash, Jack. "The Impact of Technology on Labor–Management Relations." In *Adjusting to Technological Change*, edited by Gerald G. Somers, Edward L. Cushman, and Nat Weinberg. New York, NY: Harper & Row, 1963, pp. 44–60.

Bender, Thomas. "The End of the City?" *democracy*, Winter 1983.

Bluestone, Barry, and Bennett Harrison. *The Deindustrialization of America*. New York, NY: Basic Books, 1982.

Borrus, Michael. "The Politics of Competitive Erosion in the U.S. Steel Industry." In *American Industry in International Competition*, edited by John Zysman and L. Tyson. Ithaca, NY: Cornell University Press, 1983.

Browne, Lynn. "Can High-Tech Save the Great Lakes States?" *New England Economic Review*, November–December 1983.

Business Week, April 18, 1983, p. 18.

Chaikin, Sol C. *Foreign Affairs*, Spring 1982.

Dodge/Sweets. *Construction Outlook 1984*. New York, NY: McGraw–Hill, 1983.

Harvey, David. "On Planning the Ideology of Planning." In *Planning Theory in the 1980s*, edited by Robert W. Burchell and George Sternlieb. New Brunswick, NJ: Rutgers University, Center for Urban Policy Research, pp. 213–233.

Heertje, Arnold. *Economics and Technical Change*. New York, NY: Wiley, 1973.

Heinz, Werner. "Urban Policy in the Federal Republic of Germany." In *Advanced Industrialization in the Inner Cities*, edited by Gail S. Schwartz. Lexington, MA: Lexington Books, 1981.

Henrici, Stanley B. "How Deadly is the Productivity Disease?" *Harvard Business Review*, November–December 1981.

Killingsworth, Charles C. "Cooperative Approaches to Problems of Technological Change." In *Adjusting to Technological Change*, edited by Gerald G. Somers, Edward L. Cushman, and Nat Weinberg. New York, NY: Harper & Row, 1963.

Kuhn, James W. "The Riddle of Inflation—A New Answer." *Public Interest*, No. 27, Spring 1972.

Lekachman, Robert. *Greed Is Not Enough: Reaganomics*. New York, NY: Pantheon Books, 1982.

Lipset, S.M., and W. Schneider. *The Confidence Gap*. New York, NY: Free Press, 1983.

McKenzie, Richard B. *A New Reconstruction Finance Corporation: No Cure for U.S. Economic Ills*. Washington, D.C.: The Heritage Foundation, 1983.

Magaziner, Ira C. and Robert D. Reich. *Minding America's Business: The Decline and Rise of the American Economy*. New York: Harcourt-Brace, 1982.

Meadows, Donella et al. *The Limits to Growth: A Report for the Club of Rome's Project on the Predicament of Mankind*. New York, NY: Universe, 1974.

The New York Times, April 6, 1983, p. 2.

Nobel, David F. "In Defense of Luddism II. *democracy*, Spring 1983.

Ogburn, W.F. "The Influence of Invention and Discovery." In President's Research Committee on Social Trends, *Recent Social Trends in the United States*. One-volume edition. New York, NY: McGraw–Hill, 1933, pp. 122–167.

Peet, Richard. Review. *Antipode*, vol. 14, no. 2, 1982.

"Present Tense Technology." *democracy*, Spring 1983.

Reich, Robert. "Industrial Policy of the Right. *Public Interest,* Fall 1983.

Reich, Robert B. "Why the United States Needs an Industrial Policy." *Harvard Business Review,* January—February 1982.

Salant, Walter S. "The American Economy in Transition." *The Journal of Economic Literature,* June 1982.

Schelling, Thomas. "On the Ecology of Micromotives," *Public Interest,* Spring 1971.

Somers, Gerald C., Edward L. Cushman, and Nat Weinberg. "Conclusions." In *Adjusting to Technological Change,* edited by Gerald C. Somers, Edward L. Cushman, and Nat Weinberg. New York, NY: Harper & Row, 1963, pp. 206–220.

Sorrentino, Constance. "International Comparisons of Labor Force Participation, 1960–81." *Monthly Labor Review,* February 1983.

Sternlieb, George and James W. Hughes. *Income and Jobs: U.S.A.* New Brunswick, NJ: Rutgers University, Center for Urban Policy Research, 1984.

_____. *Jobs and People: New York City, 1985.* New Brunswick, NJ: Rutgers University Center for Urban Policy Research, 1979.

_____. "A Note on Information Technology, Demographics, and the Retail Response." Prepared for the Conference on the Impact of Information Technology on the Service Sector (Wharton School, University of Pennsylvania, February 8, 1985).

Sternlieb, George, James W. Hughes, and Connie O. Hughes. *Demographic Trends and Economic Reality.* New Brunswick, NJ: Rutgers University, Center for Urban Policy Research, 1982.

Thompson, Wilbur R., and P.R. Thompson. "Hi-Tech Industry and High-Tech Places." *REI Review.* Cleveland State University, November 1983.

Thurow, Lester. "How to Rescue A Drowning Economy." *The New York Review,* April 11, 1982.

Trecsize, Phillip H. "Industrial Policy in Japan." In *Industry Revitalization: Toward a National Industrial Policy.* Elmsford, NY: Pergamon Press, 1982.

U.S. National Commission on Technology, Automation and Economic Progress. *Technology and the American Economy.* 7 vols. Washington, D.C.: U.S. Government Printing Office, 1966.

Veblen, Thorstein. *Imperial Germany.* New York, NY: Kelley, 1939.

Wolman, Leo. "Labor Groups in the Social Structure." In President's Research Committee on Social Trends, *Recent Social Trends in the United States.* One-volume edition. New York, NY: McGraw–Hill, 1933, pp. 801–856.

Index